THESE DIVIDED ISLES

by the same author

**BRITAIN ALONE:
THE PATH FROM SUEZ TO BREXIT**

PHILIP STEPHENS

THESE DIVIDED ISLES

BRITAIN AND IRELAND,
PAST AND FUTURE

faber

First published in 2025
by Faber & Faber Ltd
The Bindery, 51 Hatton Garden
London EC1N 8HN

Typeset by Faber & Faber Ltd

Printed and bound using 100 per cent renewable energy
by CPI Group (UK) Ltd, Croydon CR0 4YY

All rights reserved
© Philip Stephens, 2025

The right of Philip Stephens to be identified as author
of this work has been asserted in accordance with Section 77
of the Copyright, Designs and Patents Act 1988

A CIP record for this book
is available from the British Library

ISBN 978–0–571–38147–0

Printed and bound in the UK on FSC® certified paper in line with our continuing
commitment to ethical business practices, sustainability and the environment.
For further information see faber.co.uk/environmental-policy

Our authorised representative in the EU for product safety is
Easy Access System Europe, Mustamäe tee 50, 10621 Tallinn, Estonia
gpsr.requests@easproject.com

2 4 6 8 10 9 7 5 3 1

For my mother and for the Martin family

CONTENTS

List of Illustrations — ix
Acknowledgements — xi
Prologue — 1

1. A Divided Peace — 15
2. Best of Enemies — 47
3. A Border of the Mind — 61
4. De Valera's Ireland — 89
5. Trapped by History — 115
6. The Americans Are Back — 145
7. The Lady Turns — 163
8. Talking to Terrorists — 183
9. The End of History — 203
10. A Choice of Unions — 233
11. Past and Future — 261

Short Bibliography — 275
Notes — 281
Index — 289

LIST OF ILLUSTRATIONS

Queen Elizabeth II lays a wreath in Dublin's Garden of Remembrance. *Photo by Pool/Getty Images*
Signing the Treaty. *Photo by Topical Press Agency/Hulton Archive/Getty Images*
Proclamation of Ireland's independence. *Photo by Fotosearch/Getty Images*
Northern Ireland's first prime minister James Craig greets army officers in Belfast. *Photo by Walshe/Topical Press Agency/Getty Images*
Searched at gunpoint. *Photo by Topical Press Agency/Hulton Archive/Getty Images*
David Lloyd George and Winston Churchill leaving 10 Downing Street. *Fremantle/Alamy Stock Photo*
Michael Collins leaving No. 10 during the treaty negotiations. *Photo by Topical Press Agency/Hulton Archive/Getty Images*
The Free State crushes the IRA forces at Dublin's Four Courts. *The Print Collector/Alamy Stock Photo*
Michael Collins lies in state. *Photo by Central Press/Getty Images*
Kiltimagh, County Mayo, during the 1960s. *Gordon Standing/Irish Times*
Éamon de Valera. *Photo by Bettmann/Getty Images*
Archbishop McQuaid with de Valera. *Photo by Independent News and Media/Getty Images*
The Reverend Ian Paisley. *Photo by Bride Lane Library/Popperfoto/Getty Images*
Gerry Adams and Martin McGuinness. *Photo by Kaveh Kazemi/Getty Images*

LIST OF ILLUSTRATIONS

Harold Wilson. *Photo by SSPL/Getty Images*

Margaret Thatcher signs the Anglo-Irish Agreement with Garret FitzGerald. *Trinity Mirror/Mirrorpix/Alamy Stock Photo*

British troops fight a war on the streets they cannot win. *Associated Press/Alamy Stock Photo*

Wars past and present. *PA Images/Alamy Stock Photo*

David Trimble and John Hume. *NTB/Alamy Stock Photo*

John Major and Albert Reynolds. *Photo by Johnny Eggitt/AFP via Getty Images*

Bertie Ahern and Tony Blair. *Photo by Alan Lewis/AFP via Getty Images*

Martin McGuinness and Ian Paisley. *Photo by Peter Muhly/AFP via Getty Images*

ACKNOWLEDGEMENTS

This is the book I had long been waiting to write. I have my mother to thank for it. London-born, I first caught a glimpse of the troubled but intimate relationship between Britain and Ireland when every summer we swapped the cacophony of the great metropolis for the implacably rural County Mayo. I am privileged to be Irish as well as British. Friends spent school holidays on the English south coast. The better-off ventured across the Channel to Normandy or Knokke-le-Zoute in Belgium. My brother and I roamed free in the mountains, rivers and boglands around Kiltimagh, my mother's home in Ireland's wild west.

So I have always counted myself among those on both sides of the relationship. As a child I remember bristling at the English caricatures of 'Paddys', yet, visiting Mayo, I also quite liked the cachet that came with hailing from the big city. More recently, my spirits have been warmed by Ireland's rapid emergence as a modern, prosperous, liberal European state, even as I have lamented Britain's retreat after the self-inflicted wound of Brexit.

The sense of grievance felt by nationalist Ireland was keenly felt in what had historically been Ireland's poorest region. But the British were never less than welcome. Mayo had been a fertile recruiting ground for the Volunteers fighting the revolutionary war. But, as my mother would often remind me, nothing then or subsequently justified the merciless violence inflicted on the people of Northern Ireland by the Provisional Irish Republican Army during the Troubles. The fight for independence was one thing; the bombing of women and children utterly beyond the pale.

ACKNOWLEDGEMENTS

Personal was overlaid with professional interest when, as political editor and then chief political commentator for the *Financial Times*, I reported on the closing years of the war and the tortured peace process that finally brought the fighting to an end. During that period I travelled often to Dublin and Belfast, meeting the politicians, community leaders and, occasionally, paramilitaries who were negotiating first a ceasefire and then a political bargain that would salve the wound left by partition. For all the speculation now about a united Ireland, I am conscious the latter is still very much unfinished business.

Reporting for the *FT* gave me unique access to those determined to shed the burdens of history, whether via my conversations with John Hume and David Trimble in the members' lobby of the House of Commons or through access to the thinking of ministers and prime ministers. Politics sometimes works. British leaders such as John Major and Tony Blair had the courage and determination to doggedly pursue a resolution, with no obvious prospect of personal political reward. Albert Reynolds, John Bruton and Bertie Ahern, who stepped out of history to recognise the legitimacy of northern unionism, likewise. Much of this book draws on recollections of the hundreds of conversations with politicians and diplomats that informed my reporting and commentary during those years.

Beyond the ringside seat, the advantage that comes with writing for a newspaper as special as the *FT* is that people generally trust you to tell it as it is. I used to congratulate myself on my contacts in some of the more secret corners of Whitehall – coffees in St James's Park and such like. Later, I learned that this was not entirely a compliment on my journalistic talents. Before the opening of talks with the PIRA, these officials had messages to convey to the PIRA Army Council. They knew that reports in the *FT* about the government's intentions would be taken seriously by its leaders.

ACKNOWLEDGEMENTS

The diplomats, and occasional spook, who helped me during those years are too numerous to list here – and many of our conversations were anyhow off the record. What I remember is that visits to Dublin were always as enjoyable as they were informative; trips to Belfast and Derry a reminder of just how much was at stake. Several of these public servants have given me more of their time during the past few years, as I have sought to make sense of the emotions and impulses as well as the statecraft that mapped out a political path for Ireland's future. The contributions to the peace-making of anonymous public servants too often goes unsung. Diplomats and advisers such as Michael Lillis, Seán Ó hUiginn, Noel Dorr and Martin Mansergh come to mind, as do David Goodall, Quentin Thomas and Sir John Chilcott.

I owe special personal thanks to Dáithí Ó Ceallaigh, a veteran of Anglo-Irish relations and former ambassador in London, who offered valuable comments and corrections on early drafts of this book, and to John Holmes and Jonathan Powell, who took me blow-by-blow through the British approach to the Good Friday Agreement. Colin Wrafter has been a good friend and guide.

In searching out the private thoughts of the leading players on both sides during the century since partition, I have mined the treasure troves of the official archives to study the contemporaneous records – cabinet meetings, secret memorandums and the rest – of critical decisions and events. I have also enjoyed the many accounts supplied by the memoirs and diaries of the principal actors. I have benefited too from an abundance of rich histories, most particularly from Irish writers and scholars. I hope I have highlighted the best of these in the Select Bibliography. I have been sparing, though, in the use of endnotes throughout the text, limiting references by and large to my own archival digging, more obscure sources and to instances where the insights of one or other commentator or

ACKNOWLEDGEMENTS

historian seem particularly striking. I am conscious that the digital revolution means that familiar quotations, along with speeches and government and parliamentary papers, can be readily accessed via an online search engine.

Books are a collaborative venture. Sarah Chalfant, my agent at Wylie, has been unstinting in her encouragement, enthusiasm and insights, a rock on which to build my confidence. Laura Hassan at Faber, who kindly took me on again after steering through my last book, *Britain Alone*, was once again an invaluable guide. Fred Baty helped to order my thoughts and cut out the repetitions, while Robert Davies got the English right and Ian Bahrami added form and polish. Chris Allnutt, a colleague at the *FT*, deployed all the skills of a first-rate editor. At Faber, Kate Ward and her team pulled everything together with unruffable professionalism. Needless to say, I alone am responsible for the judgements in this book, and for any errors and omissions that have slipped through.

PROLOGUE

'*A Uachtaráin, agus a chairde*' ('President, and friends'). Opening her speech at a banquet hosted by the Irish president, Queen Elizabeth II honoured in a few words a language that the British Crown had for centuries sought to extinguish. The venue, Dublin Castle, had been the cockpit of British colonial power in Ireland. Now, in May 2011, Britain's monarch reflected on the weight of that history. 'We can all see things which we would wish had been done differently or not at all,' she said with regal understatement, addressing the 'heartache, turbulence and loss' thrown up by British rule. The day before, she had disembarked at the Irish capital's Casement Aerodrome, so named to memorialise the republican revolutionary Roger Casement. An Anglo-Irish diplomat who sought the German Kaiser's guns in the cause of Irish nationalism, Casement was hanged for treason in the months after the 1916 Easter Rising. The queen later bowed her head as she visited the city's Garden of Remembrance to pay her respects to the republican Volunteers who died alongside Casement in the fight for independence.

The monarchy could claim few friends in Ireland. Three-quarters of a century earlier, Éamon de Valera, the 'Chief' to the many who revered him as the father of the Irish state, had brusquely refused an invitation to attend the coronation of Elizabeth's father, George VI. When the soon-to-be-crowned king voiced his disappointment to the head of the Irish diplomatic mission in London, John Dulanty, he found the envoy blunt in his response. He told the king, Dulanty reported, that 'It was indisputable that the history of the two peoples consisted almost entirely of one story – the story of the attempt by the British, sustained unbroken through the centuries, to subdue and to possess Ireland. It was similarly an accepted historical fact to say that an equally unbroken resistance by us [the Irish] had defeated that attempt.' By Dulanty's account, the king did not quarrel with the characterisation.[1]

As a moment of reconciliation between the two nations, the queen's visit was an unvarnished success. Elizabeth's words and demeanour, her hosts said, were perfectly judged. Yet the trip raised a question. Why had it taken so long? After all, she was a seasoned traveller. By the time of her death she had made six formal state visits to France and enjoyed many more private stays on the other side of the Channel. She had crossed the Atlantic countless times and ventured to every corner of the Commonwealth. This would be the only trip to the Republic. It was also the first by a reigning monarch to the southern part of Ireland since that of her grandfather George V in 1911, a decade before partition and independence. The House of Windsor had waited nearly a century to bestow the royal seal of approval on the independent Irish state that emerged from the Anglo-Irish Treaty of 1921.

Here was a relationship beset by confusions, complexities and contradictions, as intimate and intertwined as it has so often been violent and traumatic. The nineteenth-century English novelist William Thackeray returned from a lengthy visit to Ireland to describe it as 'a dirty and ruinous place'. But he also observed that 'for a stranger the Irish ways are the pleasantest, for here he is at once made happy and at home, or at ease rather'. Scroll through the centuries and, in 2020, Britain's Secret Intelligence Service (popularly known as MI6) appointed a new Chief, or 'C'. Richard Moore, a distinguished diplomat, was given charge of one of the world's foremost secret intelligence agencies, the home of the fictional James Bond. A century earlier, Moore's Irish grandfather, Jack

PROLOGUE

Buckley, was serving with the IRA Volunteers fighting the British in the revolutionary war of 1919 to 1921. At one point Buckley had been an aide-de-camp to de Valera at his base in County Cork. He was given an IRA medal for his contribution to the war against the British Crown. Not an eyelid was batted when his grandson was entrusted with leadership of Britain's spooks.

Ireland is Britain's closest neighbour. The sea crossing from Scotland measures only twelve miles at its narrowest point. It was also the first possession in what became Britain's global empire. The two nations' stories have been interwoven since Anglo-Norman invaders crossed the Irish Sea during the twelfth century. During the following seven hundred years, British rule was often imposed with singular cruelty. It was one thing to conquer Ireland, the English discovered, but quite another to ensure it stayed conquered. The two peoples became deeply intermingled, thrown together by Irish emigration, colonisation, intermarriage and culture. They share the English language. William Butler Yeats was a Protestant born into Dublin's Anglo-Irish gentry (a heritage that saw him derided by a nationalist contemporary as representative of 'the English mind in Ireland'). That has not denied him the accolade of Ireland's greatest poet. Britain's towns and cities have long been home to a sizeable Irish diaspora. Taps dispensing pints of Guinness sit comfortably alongside those for English ale in Britain's pubs. The seventeenth-century plantations of English and Scottish settlers created a permanent Protestant presence on a Catholic island. Today, Irish and British citizens have reciprocal rights to vote as residents in each nation's elections.

The phrase 'beyond the pale' has its origins in the English assumption that anyone venturing beyond the region around Dublin to the Gaelic 'badlands' risked falling prey to the uncivilised habits of the Irish. The sense of superiority that came with conquest still shows itself among a certain cohort of English politicians who seem to delight in their disdain for Ireland. 'Why is he not called Murphy like the rest of them?' Boris Johnson once asked Whitehall officials before a scheduled meeting with Ireland's prime minister, Leo Varadkar. No one spoke more eloquently to English ignorance and duplicity than Johnson.

Yet for the most part British and Irish politicians and diplomats seem to like each other. Trust has often been another question. The partition that gave the Republic its independence and left Northern Ireland in the United Kingdom was intended to close the wounds of colonialism, or at the very least allow the British to escape the costly quagmire of armed occupation. Instead, it served to illuminate the deep trenches of sectarianism that had been dug in the British attempt to pacify Ireland by settling it with Protestants. This part of the narrative would be told in the roughly 3,600 lives lost to the bloody conflict that raged across Northern Ireland during the closing decades of the twentieth century.

The history is shared but viewed through different lenses. 'As nations, we often mislead and misunderstand each other,' the British ambassador to Dublin wrote in a dispatch home in 1977. 'We take the Irish for granted whereas they are obsessed with us. We don't remember the past and they cannot forget it.'[2] It was a perfect description of the enduring tension arising from the asymmetry of the relationship. Britain had written most of Ireland's history. Ireland was a troublesome footnote in Britain's imperial story. As often as it conquered it, it could not pacify it.

This book is not about the long history that began with Henry II's landing in 1171. Instead, its focus is on the century since the Anglo-Irish Treaty and on the unfinished business of partition. It is impossible, however, to understand the forces shaping the past hundred years – and indeed those that will ultimately determine

PROLOGUE

whether partition will give way to Irish unity – without reference to the tumultuous events that preceded it. Jonathan Powell, Tony Blair's chief of staff during the Good Friday peace negotiations, learned as much in talks with Northern Ireland's unionists and nationalists. Every meeting with them, he would recount, began with a history lesson, generally a catalogue of grievances. 'The nationalist and republican version of Irish history begins in the 1160s.'[3] The enduring record of repression, conquest and reconquest cannot be erased from the Irish consciousness. As for the conquerors, they never quite confronted the casual callousness with which they habitually treated their nearest neighbour. The Act of Union of 1800 notionally afforded Ireland a place in the United Kingdom. But unlike Scotland and Wales, it would for ever be treated as a colony rather than a partner.

Partition tends to be viewed entirely through the lens of the formal separation in 1920 of six of the nine counties of the ancient province of Ulster from the twenty-six counties that would form the Free State and, subsequently, the Republic. But England had long before divided its colonial possession. The story of occupation was written in two parts. Until the sixteenth century, the narrative was a familiar one of land grabs and an Anglo-Norman Ascendancy fighting local Gaelic chieftains for territory and resources. The watershed moment came with Henry VIII's break with the papacy in 1534. Scotland and Wales were receptive to the Protestantism of the Reformation. Ireland remained resolute in its Catholicism – making it a natural ally of the continental powers that retained their fidelity to Rome. The conflict about territory was thus fused with a confessional antagonism that, for the British, bestowed on Ireland a unique strategic significance as a garrison in England's fights with its Catholic enemies on the European continent. The Protestants from England and Scotland (in the latter case mostly of a Presbyterian disposition) who arrived in large numbers to settle on seized Irish lands were dispatched to defend the ramparts against a backdoor invasion of England. Protestant Ulster was born of victory at the Battle of Kinsale, when England's Queen Elizabeth I defeated the province's Gaelic lords, led by Hugh O'Neill, the Earl of Tyrone. The 'Flight of the Earls' saw their lands divided and subdivided by the settlers. This transformation of the north-eastern corner of the island from a staunchly Gaelic, Catholic province to a Protestant stronghold was completed by Oliver Cromwell with the bloody suppression of a second uprising during the late 1640s. By some estimates up to a third of Ireland's Catholics died during Cromwell's brutal reconquest. The survivors were tipped out of Ulster. The choice was 'Hell or Connacht' – the sword, or banishment to the barren lands and bogs west of the River Shannon.

William of Orange's defeat of the Catholic James II in 1690 at the Battle of the Boyne sealed the Protestant hegemony. Religious allegiance as much as economic and political rights henceforth marked out the ground between ruler and repressed, landowner and landless. The Treaty of Limerick, ratifying William's victory, had promised equal treatment for Catholics. What followed instead was a series of draconian laws calculated to extinguish the language and cultural identity of the conquered. The Education Act, the Banishment Act, the Registration Act and the Act for the Further Preventing the Growth of Popery left Catholics barred from public office, forbidden from buying land or horses and from carrying arms, prohibited from entering higher education in Ireland or abroad and facing punitive restrictions on trading and commercial activities. By 1728 Catholics had lost the right to vote and had seen their bishops and priests sent into exile. Use of the Irish language was forbidden in the transaction of public business.

PROLOGUE

The irony – and the thread that connects this distant history to the present – was that Ulster's Protestant community never felt secure in its conquest. Instead, it cast itself as a beleaguered minority in defence of 'King Billy's' victory – a mindset it has held on to during subsequent centuries and that is visibly expressed each summer during the so-called marching season. Founded in 1795 in Armagh, the exclusively Protestant Orange Order set as its lodestar hostility to Catholicism in all its forms. A vigorous defender of Protestant privilege, it was proud of its sectarianism. Its marches in celebration of William's defeat of James II captured the emerging mindset of a community that saw itself forever under siege. Known officially as the Loyal Orange Institution, it was prominent in its attacks on the nationalist Daniel O'Connell's campaign for Catholic emancipation during the 1820s. Its lodges became bastions of Protestant supremacy. Religion and loyalty to the monarch, Protestantism and unionism were inextricably joined. Two centuries later, Northern Ireland's unionists still play the same pipes and drums as they march each summer in celebration of their Britishness. They struggle still to grasp just how un-British this seems to those living in the rest of the United Kingdom.

The fight for independence that began with the Easter Rising of 1916 was a Catholic as much as a Gaelic revolution. But Irish nationalism had had its Protestant heroes. The Anglo-Irish aristocracy, descendants of the earlier generations of much wealthier settlers and inclined when left to themselves to reach rough-and-ready accommodations with the Gaelic chieftains, often had their own quarrels with English rule. Few stand taller than Theobald Wolfe Tone in the front rank of Irish nationalists. In 1791 he published a celebrated pamphlet, *An Argument on Behalf of the Catholics of Ireland*, calling for the restoration of Catholic, and Irish, political rights. Wolfe Tone was a well-to-do Protestant barrister practising in Dublin. A few years later, his United Irishmen led an abortive uprising against British rule, recruiting for a time disenchanted Presbyterians to the cause. Tone now takes a place in the pantheon of nationalists alongside O'Connell, the much-revered leader who mobilised Catholic Ireland to secure the vote a quarter of a century later.

The Great Famine of the 1840s is the event forever seared in the Irish memory. It was felt above all by the poor Catholic farmers of the west – descendants of those displaced from the richer lands of the north-east by Cromwell's Protestant plantations. What ensured that the blight of the potato crop would be a catastrophe of extraordinary magnitude was the callous indifference of Ireland's masters. Lord Russell's Whig government in London worried more about the financial health of the Exchequer than the fate of poor Irish farmers. On its instruction the export trade in corn and other cash crops from Ireland continued undisturbed even as many of the country's workers starved. Charles Trevelyan, the civil servant who headed the Treasury, spoke for an English, Protestant establishment that seemed to revel in Irish hardship. The judgement of God had sent the calamity as a lesson. To offer help would be to create the moral hazard that held that the state should be held responsible for natural misfortune. It helped, of course, that English bigotry protected the Exchequer's funds. The famine's dismissal as divine providence claimed a million lives to starvation and disease and forced up to two million souls to flee Ireland, largely for the United States. It is hard to imagine anything that could have been more calculated to fill to the brim the reservoir of Irish rebellion.

It fell to Charles Stewart Parnell, born into a wealthy Protestant family near Rathdrum, County Wicklow, to thrust the Irish question into the heart of British politics at Westminster and set in train the upheavals that would eventually force retreat. When the Liberal William Ewart Gladstone became prime minister in

1868, he promised to 'pacify' Ireland. He is remembered now as the champion of Irish Home Rule. Parnell forced the about-turn by binding the grievances of impoverished Catholic farmers to the middle-class cause of self-government for Dublin. A brilliant parliamentarian – his tactics brought the House of Commons to a standstill – Parnell was eventually laid low by a scandal surrounding an extra-marital affair. But the demand for a measure of Irish independence now burned bright in Ireland's political firmament. By the time he left the stage during the 1890s, the country was rediscovering its Irishness, as social and political – as much as economic – nationalism took hold. This flowering of Gaelic culture and tradition among a new generation of writers and poets at the turn of the twentieth century celebrated a distinctly Catholic Irishness. The revolutionaries who grew up alongside them did the same. The political and the confessional cleavages fused to make Irish nationalism an indisputably Catholic enterprise. In the reflection of the writer and politician Conor Cruise O'Brien, 'He [Parnell] was the Protestant leader of a Catholic people.'[4]

English disregard for the Irish has been a constant. Often it has seemed the English know less about Ireland than about distant colonies on the other side of the world. For the British, occupying Ireland was first a straightforward act of territorial expansion and later a matter of strategic calculation. Whenever it seemed a threat, English armies responded by creating Irish martyrs. Ireland's misfortunes under British rule were existential, measured by the flight abroad of its people. On the eve of the Great Famine, the population of the island's thirty-two counties was estimated at a fraction below 8.2 million. By the time of the last all-Ireland census in 1911, emigration had cut the number to 4.4 million. Ireland's economic fortunes, political freedoms, confessional choices and cultural identity were subject to edicts promulgated in London. All the while, the attitude of the British ruling classes veered between ignorance, irritation and indifference.

Yet enmity did not suffocate intimacy. Told by the diplomat Dulanty why de Valera was absenting himself from his coronation, King George remained comfortable enough in the Irishman's company to unburden his own dread of the ceremony:

> How would you like to pass through throngs of people for four and a half hours and to know that all the time thousands and thousands of people were staring at you. Hang it, you can't keep smiling all the time . . . As I said to my wife, all that is to happen throughout this long ceremony happens to me – everybody else gets off scot free. I have to dress and undress three times.[5]

Winston Churchill's legendary shifts in mood spoke to such contradictions. During the Boer War he was lavish in his praise of the fighting spirit of the Irish recruits to the British army. Serving in David Lloyd George's cabinet a dozen or so years later, he was unrepentant in his determination to crush republicanism. That was not to say he was an enemy of Ireland, though. As he told a pro-Home Rule rally in Belfast in 1912: 'History and poetry, justice and good sense, alike demand that this race, gifted, virtuous and brave, which has lived so long and endured so much should not, in view of her passionate desire, be shut out of the family of nations.' The contradictions were not all on the English side. Scotland joined the United Kingdom out of economic calculation, and retained its own customs, laws and culture. Ireland was forced into the union by the English with the purpose of suppressing Irishness. Yet many enterprising Irishmen went on to make their fortunes in the far-flung outposts of the British Empire. Many more were eager recruits to the imperial army. Even as Casement disembarked from a German submarine and Patrick Pearse led republican Volunteers in the seizure of

PROLOGUE

Dublin's General Post Office in 1916, tens of thousands of Irish soldiers were fighting against the Germans on Europe's Western Front. The government in London twice considered and, sensibly, then thought better of introducing conscription in Ireland, but between 1914 and 1918 an estimated 200,000 Irish men – the majority of them Catholics from the south – did not need to be told to join the British in the trenches. Nor did neutrality during the Second World War stop up to two hundred thousand young Irishmen from crossing to Britain, some to sign on for the army, others to fill the vacancies in British factories left by English conscription. With the return of peace in 1945, young women filled the boats crossing the Irish Sea, seeking a better life in Britain. The creation of the Free State in 1922 gave nationalists free rein to pursue the Arcadian Ireland of de Valera's project. Irishness, the Chief would discover, did not feed the people. There was nothing bucolic about the rural dereliction visited on Ireland during the post-war decades.

For their part, the English could never resist the temptation to supply republicanism with the martyrs it craved. The summary execution of the leaders of the 1916 Easter Rising, turning an unpopular rebellion to a sacred affirmation of Irish nationhood, was testimony to how little the English had learned. For Lloyd George's government, the partition of the island, the starting point for this book, was meant to draw a line under the Irish question. Instead, it provided half an answer. Britain's politicians judged that they had broken free from an issue that had poisoned Westminster politics for decades. The Irish henceforth could solve their own problems. Republicanism, though denied the full sovereignty demanded by Pearse's revolutionaries, was given the platform from which to achieve it – in the words of Michael Collins, the freedom to win freedom. Unionists were handed their Protestant fortress. The tragedy was that all three sides would later misread the settlement's meaning.

The British assumed they could wash their hands of responsibility for the systematic repression of Northern Ireland's Catholics. The price of neglect was the outbreak of the Troubles. Irish leaders were blind to the reality that Northern Ireland was a unionist enterprise, born as much of Protestant fear of English betrayal as antipathy towards Catholics. Ireland's leaders insisted partition was a British choice that had to be undone by Britain. Yet in building their own staunchly Catholic state in the south they gave succour to the unionist case for separation. For their part, unionists assumed they forever deserved the protection of the United Kingdom, but were never to be told what to do by a British government.

The 1998 Good Friday Agreement, eloquent testimony to the fact that, with the right circumstances and the right political leaders, the intractable can be made tractable, was in good part a reversal of these historic misjudgements. The British government abandoned once and for all the fiction that, as for Scotland or Wales, the affairs of Northern Ireland were the exclusive preserve of the United Kingdom. The Republic acknowledged that Irish unity was not in Britain's gift. A united island, it agreed, required the backing of the people of Northern Ireland. Unionists finally agreed to share power.

The accord was never going to erase the anger, resentments and mistrust of the past. It was an armistice as much as a peace. The queen's visit to Dublin, however, spurred a reasonable hope that the passage of time would apply its balm. The close Anglo-Irish cooperation that had brought an end to Northern Ireland's sectarian violence would allow for a period of stability. As a modern, economically vibrant European nation, Ireland no longer defined its identity by the grievances of history. Shared membership of the European Union recalibrated the relationship. As for eventual union, why hurry things? A government in Dublin rhetorically committed but pragmatically ambivalent showed no inclination to force the pace. There was no need to rush deciding between whether Northern Ireland was content to remain a part of the United Kingdom or whether fading memories and an economic logic mapped the path to a united Ireland.

Such calculations were thrown into the air by Brexit. The British decision to leave the European Union at once loosened the constitutional bonds of the United Kingdom, injected new tensions into Anglo-Irish relations and jeopardised the delicate political balance between unionist and nationalist identities that had been embedded in the Good Friday Agreement. Brexit confronted unionism with the exceptionalism it had long disavowed. The post-Brexit trade deal struck with Brussels by Boris Johnson's government promulgated one set of rules for mainland Britain and another for Northern Ireland. Faced with a choice, a Westminster government again elevated what it saw as the interests of Britain – in Johnson's case, England – above those of the province. The Conservatives still styled themselves as unionists, but had reinvented themselves as the party of English nationalism.

The political leaders of Fianna Fáil and Fine Gael, the two governing parties that emerged from independence, always found it easier to frame unity as an aspiration rather than a tangible goal. It was simpler to make the case for Irish unity than try to achieve it. The dislocation of Brexit and the emergence of Sinn Féin as a powerful political force in both Northern Ireland and the Republic gave the issue a new immediacy. The answer to the Irish question, however, has remained elusive. The nationalist leaders who won independence for the south and the unionists who walled off the island's north-eastern corner would not recognise today's Ireland. The inward-looking, rural, intensely Catholic state built by Éamon de Valera has made way for a prosperous, internationalist and increasingly secular society. The walls of the fortress established by the Protestant leader Edward Carson have fallen. Unionist hegemony was broken by the Good Friday Agreement, and Protestants are now outnumbered by Catholics. What's missing is a sense of what might replace the settlement enshrined in the 1921 Anglo-Irish Treaty.

The distinguished Irish historian F. S. L. Lyons observed that to understand the past is to cease to live in it. To understand Anglo-Irish relations during the past century is to take several lessons, some already learned, some still to be properly absorbed. Though sovereignty still resides exclusively with Britain, for the foreseeable future the governance of Northern Ireland will remain to all intents and purposes a joint enterprise. For the future, whatever the constitutional path taken by the province, whether continued separation, unification or something in between, Britain cannot simply walk away from its responsibility. A couple of generations of peace will not wash away centuries of accumulated resentments. For nationalism to think unity requires only a narrow majority of voters in the north would be to risk piling new grievances on old. If the island of Ireland is to prosper in peace and security, there can be no 'victory' of one community over another. The beginning of understanding the events of the past century is to recognise that it is much easier to imagine a united Ireland than to design such a state.

1 A DIVIDED PEACE

There was a theatrical quality to the ultimatum issued by David Lloyd George. The new parliament in Belfast was to reconvene the following day. A Royal Navy frigate, the prime minister told his interlocutors, was standing by to take news of the outcome of their deliberations to the unionist government. After months of arguing, the choice the prime minister presented to the republican negotiators in Downing Street was between accepting the accord before them or bearing responsibility for the 'terrible war' Britain would otherwise unleash within days to crush their rebellion. At a little after 2 a.m. on 6 December 1921, the Sinn Féin delegation of Arthur Griffith, Michael Collins, Eamonn Duggan, George Gavan Duffy and Robert Barton signed the articles of agreement for a treaty between Britain and Ireland. The war that had begun nearly three years earlier when Volunteers of the Irish Republican Army had launched a lethal attack on the police in Soloheadbeg, County Tipperary, was over.

When the Downing Street conference had first met in October, the prime minister's officials had set a wide table between the two delegations. They were fearful of embarrassment should one of the attending British ministers refuse to extend a hand to the leaders of what they regarded as a lawless insurrection. Now, the seven-strong British side – counting among them Austen Chamberlain and Winston Churchill – walked around to clasp hands with the leaders of a new Irish state. Lloyd George had almost certainly been bluffing. He had indeed promised to send an update on the progress of the talks to the Ulster leader James Craig. He had played his hand skilfully – even to the point of drafting a statement explaining the breakdown of the talks. The Irish side, this said, had presented to the British 'proposals which would break the empire in pieces, dislocate society in all its self-governing nations and cancel forever the hope of national unity in Ireland itself'.[1] But there was no immutable deadline. Rather, Lloyd George considered he had exhausted his political room for compromise. The ultimatum was a last throw.

The rock-strewn path to the treaty and the partition of Ireland was marked out with blood, prejudice, political opportunism and deception, culminating in the armed uprising that began in Limerick. Peace had taken its time. The Tory statesman Benjamin Disraeli had defined the challenge in 1844, during a speech to the House of Commons on the eve of the Great Famine:

> A dense population, in extreme distress, inhabit an island where there is an Established Church, which is not their Church, and a territorial aristocracy, the richest of whom live in foreign capitals. Thus you have a starving population, an absentee aristocracy, and an alien Church; and in addition the weakest executive in the world. That is the Irish Question.

The Liberal statesman William Gladstone had tried to offer an answer with his proposals during the 1880s for Home Rule. His premiership had been broken by the endeavour.

The promise of the treaty was to set both nations free – the twenty-six counties of the Free State from seven centuries of violent repression; and the British from the disruptive intrusion into the affairs of the empire that came with ruling a nation that did not want them. Partition, its authors hoped, would draw a line not just across Ireland but under a conflict Britain had come to understand it could not win. The new Northern Ireland's place in the United Kingdom would be unique: separated but attached, Irish but still

British. For Michael Collins, the military commander of the IRA Volunteers whose war had brought Lloyd George's coalition government to the negotiating table, the treaty was an imperfect outcome, but one that put Ireland on the path to the freedom it craved. Lloyd George's adviser Philip Kerr caught the British mood when he remarked that the agreement would achieve two vital objectives: 'It would take Ulster out of the Irish question which it has blocked for a generation and it would take Ireland out of English party controversies.'[2] For the following half-century, Kerr might have argued he had been right. But then, as Northern Ireland fell to violent conflict, it was revealed as a truce rather than a peace.

For Irish nationalism, the loss of most of Ulster was proof of immutable English perfidy. The very existence of Northern Ireland (unionists would have preferred to call it Ulster) was a baleful reminder of the legacy of colonisation. But then for Lloyd George's government, partition was not so much a principled plan as another chapter in the narrative of political expediency that guided British policy towards Ireland. It was shaped by English politics rather than Irish geography. The bargain fell far short of the republicans' aspirations for an independent, sovereign and united Ireland because a British prime minister considered that Dominion status within the empire for the twenty-six counties was as much as he could offer the revolutionaries without forcing a confrontation with Craig's unionists and provoking the collapse of his own coalition government. If Collins would characterise the treaty as a stepping stone to full nationhood, for Britain's ruling class it was counted as a blessed release.

The Government of Ireland Act that had been passed into law by Herbert Asquith's Liberal government seven years earlier had for a moment seemed to map a political accommodation between London and Dublin. Asquith had succeeded where Gladstone had failed in piloting through the Westminster parliament an arrangement to reconcile Irish demands for self-government with the British imperative that Ireland remain within the family of the empire. In truth, the plan for a new Dublin parliament that kept Ireland firmly within the bounds of the empire was always set to fail. As so often in the history of Anglo-Irish relations, the terms of the proposed settlement were crafted without reference to political realities in Ireland. What might have met the demands of the celebrated Irish nationalist Charles Stewart Parnell during the 1880s had been overtaken by events. As it turned out, the onset of war with the Kaiser in 1914 ensured the attempt to implement Asquith's plan would be suspended for the duration of hostilities with Germany. But anyway it was out of time. Falling short of the aspirations of nationalism, it was also anathema to a Protestant population in the north-east that had circled the wagons of implacable unionism against any accommodation with the Catholic south. John Redmond, the leader of the constitutional nationalists in the Irish Parliamentary Party (IPP), had acquiesced in Asquith's plan, albeit with great reluctance. Edward Carson, the fiery Dublin-born lawyer who dominated the unionist politics of the north during the decade after 1910, had railed against the act as 'a sentence of death with a stay of execution'.

Lloyd George's peace treaty was nothing if not true to the organising impulse of British, or more accurately English, attitudes to Ireland: the balance of interests and votes at Westminster took precedence over the force or the justice of any of the arguments heard in Ireland itself. Gladstone's attempts to deliver a measure of self-government had foundered in the face of Conservative hostility and divisions in his own party between Home Rulers and self-proclaimed Liberal unionists who shared Tory fears that concessions to Irish nationalism would strike at Britain's global standing. In

1895 Gladstone's departure saw the Liberals swept from office by Lord Salisbury's Conservatives. Parnell's IPP, which for a decade had contrived to set the agenda of politics at Westminster, fractured. Disgraced by public disclosure of an affair with the married Kitty O'Shea, Parnell died prematurely in 1891. Robbed of its charismatic leader, the party fell into internal squabbles.

For a handful of Conservatives, opposition to Irish Home Rule reflected family background, typically infused with visceral disdain for the native Irish. Andrew Bonar Law, who led the party's battle against Asquith's Home Rule bill, hailed from a staunchly unionist family. He belonged to those who shared the opinion of the writer and historian James Anthony Froude that the fault in Ireland lay in the deeply flawed character of the Irish people: 'a race which seemed incurable', as Froude put it. Others in the party were driven by a broader but deep-seated anti-Catholic prejudice. What pulled the various factions together was the wider fear, shared by Liberal Party unionists and heightened by the Boer rebellion in southern Africa, that concessions to Irish nationalism would signal weakness. The loss of Ireland, they concluded, would risk the unravelling of Britain's great empire. What clinched the argument was cynical electoral calculation. 'Ulster will fight, and Ulster will be right': Randolph Churchill's notorious unionist rallying cry against Irish nationalism in 1886 had owed nothing to political principle. The purpose was to destabilise Gladstone. So it was with Tory backing for Carson's insurrection against Asquith's plan thirty years later. Leading a party that had been divided by arguments about imperial trade preferences and protectionism, Bonar Law saw a way to cement at once his own position and force the Liberals from office. Political calculation counted above the risk of civil war in Ireland.

For a short period after Parnell's death, it seemed Ireland might slip back into the shadows of British political life. The respite was illusory. While Britain looked away, the nationalist cause was gaining force. Parnell's campaign had harnessed to nationalism the deep resentments of the Catholic majority at punitive landownership and tenancy laws. His cause was essentially economic. The intention was that a Home Rule parliament would offer continued allegiance to the British Crown. Irish control of domestic affairs would thus do nothing to undermine the empire's authority over foreign and defence matters, trade and, ultimately, economic policy. As the Victorian made way for the Edwardian age, however, the world was changing. Irish nationalism took on a more radical hue. Parnell had spoken to the need for constitutional adjustments. The new nationalism tapped deeper emotions, rooted in tradition, language and culture. The cultural renaissance that spilled over from the 1890s into the opening decade of the twentieth century called for Ireland to recover its Celtic character. In the description of William Butler Yeats, this 'modern literature of Ireland, and indeed all that stir of thought which prepared for the Anglo-Irish war, began when Parnell fell from power'.[3] The rise of this political nationalism had been prefigured in the inaugural speech delivered by the first president of the Conradh na Gaeilge, or Gaelic League, in 1892. Douglas Hyde, who decades later would become Ireland's first president, set as his text 'The Necessity of De-Anglicising the Irish Nation'. His particular passion was the reinstatement of Gaelic as the national language, but de-Anglicising also meant the restoration of Irish music, literature and dance. A generation of Irish writers, poets and playwrights rose to the ambition. The Gaelic Athletic Association (GAA), founded in 1884, set itself the same nationalist ambition, promoting traditional sports such as Gaelic football and hurling over the English imports of cricket, soccer and rugby. Unashamedly discriminatory, the GAA barred from membership anyone who also bowled a cricket ball or pulled on a rugby shirt. The mission of the celebrated Abbey Theatre, founded by Yeats and the folklorist Isabella Augusta, Lady Gregory, was 'to bring upon the stage the deeper emotions of Ireland'.

Gaelic was the language of only a small minority, particularly in cosmopolitan Dublin. Yeats wrote his poetry in English. For all that, the capital's bustling literary salons and theatres were the crucible for a sharper definition of Irish identity. Culture acted in turn as a recruiting sergeant for the radical republican societies that sought the physical overthrow of British rule. Éamon de Valera, Michael Collins and Patrick Pearse were among the many future revolutionary leaders who as young men held membership cards for the Gaelic League. They and others drew inspiration from the Young Ireland movement, which had staged an abortive rebellion when much of Europe turned to revolution in 1848. In its aftermath, the Irish Republican Brotherhood (IRB) and its allies among the Irish diaspora in the United States, the Fenian Brotherhood and Clan na Gael, staged sporadic attempts at uprisings. After the collapse of Parnell's Home Rule plans, they were joined by other secret societies and paramilitary groups, including the Irish Citizen Army and the women's militia Cumann na mBan. By the time the writer and newspaper editor Arthur Griffith founded Sinn Féin (Ourselves Alone) in 1905, nationalist ambitions had made way for violent republicanism.

Asquith's plan was no longer enough for Irish nationalism and too much for Protestant unionism. In Ulster traditional unionism merged with the militant loyalism of the Orange Order. For Edward Carson, the establishment of an Irish parliament, even one within the bounds of empire, was the beginning of an inevitable slide to republican, and Catholic, rule. The tens of thousands who dressed up in their Sunday finery to march every July in celebration of William of Orange's victory over James II judged power transferred to Dublin as power surrendered to Rome. Nationalism and popery were indivisible. Protestants, under Asquith's plan, would soon be ruled by Catholics. The confessional divide was entrenched by contrasting economic fortunes. The most important economic event in the south during the previous century had been the death and depopulation wrought by the Great Famine. The north, and Belfast in particular, had prospered greatly from Britain's Industrial Revolution, sharing in the manufacturing and trade boom that came with the expansion of empire. By the turn of the twentieth century Protestants counted for barely 10 per cent of the population in the three ancient provinces of the largely agrarian south. In the nine counties of Ulster they measured half.

The unionists' anti-Catholic fervour joined with deep mistrust of the United Kingdom government to which they formally pledged allegiance. In 1911 fifty thousand gathered to listen to Carson's fiery rhetoric at the Craigavon estate of fellow unionist James Craig. If Asquith pressed ahead, Carson declared, unionism would take control of the 'Government of the Protestant Province of Ulster'. The threat was made explicit in September of the same year, when Ulster was brought to a standstill for the public signing of a 'Solemn League and Covenant'. Some 470,000 Protestants put their name to the pledge to use 'all means which may be found necessary' to preserve Ulster's place within the United Kingdom – even if that meant defying the parliament of that same United Kingdom. Backing the pledge, Charles Frederick D'Arcy, a bishop in the Church of Ireland, acknowledged the inherent contradiction: 'We hold that no power, not even the British Parliament, has the right to deprive us of our heritage of British citizenship.'[4] Within a year the unionists had armed a ninety-thousand-strong Ulster Volunteer Force (UVF).

The unionists had friends in the highest ranks of the Tory party. Its leaders looked the other way as guns – twenty-five thousand rifles and five million rounds of ammunition – were shipped into the north from the Kaiser's Germany to arm the UVF. Determined to oust Asquith, Bonar Law was unperturbed by this threat to overturn Britain's constitutional order. For the Tory leader what mattered was that Ireland promised to bind the wounds of division in his party over imperial trade preferences. Carson had allies too in the senior ranks of the army. When Asquith's government considered sending in troops to confront the unionist militias, British officers at the Curragh barracks in County Kildare all but mutinied. They threatened to resign their commissions rather than march north to face down the UVF. The officers found a powerful sponsor in General Henry Wilson, the army's director of military operations and a future chief of the imperial staff. Wilson, whose family boasted an ancestor who had arrived in Antrim with William of Orange, conspired openly with Carson and the UVF. He would later boast that 'we soldiers beat Asquith and his vile tricks'. When Lloyd George called the truce with the republicans in 1921, Wilson accused him of 'rank, filthy cowardice'.[5]

Shocking as Bonar Law's backing for an armed coup against the elected government was, the Conservatives were not alone in putting politics before principle. When Asquith first reached Downing Street in 1908 he showed little interest in reviving his party's support for Home Rule. It took electoral arithmetic to bring a change of heart. After a series of bruising encounters with the Tory-dominated House of Lords and a failed gamble on a general election, by 1910 he found himself dependent for his House of Commons majority on the votes of the seventy-odd MPs of the IPP, now under the leadership of John Redmond. Reviving the deal Gladstone had struck with the nationalists was a matter of simple political expediency: Home Rule in return for the Irish votes at Westminster that would allow him to break the stranglehold on his government exercised by a Tory-dominated House of Lords. It was too late, though, for half measures.

The rebellion that began on Easter Monday 1916 would enter Irish history as a daring revolutionary act that read the rites over seven centuries of British oppression. It seemed otherwise at the time. The occupation of Dublin's General Post Office and several other buildings in the centre of the capital had been planned by the Irish Volunteers, effectively the military wing of the IRB, as part of a nationwide uprising. Alongside the Irish Citizens' Army, the trade-union-based militia led by James Connolly, and the women of the republican Cumann na mBan, the rebellion was planned to inflict a decisive blow on British rule. The Volunteers were republicanism's answer to Carson's Ulster militia. The operation's planning, however, fell foul of disputes about strategy within the republican leadership. On the very eve of the uprising, local commanders across the country were ordered by the movement's political leadership to stand down. Radicals led by Patrick Pearse pressed ahead.

The proclamation of the Republic was read by Pearse on the steps of the Post Office on Easter Monday. It allowed no doubt as to its revolutionary intent:

> In the name of God and of the dead generations from which she receives her old tradition of nationhood, Ireland, through us, summons her children to her flag and strikes for her freedom . . . [We] hereby proclaim the Irish Republic as a Sovereign Independent State, and we pledge our lives and the lives of our comrades in arms to the cause of its freedom, of its welfare, and of its exaltation among the nations.

A DIVIDED PEACE

Pearse was declared the first president of the Provisional Republic and some 2,500 printed copies of the proclamation were distributed around the capital. But save for sporadic attacks by Volunteers on police stations and public buildings in the rest of the country, the 1,500 fighters in Dublin found themselves alone. They held their positions for a week against overwhelmingly superior British forces, countering heavy artillery with rifles and home-made bombs. The eventual surrender was inevitable. For all the cordite, in the phrase of historian Roy Foster, the rebellion had been the work of 'a minority of a minority'. Initially, the national mood reflected this. Opinion was largely critical. The *Irish Independent*, a pro-Home Rule newspaper, spoke for the nationalists among Dublin's middle classes when it said that the rebellion had 'not a shred of public sympathy'. Under the headline 'Criminal Madness', its editorial declared that 'no terms of denunciation ... would be too strong to apply to those responsible for the insane and criminal rising of last week'. The rebels, it continued, were 'willing dupes' of Prussian plotting, 'out, not to free Ireland, but to help Germany'.[6]

It fell to the British to turn military victory into political defeat. That the uprising was soon written indelibly into Ireland's nationalist folklore was due for the most part to the British government's summary response once the rebels had been bombed into surrender. After a series of brief court martials, dozens of the leaders faced a sentence of execution. Some three thousand suspects were arrested and many of them were sent to England for internment. Michael Collins was among those who found himself in a prison camp only recently vacated by German prisoners of war. On the orders of Sir John Maxwell, at the head of British forces in Ireland, fifteen rebels, including the commandant Pearse, were summarily shot. They included the seven signatories to the proclamation: Thomas J. Clarke, Seán MacDiarmada, P. H. Pearse, James Connolly, Thomas

MacDonagh, Éamonn Ceannt and Joseph Plunkett. The hanging of Roger Casement, the celebrated Anglo-Irish diplomat who had tried and failed to recruit the Kaiser to the republican cause and been apprehended after landing on the west coast by way of a German submarine, followed a few months later.

The execution of the rebel leaders was met with an international outcry, with British diplomats in Washington reporting deep dismay in President Woodrow Wilson's administration. By the time Lloyd George's government responded by commuting the remaining death sentences, it was too late. Irish nationalism had been gifted another set of martyrs. The 'blood sacrifice' had long held a special place in the nationalist cause. Now it was fixed front and centre. And the republicans were adept propagandists. The proclamation became a sacred text, setting armed defiance – and willing martyrdom – as the unavoidable route to the restoration of Ireland's liberties and nationhood. Some 485 died during the uprising, including 64 of the rebels and 116 soldiers on the British side. The rest were civilians caught in the crossfire. It was the executions that changed everything. The prominent MP John Dillon, a champion of the peaceful transition to self-government favoured by the Irish Parliamentary Party, rose in the House of Commons to accuse the government of 'washing out our whole life work in a sea of blood'. For Yeats, the killing of the rebel leaders unleashed an irresistible force:

> Now and in time to be,
> Wherever green is worn,
> All changed, changed utterly:
> A terrible beauty is born.

The impact was momentous, transforming the framing of the nationalist cause in Ireland's public mind. Dillon's constitutional nationalism was elbowed aside by revolutionary republicanism that demanded a complete break with the British colonialists. The economic nationalism of the Home Rulers was replaced by the more powerful emotional pull of a republicanism rooted in Celtic identity and Catholicism. God was on the side of the rebels. The republicans coalesced around Sinn Féin, the organisation established a decade earlier by Arthur Griffith. Griffith, an intellectual, had previously championed the idea of a joint Anglo-Irish monarchy modelled on the Habsburg arrangement for the Austro-Hungarian Empire. Leadership of the new movement fell to Éamon de Valera. Alone among the Easter Rising's senior commanders in escaping execution, de Valera became president of both Sinn Féin and the Volunteers, the latter soon to become the Irish Republican Army. General Maxwell was among those who belatedly recognised the wider impact of the retribution he had exacted. 'There has been a growing feeling that out of rebellion more has been got than by constitutional methods,' he reported to London. 'It is becoming increasingly difficult to differentiate between a Nationalist and a Sinn Féiner.'[7]

Just as the Easter Rising replaced constitutional with revolutionary politics, it sealed the essentially Catholic nature of nationalism. The Catholic Church hierarchy's immediate response to the seizure of the Post Office reflected Rome's reflex fear of all revolutionary movements. The Church, an essentially conservative institution, leant towards authoritarianism. The Vatican instructed the Irish bishops to cooperate in the restoration of civil order. The archbishop of Armagh and primate of all Ireland Cardinal Michael Logue telegraphed reassurance to Rome: 'Insurrection happily terminated. Insurgents have surrendered unconditionally. Hope peace soon reestablished.'[8] Younger priests, and particularly those serving rural parishes in the west of the country, took a more sympathetic view of the rebels. Pearse understood the importance of attaching faith to the independence cause. The Provisional Government's proclamation placed 'the cause of the Irish Republic under the protection of the Most High God'. The rebels had worn their piety on their sleeves. Austere and authoritarian, de Valera, it would later be said, was never more comfortable than when in the company of priests. In many local churches those executed were all but canonised. Maxwell caught the change in the wind, lamenting the ubiquity of 'mourning badges, Sinn Féin flags, demonstrations at requiem masses'.[9] The rising was bound into the public consciousness as what Roy Foster called a 'sacrificial insurrection', appropriating the iconography and mysticism of Catholicism. Ireland's demand was for a sovereign and Catholic state.

The Liberal David Lloyd George, who from 1916 replaced Asquith as leader of Britain's wartime coalition with the Conservatives, hoped at first that the Irish question would go away. The empire was engaged in an existential struggle with Germany. Hundreds of thousands were dying on the Western Front. Ireland could surely look after itself? Carson had joined the coalition. The nationalist Redmond urged the young men of Ireland to join the English in the fight against Germany. In 1914 the government briefly considered extending conscription to Ireland. They then forgot about it. The historian Ronan Fanning counted only one substantial cabinet discussion about Ireland during the fourteen months from January 1917 to March 1918.[10] Such was the distance between the thinking in London and the realities in Ireland that in the early months of 1918 the prime minister returned to the idea of compulsory conscription to make up for troop shortfalls on the Western Front. The public furore hardened further the rising support for republicanism, and Lloyd George backed down. The rude political awakening, though, came soon after the Armistice in the general election of December 1918. The results at once buried constitutional nationalism and in British minds determined that, whatever the arrangement offered to Irish republicanism, it would exclude the Protestants of Ulster.

Sinn Féin, on a platform demanding full Irish sovereignty, took seventy-three Westminster seats, many of them won by candidates in prison or on the run. Redmond's constitutional nationalists were left with only six. Unionists claimed twenty-three, concentrated in Ulster. Lloyd George returned to Downing Street as leader of the Liberal–Conservative coalition. His victory, however, disguised a sweeping shift in the balance of power. Strong Tory gains and steep Liberal losses meant that, de facto, it was now a Conservative–Liberal alliance. Two-thirds of the MPs upon whom Lloyd George depended to stay in Number 10 were Tories. In the biting description of the press baron Lord Beaverbrook, he was a prime minister without a party. The corollary for the Irish question was that he could do nothing without the support of a partner that, during the fight over Home Rule, had rechristened itself the Conservative and Unionist Party.

Lloyd George's abiding preoccupation was self-preservation. His character was well suited to the task. The prime minister was as supple a politician as there was to be found. His political fortunes had been built on ruthless opportunism. During the 1912 Home Rule crisis he had been among the first in the cabinet to press Asquith to recognise that an Irish settlement would require separate terms for the unionists. Now prime minister, he had no love for Carson's party. His private secretary Thomas Jones recorded in his diary that Lloyd George considered unionists as 'pugnacious' and 'stubborn'. They were not to be counted in terms of loyalty alongside the English, Welsh and Scots. 'We [the British] are only behind them to the extent that we cannot allow civil war to take place at our door which will embroil our own people.'[11] And behind them,

Jones might have added, in order to keep the Tories inside the coalition and Lloyd George in Downing Street. Whatever the forces for change in Ireland, his priority as prime minister was to manage the politics of his government. Ireland had broken Gladstone, and Lloyd George did not intend to see history repeat itself. Much later, the politician and writer Roy Hattersley offered a succinct assessment: Pitt, Peel and Gladstone tried and failed to do what was right; Lloyd George achieved what he deemed to be possible.

Ireland was in no mood to wait. Elected with a promise to boycott Westminster, the new Sinn Féin MPs gathered instead at Dublin's Mansion House for the opening of Ireland's own parliament, Dáil Éireann. Republicans then set about laying the foundations for their own state. Defiance of the British authorities bled into armed ambushes of the Royal Irish Constabulary and the requisitioning of public buildings in towns across the country. Sprung from his cell in Lincoln jail and duly elected president of the Dáil, de Valera crossed the Atlantic to raise Irish American funds for the cause. Michael Collins took effective charge of the IRA Volunteers to wage war on the agents – civilian as well as police and military – of the British state.

The international pressures on Lloyd George were powerful. In June 1919 the Treaty of Versailles sanctified the doctrine of national self-determination enunciated by US President Woodrow Wilson in his celebrated 'Fourteen Points' speech setting the framework for a new global order. The First World War had marked the beginning of the end of the age of sprawling empires. The Austro-Hungarian and Ottoman empires were being broken into new independent nations. Setting itself as the champion of democracy, Washington led the international chorus for decolonisation. Inconveniently, Britain's stubborn defence of its own empire collided with Wilson's clarion call for national self-government. Irish

Americans were assiduous political organisers. They translated a concentration of votes in a handful of north-eastern cities and states into significant clout in Congress. In Europe and the Middle East, populations were being moved across borders to create new, homogeneous sovereign states. For all that it was one of the victors of the war, Britain was not immune from the temper of the times.

Ireland had become a vital piece in the imperial chess game. In geographical spread, the British Empire had never reached further than during the early 1920s. Many of the colonies, however, chafed at British rule. In September 1920 India's nationalist leader Mahatma Gandhi called for a strategy of non-cooperation with the Raj. The Indian pro-independence movement announced a boycott of British goods. The nationalist cause in Ireland claimed its own international headlines. So did British efforts to quell the rebellion. The recruitment into the Royal Irish Constabulary of the so-called Black and Tans – an undisciplined force of demobbed soldiers – saw the British abandon traditional military restraint. Alongside a new Auxiliary Division, recruited from former officers in the British army, the strategy of the Black and Tans was to meet violence with more violence, terror with more terror. The arbitrary execution of suspected republican sympathisers became as commonplace as reprisals against innocent civilians after IRA attacks. 'We are getting an odious reputation,' the war minister Winston Churchill admitted, 'poisoning our relations with the United States.'[12] In October 1919 Lord Edward Grey, on temporary assignment as ambassador to the United States, telegraphed from Washington: 'In Anglo-American relations one comes on the Irish difficulty everywhere. It poisons the atmosphere. A statement of Irish policy on self-government lines is now very desirable.'[13]

Partition was never part of a grand design for a new constitutional settlement in Ireland. Rather, it was the product of the iterative effort to reconcile the competing demands of nationalism and unionism in a way that suited politicians at Westminster. Ultimately, it would represent in turn the sum of Liberal dependence on the votes of Irish nationalists, Conservative determination to use Ireland as a stick with which to beat the Liberals, the threat from unionists to take up arms in defence of Protestant rule, republican rebellion and British exhaustion. As early as 1912, some form of separation had begun to look like an unavoidable price for a settlement in the south. Churchill and Lloyd George had nudged Asquith towards partition. Carson's threat of open rebellion hardened the case. Asquith toyed initially with offering each of the nine counties of Ulster the right to opt out of Home Rule. Opposed as he had been to the establishment of any parliament in Dublin, Carson saw the creation of a Protestant citadel in the north-east of the island as a fallback. For his part, Asquith's assumption was that any division would be temporary – lasting perhaps six years. Militant unionism would not countenance anything but a permanent divide, but Redmond's Irish nationalists were assured by the prime minister that unity remained within their grasp. The assumption was that the passage of time, shared economic interest and the accretion of mutual trust would bring the two sides together. The *sine qua non* was that Ireland would remain within the bounds of the British Empire.

By 1920 all this had been rendered irrelevant by Sinn Féin's demand for an 'Irish Republic as a Sovereign Independent State'. That in turn hardened the resolve of unionists. Carson had friends in high places. The former prime minister and senior cabinet minister Arthur Balfour spoke for Tory diehards in Lloyd George's coalition when he contrasted a 'loyal and Protestant north' with the 'disloyal and Roman Catholic south'. Balfour's particular preference for full integration of Ulster into the United Kingdom was not widely shared, but for the partners in Lloyd George's coalition absolute guarantees for the unionists were by now non-negotiable.

Confronted with the competing demands, Lloyd George sought political cover by choosing Walter Long, a former leader of the Ulster unionists well trusted by the Conservatives, to chair the cabinet committee charged with navigating a course out of the quagmire. Its blueprint for a settlement, laid out in the 1920 Government of Ireland Act, would pay homage to the balance of power at Westminster. By appointing Long, Lloyd George had sought immunity against any charge of selling out to Irish nationalism. There was one proposition all sides could sign up to. They had for too long been prisoners of unrest in Ireland. Long's committee set as its organising ambition 'the complete withdrawal of British rule from all of Ireland in all measures not especially reserved'. In the historian Ronan Fanning's formulation, the goal was now to take Ireland out of British politics by taking Ulster out of the Irish question.[14]

The Ireland Act marked the decisive step in this direction. The legislation provided for two new parliaments, in Dublin and Belfast, empowered to oversee Ireland's domestic affairs. Six counties in Ulster – Antrim, Armagh, Down, Fermanagh, Derry and Tyrone – would continue to send thirteen MPs to Westminster. The nationalist-majority counties of Donegal, Cavan and Monaghan, with the blessing of Carson's unionists, would remain part of the south. The unionists now had their citadel. For how long? Until the Irish, north and south, agreed otherwise. The act made provision for an all-Ireland council as a pathway to eventual unity, but it would be for nationalists in the south to win over northern unionists to the idea. The assumption in London was that at some point they would succeed, but the act offered neither a timetable nor incentives. In truth, earlier assumptions of an all-Ireland settlement had all but evaporated. The six-year time limit on the life of the Belfast assembly envisaged by Asquith was no more. The future of the new Stormont assembly would be open-ended until the people of Northern Ireland decided otherwise. The principle of unionist 'consent' to political arrangements on the island of Ireland – and 'consent' was a word that would echo down the decades – had been set in legislative stone. Speaking in the House of Commons in December 1919, Carson declared the determination of unionists to ensure that such authority would never be offered: 'You cannot knock parliaments up and down as you do a ball, and once you have planted them there you cannot get rid of them.' When the Stormont parliament first met in the summer of 1921, one of the first acts of the unionist majority was to introduce measures to further entrench the Protestant hold on power. If the proposed Council of Ireland ever met, it would do so without the presence of unionists. The British had created the border but, in Fanning's telling phrase, 'The ending of partition would be a matter for the Irish.'[15]

Sinn Féin, waging an increasingly bloody insurgency, was not afforded a place in the British deliberations. It would have no truck with any arrangement that allowed the British to remain in the island of Ireland. Yet the nature of its military campaign reflected its own focus on winning the south. Northern Ireland faced escalating sectarian violence, with the bloodiest losses inflicted on Catholics by unionist militias. The Royal Irish Constabulary, responsible for keeping the peace, abandoned all pretence at even-handedness by recruiting directly from the ranks of the sectarian Ulster Volunteer Force. But the southern support for nationalists from the IRA was limited. Its operations in the north were less than spectacular, avoiding a head-to-head confrontation with loyalists. By contrast, republican attacks on the British were increasingly audacious. In

November 1920 the killing of fifteen suspected British intelligence agents in Dublin, which would become known as Bloody Sunday, was followed a week later by the ambush of a force of eighteen Auxiliary troops in Kilmichael, County Cork, and the next month by an attempt to assassinate Field Marshal Sir John French, the lieutenant general of Ireland.

The reports to the politicians from senior military commanders forever predicted victory around the next corner, even as they asked for more battalions and pressed for the widespread imposition of martial law to contain the insurrection. Lloyd George was momentarily persuaded. Speaking at London's Guildhall only weeks before the spectacular IRA strikes in November, he boasted that 'we have murder by the throat'. The reality was that the military campaign was being lost even as the generals insisted it could be won. The IRA's hit-and-run tactics – assassinations, raids on police and army posts, bank robberies – sapped the morale of the police. Under the overall command of Sir Henry Wilson, promoted to chief of the general staff, the response of the British was to tighten the screw of coercion. Martial law was imposed in the most troublesome counties. The lesson of the Easter Rising was ignored. Each time the British turned the ratchet of repression, they widened support for the rebels among local populations. Just as the shooting of the leaders of the 1916 rebellion provided the oxygen for revolutionary republicanism, reprisal killings of innocent civilians increased support for the IRA.

As the insurrection spilled over into 1921 it was irrefutably clear that Sinn Féin would never settle for the terms that had been offered to the constitutional nationalists in 1914. That version of Home Rule had left Ireland's foreign and defence policies entirely in Britain's hands, safeguarding its strategic interests and upholding the legitimacy of the empire. It was also evident that without wholesale slaughter, the uprising could not be put down.

Looking over his shoulder at the Tory diehards, Lloyd George edged towards compromise. The logical next step was to offer the republicans the Dominion status within the empire enjoyed by Canada, Australia and New Zealand. But how far could he go? Would Dublin, the prime minister worried, demand its own army and navy, the right to impose duties on imports of British goods, and establish its own diplomatic representation in Washington? And what about Ireland's harbours, vital to protect the Atlantic sea lanes and the waters around Great Britain in the event of war?[16] Peace would have to be on terms acceptable to his Tory cabinet colleagues and their unionist friends. The results of the first election to the new Belfast parliament in May 1921 spoke vividly to the new Protestant hegemony. The Ulster unionists, now under the leadership of James Craig, took forty of the northern assembly's fifty-two seats. The remainder fell to nationalists and republicans. In the elections in the south, Redmond's nationalists stood back. Unopposed, Sinn Féin won 124 of the 128 seats. The remaining four, reserved for the staunchly Protestant Trinity College, went to independent unionists. The sectarian line between north and south could scarcely have been more sharply drawn. Politically, however, this polarisation presented an opportunity. The challenge for Lloyd George was to strike a bargain with Irish nationalism that would at once satisfy Sinn Féin and win the acquiescence of northern unionism. The more unionists were assured of an iron grip on Stormont, the more room there was for the British government to reach an accommodation with nationalism.

That spring, the mood in the cabinet began to shift. A year before, Churchill had spoken confidently of crushing the rebels. Now, he edged towards conciliation. He was increasingly convinced that military victory was possible only at a terrible cost in blood and treasure. Britain's standing in the world would pay the price.

Having switched from the war ministry to become secretary of state for the colonies, he was conscious of the rising tide of international condemnation of British policy. By early summer he was in favour of a truce with the rebels. A readiness to negotiate with republicanism, he argued, would allow the government to take the moral high ground. And if talks broke down, the IRA would struggle to regain its military momentum. There was a softening too among senior Conservatives. A handful of diehards would never budge, but now unionism was safe, others began to doubt whether the victory promised by the military commanders would ever be possible. Jones, the prime minister's private secretary, noted in his diary that prominent Tories including Arthur Balfour, Austen Chamberlain and Lord Birkenhead had begun to recognise the realities. Bonar Law would never be reconciled – he thought the Irish an 'inferior race' – but others might be ready to put their hands in the blood of compromise. The key was a settlement that upheld the authority of the Crown. The king lent encouragement to the peacemakers. Delivering the opening address at the inauguration of the Stormont parliament in June 1921, George V noted that the 'eyes of the empire' were on Ireland. His call was for reconciliation. 'May this historic gathering be the prelude of a day in which the Irish people, North and South, under one parliament or two, as those parliaments may themselves decide, shall work together in common love for Ireland upon the sure foundations of mutual justice and respect.' His words, coordinated in advance with Downing Street, were followed on 11 July by a ceasefire.

Lloyd George's offer of talks with the republicans was carefully framed. The invitation to de Valera set out a process that would see Ireland 'take her place in the great association of free nations over which His Majesty reigns'.[17] Ireland, in other words, would remain within the imperial family. Restating republican demands for complete independence, de Valera protested that Britain sought to set aside partition as 'an accomplished fact'. There were deep suspicions among republicans as to the seriousness of British intent. The prime minister was facing difficult negotiations with Washington about naval disarmament. Harry Boland, a senior Sinn Féin representative in the US capital, wrote to de Valera of his impression that 'behind the overtures of Lloyd George there is an ulterior purpose':

> It might well be that England is endeavouring to create a favourable atmosphere here in America, and particularly in Washington, for the forthcoming disarmament parleys. It is not too much to assert that the English delegates would find it impossible to come to this conference if She had continued her bloody work in Ireland.

For all that, on 14 July the Sinn Féin president and republican fugitive crossed the threshold of Downing Street.[18] In the acid, private judgement of the prime minister, the British were confronting an 'uncompromising fanatic'.[19] Lloyd George was careful not to let his feelings show when de Valera arrived at Number 10. Instead, he recalled his own Welsh ancestry. In the description of his private secretary, Jones, 'Mr Lloyd George, never a greater artist than in the first moments of a fateful interview, received the Irish Chieftain cordially as a brother Celt.'[20]

De Valera laid out his demands in a letter sent to the prime minister the following month. The republic sought by Sinn Féin could be neither divided nor shackled by any association with Britain. 'Ireland's right to choose for herself the path she shall take to realise her own destiny must be accepted as indefeasible.' 'Amicable but absolute separation' was the only route to true friendship.[21] The chink of light from the British perspective was that de Valera would choose to absent himself from the face-to-face negotiations – delegating them to a team of plenipotentiaries led by Arthur Griffith and Michael Collins. Both men were implacable republicans. 'I am just a representative of plain Irish stock whose principles have been burned into them,' was Collins's self-description.[22] Neither, however, showed the same, almost mystical commitment as de Valera to an Ireland detached from all things British. The bargaining that followed saw Lloyd George deploy every ounce of the guile, charm and resilience to which he owed his political fortunes. Above all, in navigating the shoals between republicanism and unionism, the British side displayed a talent for calculated ambiguity.

The immoveable pillars of the British negotiating stance were that any new state would maintain constitutional ties to the empire and that Northern Ireland would be free to make its own choice. The question was whether ambiguity could be found in sufficient quantities to render this acceptable to the Irish negotiators. During the spring Lloyd George had recoiled from making an offer of Dominion status. By the autumn he felt sufficiently confident of his cabinet to propose just that. The required oath of allegiance to the British Crown would be '*de minimis*', the Irish negotiators were told. Ireland's government would defer to the king only in his 'capacity as head of the state and empire'. Three of Ireland's seaports would remain in British hands, but the new Irish Free State would have its own armed forces and the right to build its own coastal defences. As for Northern Ireland, 'Ulster does not want [to join] and we will not force [it]', the prime minister told the cabinet.[23] This did not preclude the application of pressure on Craig to accept an All-Ireland Council to develop cooperation between north and south. The new Northern Ireland, Lloyd George pointed out, needed British money. Jones, who emerged during the talks as much mediator as note-taker, applied the best possible gloss in his contacts with the

Sinn Féin delegation. If republicans seized the opportunity, Jones told Griffith, 'We might have Ulster in before many months.'[24]

The British side was held together by a shared exhaustion with war. In the Irish cabinet, established by Sinn Féin after the May elections, de Valera led a hardline grouping that pressed for the sovereign republic declared by Pearse. Born in New York to an emigrant Irish mother and Spanish father, de Valera had been brought up in rural County Limerick by his mother's family, before winning a place at Blackrock College in Dublin. A mathematics teacher by training and the person for whom the adjective 'austere' might have been invented, he joined the Gaelic League in 1908 and the IRB's Volunteers five years later. Folklore had it that, as the commandant of the Volunteers who seized Dublin's Boland's Mill during the Easter Rising, he had escaped the firing squad only because of his American citizenship. The US State Department certainly recorded that one of its officials in Dublin had been in contact with the British military authorities at the request of his family. Less clear was whether the intervention was decisive. Tall and slim, Sinn Féin's president had an earnest and fiercely Catholic temperament, mirrored by his preference for dark suits and overcoats. The long (or tall) fellow, he was often called. What set him apart was the cultural and religious as much as the political depth of his nationalism. De Valera's republicanism was rooted in the ideals of the Gaelic revival and a passionate personal quest to rescue the Irish language. An independent Irish state would mark only the beginning of the nation's journey. After so many centuries of English occupation, the recovery of Irish identity demanded the comprehensive de-Anglicisation sought by Douglas Hyde's Gaelic League. An alien language and culture would be banished to make room for Irish tradition. Ireland's heart, as Hyde put it, was found in its past.

Griffith and Collins were cut from different cloth – the one quiet and considered, the other with a boom in his voice to match his considerable physical frame, but both, crucially, practical revolutionaries impatient to start building the new state. A former journalist, Griffith had founded Sinn Féin with a call for nationalist MPs of the Irish Parliamentary Party to withdraw from Westminster. Absent from the 1916 rebellion but arrested immediately afterwards, he showed his political acumen in gathering up the various strands of republicanism into a reorganised Sinn Féin. He was the architect of Sinn Féin's policy of abstentionism. He put it into practice when he was elected to Westminster from a cell in Gloucester prison during a second spell of internment in 1918. A year earlier, he had ceded the presidency of Sinn Féin to de Valera, but the latter's extended fundraising campaign in the United States led Griffith to serve as acting president during much of the war of independence. A critical Irish voice in the forging of the treaty with the British, he would be neglected by history. Collins would be immortalised. The architect of the IRA's military campaign, Collins, as instinctively bold as de Valera was ascetic, would prove an astute political organiser as well as an accomplished insurgency commander.

Lloyd George had struggled to find the measure of de Valera – bargaining with the Sinn Féin president, he remarked, was like 'picking up mercury with a fork' – but he warmed to Collins's realism. The energy Churchill had once directed towards military victory was now concentrated on securing a settlement. During weeks of talks, drafts and counter-drafts were pushed across the table and brinks were approached and then stepped back from, the Irish delegates travelling to and from Dublin for consultations with the Sinn Féin cabinet. The British knew Ireland was lost. It was the integrity of empire that mattered. For the Irish, the question was how to define national sovereignty. Was it to be absolute – the pure sovereignty sought by de Valera – or could the new state accept an arrangement that would set it alongside the Commonwealth Dominions? How could Ireland be free of its colonial master and still pay fealty to its monarch? As for the north, the unionist parliament was an unavoidable fact, but was it permanent?

By the beginning of December the British side considered that negotiations had run their course. For his part de Valera proved immoveable on the question of sovereignty, above all on whether the new state would be bound by an oath of allegiance to the Crown. To his mind sovereignty was lost for as long as Ireland remained in the family of empire. As far as he would go was the offer of an 'external association' with Britain and its empire. Britain's last throw was an offer of what Lloyd George presented as a pathway to Irish unity. The treaty would establish a boundary commission to reconsider the border between north and south. Implicit in the offer was an assumption that a review would shrink Northern Ireland at birth. Taken together the six counties produced a sizeable Protestant majority, but in the two closest to the border Catholics held sway. The British negotiators suggested – though never quite promised – that a Northern Ireland shorn of its preponderantly Catholic areas would soon enough be driven into the arms of the Free State. In the north, James Craig, who had for the most part been sidelined during the negotiations, railed against the idea, warning that any decision to redraw the border in the nationalists' favour would provoke a loyalist insurrection. Carson condemned the plan when the House of Lords debated the treaty. But the political calculus in London had changed. Lord Birkenhead, a staunch unionist turned pragmatist during the course of the negotiations with Griffith and Collins, delivered a celebrated putdown in the House of Lords: 'As for the speech of

Lord Carson, as a constructive effort at statecraft, it would have been immature on the lips of a hysterical schoolgirl.'

Michael Collins arrived in Downing Street at 9.30 a.m. on 5 December for the last round of talks. At a Sinn Féin cabinet meeting in Dublin two days earlier de Valera had spoken out against compromise. But Griffith and his colleagues were plenipotentiaries, free to make their own judgement. They signed. 'I may just have signed my political death warrant,' the Tory Lord Birkenhead famously remarked, anticipating charges of betrayal from unionist diehards. 'I have just signed my actual death warrant,' Collins replied.

De Valera disowned the treaty, putting himself at the head of those in the IRA determined to continue the fight. His denunciation found echoes among Protestant leaders in Belfast. The unionist *Belfast Telegraph* branded the British negotiators as 'the men who have engineered the beginning of the downfall of the British empire'. For the *News Letter* they were 'men without conscience'. The public mood in the south was otherwise. The crowds that gathered in Dublin wanted peace. The debate in the Dáil began on 14 December and continued, with a break for Christmas, until 7 January. The final vote was close. Sixty-four backed the treaty, fifty-seven were against. The national mood was receptive to the sentiment voiced by Collins during the Dáil debate. Ireland had won statehood, with 'immense powers and liberties'. Britain's troops would depart. The Free State was 'defined as having the constitutional status of Canada, Australia, New Zealand, South Africa'. And the agreement did not mark the final destination: it offered 'not the ultimate freedom that all nations desire and develop to, but the freedom to achieve it'.

On 16 January Collins, nominated as chair of the Provisional Government, was handed the keys to the British citadel of Dublin

Castle. De Valera was replaced by Griffith as president of Dáil Éireann. Lloyd George's government transferred the Auxiliaries from Ireland to support the British security forces in Palestine, another troubled corner of the empire. In March the IRA formally split. Three months later, the implacable unionist Sir Henry Wilson was assassinated by anti-treaty republicans. Faced with the threat that British forces were preparing to intervene, Collins borrowed British artillery to end the occupation by IRA rebels of Dublin's Four Courts buildings. In August he was killed when his convoy was ambushed by anti-treaty forces in County Cork. Lloyd George would lament the passing of 'a gallant young Irishman' who 'fell to a treacherous blow when he was endeavouring to restore ordered liberty to his country'. Arthur Griffith had died of heart failure two weeks earlier. Collins's legacy, though, was secure. Ireland had begun its journey to independent statehood. Soon enough it would drift out of the British consciousness.

Partition threw up awkward truths. The organising grievance of Irish nationalism could not be gainsaid. Whatever might be said about the rights of those who in 1921 preferred allegiance to Britain over an Irish state, the division of the island of Ireland was ultimately the work of British colonial rule and settlement. North and south were different because the English had thrown the native Irish from their lands to make way for English and Scottish Protestants. Sinn Féin's mistake was to believe this long history could be rewritten in the opening decades of the twentieth century. Like Redmond's constitutional nationalists before it, Sinn Féin was reluctant to properly confront the political forces at work in the north-eastern counties. When Carson backed partition, he abandoned Protestants living in the south. In defiance of its rhetorical commitment to Irish unity, republicanism did something of the same with regard to Catholics in the north. De Valera paid only sporadic attention to the northern counties after the Easter Rising. The energy and focus of the anti-British insurgency were concentrated in the south. Republicanism in the north was a poor relation, mostly neglected by the leadership in Dublin. Sinn Féin theology said that the division of the island was a calumny engineered by the British. From this standpoint, all that was required of Lloyd George in 1921 was to agree to coerce the Ulster unionists into a united Ireland. What the analysis missed – and this had been demonstrated by the arming of the UVF during the passage of the Home Rule bill – was that Carson and then Craig were ready to defy the British as well as fight the nationalists. Much as Lloyd George's answer to the Irish question was rooted in the search for a political escape route, it was not in his gift to transfer Northern Ireland to a new Irish Republic against the will of 800,000 unionists.

The curiosity of the outcome was that even if the break with the six counties disfigured the republican vision of sovereign independence, time would show that it also empowered the effort to create the Irish state envisaged by the revolutionaries. Partition was the route taken by Britain to get out of Ireland with minimum damage to itself and its standing in the world. It was also the reason that a new government in Dublin had free rein, for good or ill, to build de Valera's Ireland. The deeply conservative, inward-looking society that described the nature of the first half-century of the new Irish state was possible only because it had no need to accommodate northern Protestants.

2 BEST OF ENEMIES

Arthur Griffith heads the list of Irish signatories to the treaty sealed in 10 Downing Street. Michael Collins, the architect of Ireland's revolutionary war, takes second place. On the British side, Winston Churchill ranks fourth behind David Lloyd George, the Conservative leader Austen Chamberlain and the lord chancellor, Lord Birkenhead. Lloyd George was guile itself in marking out the territory for the negotiations and choreographing the steps that brought them to a conclusion. In one dimension the bravest of the negotiators was Griffith, as taciturn as Collins was flamboyant. As head of the Irish side it was his resolve during the last days that persuaded the doubters to sign. 'A braver man than Arthur Griffith I never met,' Birkenhead would say.

Yet the two figures who often loomed largest, the source first of organising energy during the talks and then, after the signature, the implementation of the bargain, were Collins and Churchill. These two men could never be close. Collins, born to a Catholic farming family in nationalist Cork, had devoted his adult life to the cause of Irish independence. He joined the Gaelic League and IRB while working during his teens as a trainee clerk in London. After returning to Ireland to escape the British call-up to war, he became instead a member of the IRB's Volunteers. By the time he helped garrison the General Post Office during the Easter Rising, republicanism was his life. Soldier as much as politician, he would become, in Griffith's description, 'the man who won the war'. Griffith was a cerebral figure, well read in politics and history. In the description of Lloyd George, Collins was a figure with 'a swaggering gait, loud voiced and with noisy laughter . . . None could mistake his nationality. Irish through and through . . . full of fascination and charm – but also of dangerous fire. That was Michael Collins, one of the most courageous leaders ever produced by a valiant race.'[1]

On the other side of the table Churchill could claim Irish roots of a sort. He had made a first public appearance in Dublin in 1878 at the age of three, when a painting of the infant Winston by his American-born socialite mother, Jennie, was displayed in a fashionable gallery. His father, Randolph, infamous for his role in stirring up unionist insurrection, served as aide to John Winston Spencer Churchill, the 7th Duke of Marlborough and lord lieutenant of Ireland. The Churchills, one might say, kept it in the family. Much as in later life he would often express a fondness for Ireland and the Irish, Winston's abiding preoccupation remained the preservation of the empire. The Irish were to be respected only to the extent that they did not get in the way of England's global destiny. It is not obvious that Churchill and Collins much liked each other – though after Collins's death Churchill offered personal condolences by way of booking a railway compartment to take Collins's sister Hannie back to Dublin from London. During the treaty talks they met socially as well as around the negotiating table, often at the London home of the Irish painter John Lavery. Churchill deployed flattery as well as charm. Collins, as conscious as any of the power of his own myth, became something of a celebrity – in demand in the fashionable salons of Belgravia, filling the front pages of the tabloid press and intriguing the broadsheets. Publishers clamoured for his memoirs – one was reported to have offered £10,000 – and the society magazine *Tatler* sought a photoshoot. Even the stolid *Financial Times* was moved to describe him as the 'popular hero of the hour', preferring to point out that he had worked as a young man for a firm of London Stock Exchange brokers than to dwell on his exploits killing British soldiers. What gave the two men influence, though, was a shared temperament. They were both, as the cliché runs, 'men of action'. They were willing to take risks. And realism sat above high idealism. Churchill would later say that Collins's 'qualities of action and personality' were essential to the foundation of Irish nationhood. The treaty marked the reconciliation of their competing ambitions. For Collins the agreement was a starting point; for Churchill it was an escape.

Churchill's political career was punctuated with somersaults, and his views of Irish nationalism never lacked for inconsistency. At one moment the aspiration of nationhood was to be lauded, at the next, to be crushed. As a Tory MP at the turn of the century he started out as a conventional unionist, signing up to the belief that Irish self-rule would unpick the threads of empire. After he switched parties to join the Liberals in 1904, his views were moulded by the parliamentary arithmetic that led Herbert Asquith into the embrace of the Irish Parliamentary Party and the cause of Home Rule. By 1912 Churchill was braving Protestant anger to share a platform with IPP leader John Redmond in Belfast. He had intended to speak at the unionist temple, the Ulster Hall, but, jostled and jeered by angry unionist crowds, he had been refused the platform from which his father had delivered his inflammatory 'Ulster will fight' pledge. Instead, his declaration of affection for a people 'gifted, virtuous and brave' was heard in a marquee erected at the football ground in nationalist west Belfast.

When Asquith's cabinet grappled with Home Rule, Ulster's unionists threatened armed rebellion and the army threatened mutiny, Churchill was among the first (along with Lloyd George) in the cabinet to propose at least a temporary derogation for Ireland's north-eastern counties. To his mind, this was practical politics, a way to settle the Irish question. He had been notably belligerent in his response to the threats of insurrection from unionists, at one point arranging for a Royal Navy battlecruiser to be dispatched to Ulster's coastal waters, but his backing for Home Rule was always conditional. An admirer of the fighting spirit shown by Irish regiments in the imperial army, he backed the abortive attempts to extend conscription to Ireland during the First World War. Yet, like most in the cabinet, Churchill failed to understand how the harsh treatment of the leaders of the Easter Rising had transformed the political dynamics of Irish nationalism. Once the IRA rebellion began, first as secretary for war and then secretary for the colonies, he presided over the brutal, and once again counterproductive, effort to suppress the insurgency. The deployment of the Black and Tans and the Auxiliaries was calculated to demonstrate, in Churchill's words, 'the most unlimited exercise of rough-handed force'. In May 1920 Churchill complained that it was 'monstrous that we have had some 200 [IRA] murders and no-one hanged'.[2] How was it that a great empire could be made to dance to the tune of a few thousand Irish gunmen? At other moments he seemed almost to blame the Irish for Britain's conquest. 'How is that she [Ireland] has forced generation after generation to stop the whole traffic of the British empire in order to debate her domestic affairs?'[3] This was the view of empire popularised by the English writer and poet Rudyard Kipling: the conquered should thank the ever-munificent English for conquering them.

At times, Churchill imagined the threat from Irish rebellion to be existential, with enemies of the empire conspiring against it in Egypt, India and beyond. 'The rascals and rapscallions of mankind are now on the move against us. Whether it is the Irish murder gang or the Egyptian vengeance society, seditious extremists in India, or the arch-traitors we have at home, they will feel the weight of the British arm. It was strong enough to break the Hindenburg line.'[4] It did not, though, seem sufficient to defeat the IRA. By 1921 Britain's military commanders despaired of victory without significant reinforcements and the imposition across most of Ireland of martial law. Such a strategy would have stirred an international outcry. In his calmer moments Churchill understood the public revulsion at home at the tactics being deployed by British forces.

For his part, Lloyd George sensed the shift in the mood of the unionist diehards in the cabinet, opening up the possibility of talks with the republicans. What followed was, in Churchill's description, the most complete and sudden policy reversal in modern memory. 'In May the whole power of the State and all the influence of the Coalition were used to "hunt down the murder gang"; in June the goal was lasting reconciliation with the Irish people.'[5] Churchill, no novice in the game of changing political horses, adapted quickly to the new approach. He was unapologetic about the reversal. The much-revered Gladstone, he would point out, had made his own about-turn – pledging to fight Irish nationalism before picking up the standard of Home Rule.

Once talks were under way, the thirty-one-year-old Collins was recognised as the most influential figure on the Irish side. The other members of the Sinn Féin delegation travelled to London three days early to set up a base in Belgravia's Hans Place. Collins arrived separately on the eve of the talks, establishing his own operation at nearby Cadogan Gardens. Four Volunteers took it in turn to guard the doorway. The main delegation had been mobbed by cheering crowds when it arrived at Euston station. Collins slipped in without fanfare. Asked by a reporter how he had arrived without being noticed, the revolutionary responded with a clue to his success in the ruthless war he had only recently led against British intelligence agents in Ireland: 'I always watch the other fellow instead of letting him watch me.'[6]

Robert Barton, the member of the Irish side perhaps closest to de Valera's views, would observe that 'it was clear from the outset that the English interest centred on Michael Collins'. Chamberlain described him as belonging 'to the open spaces and the rough life of frontier settlements and mining camps'. That might have been a touch unfair, but in any event, the man widely condemned as a terrorist only months earlier was now a prized guest at society soirées.[7]

Griffith, an intellectual more than a warrior, was judged by the British as potentially amenable to compromise. If England, he declared in his opening statement to the conference, was willing to change its 'policy of subordinating Ireland to English interests', a settlement was possible. His judgement spoke to the mood among Irish nationalists. They wanted independence but had tired of war. The calculation on Lloyd George's part was that if Collins could also be swayed, there would be little option but for the three other Irish plenipotentiaries to fall into line. Griffith's description in the Dáil of Collins's pivotal role in the war was only a slight exaggeration. As finance minister, head of the Volunteers' intelligence network and president of the Irish Republican Brotherhood, he was the organising force. De Valera spent much of the war fundraising in the United States. Collins commanded the troops. His nickname – the Big Fella – had been earned. It never ceased to irritate de Valera.

The IRA's commander absorbed the military lesson of the republicans' defeat in the Easter Rising. They could not win in fixed battles against such a numerically superior and better-equipped British army. The uprising that began in January 1919 was organised around hit-and-run attacks on the agents of British authority – whether the police or judges, army officers or secret service agents. The Volunteers' intelligence network identified the targets for assassination by the 'Squad' or 'Twelve Apostles'. This was the team, under the direct control of Collins, charged with the killing of fifteen British intelligence agents and army officers in November 1920. Collins was unrepentant about the tactics: 'For myself, my conscience is clear. There is no crime in detecting in wartime the spy and the informer. They have destroyed without trial. I have paid them back in their own coin.'[8] The damage inflicted on the British by the assassinations was duly amplified by the reprisals of the Black and Tans.

For all his ruthlessness in the prosecution of the war, by the summer of 1921 Collins understood that outright victory was beyond reach. 'We had not beaten the enemy out of our country by force of arms,' he would say in explaining the peace treaty. The British had unmatched military resources. The IRA lacked the rifles and ammunition to equip its soldiers. Collins had no enthusiasm, though, for the role of negotiator. When de Valera suggested he join the team that would bargain with Lloyd George as Griffith's deputy, he protested that he was a soldier, not a politician. Doubtless he also understood that the negotiators would be asked to sip from a poisoned chalice.

During the weeks following the truce de Valera had refused to budge from the demand for full independence from the British Crown. Visiting London to attend an imperial conference, Jan Smuts, the South African leader, offered himself to Lloyd George as a mediator. When he returned to London from Dublin he reported that the Sinn Féin president 'spoke continually of generations of oppression and seemed to live in a world of dreams, visions and shadows'.[9] The prime minister knew that there was one river that the Conservatives in the coalition would never cross – a break with empire. Instead, in a final offer to the Sinn Féin president sent in September, Lloyd George proposed that the negotiations turn on the question of how 'the association of Ireland with the community of nations known as the British Empire may best be reconciled with Irish aspirations'. De Valera accepted. To Collins's mind, the die had been cast. A note written to a friend in Dublin on the opening day of the London talks might have been a premonition. 'You know the way it is. Either way it will be wrong. Wrong because of what has come to pass. You might say the trap is sprung.'[10] The British had chosen the field on which the battle would be fought. A fully sovereign republic had been taken off the table. Collins also knew well that many in Sinn Féin and the IRA would repudiate anything that fell short of Pearse's republic. 'It was the acceptance [by de Valera] of the invitation that formed the compromise,' Collins would say when the treaty was debated in the Irish parliament. As for partition, republicans were bound by previous commitments. They had stated in advance that 'we would not coerce the North East'. Griffith insisted that the negotiators had done 'the best we could for Ireland', providing an opportunity to rebuild the 'Gaelic civilisation' that had been broken at the Battle of Kinsale more than three centuries earlier. 'I know and you know that I can't bring back a republic,' Griffith had told de Valera before the start of negotiations.[11] With the treaty signed, he pointed out that de Valera could have chosen to lead the Irish team: 'Other men were asked and other men refused,' he told the Dáil.[12]

For his part de Valera offered different explanations for his reluctance to lead the Irish delegation, even though the British side was headed by his counterpart Lloyd George. Collins could be forgiven for the suspicion that the Sinn Féin leader was dodging the opprobrium for the inevitable compromise. It had been obvious since his return from the United States in December 1920 that de Valera resented the authority that had accrued to Collins as leader of the military campaign against the British. Collins rebuffed a suggestion that he embark on his own American tour, but de Valera had excluded him from the delegation that met Lloyd George in July. By staying in Dublin rather than leading the Irish in the autumn talks, de Valera preserved his own reputation. As plenipotentiaries rather than delegates, the negotiators had the authority, after consulting the Irish cabinet, to make their own decisions. This in turn gave de Valera the distance to disown them.

Disown them he did. Unionism may have declared that the treaty was a victory for the republicans, but de Valera was scathing. By accepting Dominion status and the attached oath of allegiance to the Crown, he thundered during the Dáil debate, the negotiators were guilty of 'a surrender which was never heard of in Ireland since the days of Henry II'. The treaty cast aside the 'independence of our people' and condemned the Irish to taking 'the British monarch as their king'. As for the popular support for the agreement: 'A war-weary people will take things which are not in accordance with their aspirations.'[13] It was largely bluster, but no less potent for that among republican diehards. De Valera's own complicated formula for a settlement – an arm's-length 'association' of the new state with the empire, in which the monarch would be acknowledged as leader of the association – was not markedly different from the wording in the treaty. The modifications owed more to semantics than substance. A 'quibble of words', Griffith called it during the Dáil debate. The Irish people knew that 'a treaty that gives them their flag and their free state and their army is not a sham treaty'. Collins's case that freedoms comparable to those enjoyed by Canada, Australia, South Africa and New Zealand mapped the path to full sovereignty did not soften the anger of purist republicans. Séumas Robinson, an anti-treaty member of the Dáil, called the treaty an 'act of high treason and betrayal'. The language of others was still more colourful. Yet Richard Barton, a staunch republican who had signed the treaty only with great reluctance, agreed with Collins's analysis. 'The English refused to recognise us as acting on behalf of the Irish republic and the fact that we agreed to negotiate at all on any other basis was possibly the primary cause of our downfall. Certainly it was the first milestone on the road to disaster.'[14] Those who condemned Collins as a traitor spread bizarre rumours of an affair with the king's daughter, Princess Mary, that would lead to his appointment as governor general of Ireland. Republicanism split. The war of words in the Dáil prefigured a conflict more bloody in its way than had been the war with England – only this time, Collins and Churchill were on the same side.

Handed cabinet responsibility for overseeing the passage and implementation of the agreement, Churchill saw his task during the opening months of 1922 as holding Collins to the terms of the bargain. Such was the eagerness of British politicians to rid themselves of the Irish question that the House of Commons voted by 401 to 58 in favour of the treaty. The House of Lords, more sympathetic to unionism, backed it 166–47. In the reckoning of former prime minister Asquith, the treaty offered a 'new compact between two peoples, giving, as it does, to Ireland complete local autonomy, and at the same time, what is equally important, preserving for Irishmen a full share of free citizenship throughout the British Empire'.[15] For Churchill, the promise was of liberation, not simply for Ireland but for the empire:

> Whence does this mysterious power of Ireland come? It is a small, poor, sparsely populated island, lapped about by British sea power, accessible on every side, without iron or coal. How is it that she sways our councils, shakes our parties, and infects us with her bitterness, convulses our passions, and deranges our action? How is it she has forced generation after generation to stop the whole

traffic of the British Empire, in order to debate her domestic affairs? Ireland is not a daughter State. She is a parent nation. The Irish are an ancient race.[16]

Two months later, during the House of Commons debate on ratification of the agreement, Churchill was still dwelling on Northern Ireland's baleful influence:

> As the deluge [of the First World War] subsides and the waters fall short we see the dreary steeples of Fermanagh and Tyrone emerging once again. The integrity of their quarrel is one of the few institutions that have remained unaltered in the cataclysm which has swept the world.[17]

Parliament should now be satisfied with the bargain struck with republicanism:

> The position of the Imperial Government has also become greatly improved. It is very desirable that the great affairs of the British Empire should be increasingly detached from the terrible curse of this long internal Irish quarrel, and that the august Imperial authorities should stand on a more impartial plane.[18]

By handing the Free State control over its own trade and defence policies, Lloyd George had reached well beyond the lines drawn by Tory diehards. Even as de Valera condemned Collins in Dublin, Carson branded the foreign secretary Lord Curzon a 'traitor'. Unionist protests in Northern Ireland were followed by sectarian attacks on Catholic communities and nationalist boycotts of unionist-dominated industry. But Britain had washed its hands of Ireland.

The vote in favour of the treaty in Dublin, at 64–57, was much narrower than that at Westminster, offering succour to de Valera's hopes that it might yet be overturned. He was replaced by Griffith as president of the parliament, and Collins was appointed head of a new Provisional Government. But many IRA Volunteers refused to come to terms with the treaty. Churchill's concern was that the deal would unravel as Collins sought to appease them – a fear amplified when armed anti-treaty republicans seized control of Dublin's Four Courts, the administrative centre of the Irish legal system, and Collins and de Valera reached an electoral pact on the fielding of pro- and anti-treaty candidates for the post-treaty Dáil. Publicly, Churchill struck an optimistic note. He told the House of Commons in February that 'for generations we have been wandering and floundering in the Irish bog but at last we think that in this treaty we have set our feet upon a pathway'.[19] Privately, he feared civil war in the north and a break with the treaty in the Free State. Collins did little to assuage such fears. He had the country behind him, but many, if not most, of the IRA Volunteers against him. Having compromised with the British, winning the war at home demanded he reaffirm his Irishness.

The future of the north was pushed into the background during the long Dáil debate on the treaty. Even as he raged against the oath of allegiance, de Valera offered little in the way of an alternative to the arrangements for partition. In the decades to follow he would not resile from the conviction that the problem would be solved by British withdrawal. The reality was always otherwise. Collins admitted that the Free State was pledged not to coerce the north into unity. He put his faith in the boundary commission promised by Lloyd George. Alongside its provision for the Stormont parliament to opt out of the new Irish state, the treaty stated that such self-exclusion by the north would be an automatic trigger for the commission to begin its work. The pressures on Collins in the early months of 1922, however, were immediate. His response was to sanction IRA attacks on the north. For a time, the IRA hit-and-run operations and continued loyalist attacks on nationalists threatened to tip the province into civil war, while occupation of the Four Courts gave the anti-treaty Volunteers a centre of power in Dublin. Twice Churchill felt compelled to summon the two sides and negotiate a truce between Collins and the Northern Ireland prime minister James Craig. After an outbreak of communal violence in March 1922, Churchill organised a meeting and the three men issued a joint communiqué. 'Peace is today declared,' it began with an unbridled optimism far distant from the realities on the ground. 'From today, the two Governments [Dublin and Belfast] undertake to co-operate in every way in their power with a view to the restoration of peaceful conditions in the unsettled areas.'[20] It was a pipe dream. The constitution for the Free State drafted by Collins – stretching the terms of the treaty to the limits – added to the sense of crisis. Then, in June 1922, Henry Wilson, the former chief of the general staff turned military adviser to diehard unionists, was assassinated on the doorstep of his house in Belgravia's Eaton Place. Enough was enough. Churchill told Collins that unless he reasserted his authority, British troops would be used to clear the Four Courts. Two days later, Collins's new National Army deployed British artillery to drive out the anti-treaty rebels. The civil war would last ten months. The recriminations would tumble down through the decades, defining for the rest of the twentieth century the essential divide in the politics of the south.

For Churchill, the civil war's opening shots were reassurance. The treaty would endure. 'All is changed,' he said in a letter to Collins.

> Once the national army establishes order in the south . . . a new phase will begin far more hopeful than anything we have hitherto experienced. In this phase, our objective must be the unity of

Ireland. How and when this can be achieved I cannot tell, but it is surely the goal to which we must look steadfastly.[21]

It would not be a shared endeavour. Within a month Collins would be dead, cut down in an ambush by the anti-treaty IRA at Béal na Bláth, in his home county of Cork. Ten days earlier, Arthur Griffith, exhausted by the negotiations and the battle within Sinn Féin, had succumbed to ill health. Griffith was widely mourned. In his message of condolence to Griffith's wife Maud, Collins had described himself as one of Griffith's 'true disciples'. Now, the emerging Free State had lost its most prominent leaders. The grandeur and crowds at Collins's state funeral spoke to his unique stature. An estimated 500,000 people – about a fifth of the entire population – crowded the streets of Dublin to pay homage to the hero of the revolution. British soldiers joined republican leaders and foreign dignitaries in paying their respects during the three days his body lay in state. Lloyd George's statement to the press spoke of a 'gallant young Irishman' who 'fell to a treacherous blow when he was engaged in endeavouring to restore ordered liberty to his country'.[22] Churchill called him 'an Irish patriot true and fearless'. Later, he claimed to have earned his adversary's respect. A message – 'Tell Winston we could not have done it without him' – had been passed to him by an intermediary, he said. Collins had been less complimentary in a pen portrait drawn during the treaty negotiations. Churchill 'will sacrifice all for political gain . . . Inclined to be bombastic. Full of ex-officer jingo or similar outlook. Don't actually trust him.' This was kinder, though, than his assessment of the 'particularly obnoxious' Lloyd George: 'All craft and wiliness, all arm around the shoulder . . . not so long ago he would joyfully have had me at the rope's end.'[23]

3 A BORDER OF THE MIND

It fell to the man who had so violently denounced him to supply the proof that Michael Collins had been honest in his legacy. After being defeated in the civil war, it would take time for Éamon de Valera to leave behind the angry recriminations. Then he would lead Ireland to Collins's summit. The new constitution for the Irish state, renamed Éire, unveiled by de Valera in 1937 proclaimed a republic in all but name. As his comrade-in-arms had predicted, the treaty had provided the freedom to achieve freedom. There is no record of de Valera admitting he had been wrong.

Inaugurated in December 1922, the anniversary of the treaty's signature, the Irish Free State was led by William T. Cosgrave as the president of the Irish Executive Council, a title later to be shortened to Taoiseach. A veteran of the Easter Rising, Cosgrave was at the head of Cumann na nGaedheal, set up by Sinn Féin supporters of the treaty. Cosgrave's immediate challenge was evident enough. He had to build the infrastructure of a new state from the remnants of British rule and the rubble of two wars. More than that, the imperative was a nation that proclaimed its Irishness and its permanent escape from the shackles of colonialism.

The retaking by pro-treaty forces of the Four Courts had been a harbinger. The anti-treaty IRA had lost the civil war almost as soon as it had started. It was soon outnumbered and outgunned by the National Army created by Collins. The British government, anxious that the new settlement should hold, was generous in its supply of weaponry. Driven from the cities and towns, the anti-treaty republicans deployed the hit-and-run tactics honed by Collins during the war of independence. But now they faced a foe who had written the rule book for insurgencies. Critically, the National Army could rely on wide support among the population. 'His death is a disaster for Ireland,' the *Irish Times* had recorded after the death of Collins. 'The Irish Nation will be shocked beyond measure at this awful news. General Collins stood for stable government and the restoration of civilised conditions to our distracted country.'[1]

Stable government and civilised conditions. There lay the key to the victory of the pro-treaty forces. Ireland had tired of war. The people wanted peace. The fighting spluttered on into 1923, but in May de Valera and the IRA's military command bowed to the inevitable and gave the order to 'dump' arms. Estimates of the numbers killed during the conflict range up to about 2,000, compared to the 1,400 or so who had died in the war of independence. The legacy of bitterness ran deeper. There was something visceral, elemental about the hatred that separated pro-treaty realists from purist republicans. Summary executions were commonplace. The forces of the Free State displayed a ruthlessness and disregard for due legal process of which Churchill in 1920 would have been proud. The Taoiseach Cosgrave was unrepentant: 'I am not going to hesitate and if the country is to live, and if we have to exterminate 10,000 republicans, the three million of our people are bigger than the 10,000.'[2] Communities, and sometimes families, would hold on to the rancour for generations to come. Some would fight on. For all the subsequent vicissitudes and splits, the IRA never completely went away. The fighting had stopped, but as Northern Ireland learned half a century later, the tradition of armed republicanism endured.

The war created its own, peculiarly Irish, political fault lines. Democratic politics elsewhere in Europe operated on a left–right axis. The argument was about the role of the state, the level of taxes, the economy, social mores and foreign policy. Ireland's identifying markers were set by the civil war, by the pro- and anti-treaty camps. Cumann na nGaedheal (and its successor Fine Gael) would forever be associated with those who had followed Collins in seeking peace. Fianna Fáil, the party that would be established by de Valera on his return to constitutional politics in 1926, claimed the mantle of anti-treaty republicanism. The strange thing was that while Fine Gael (Family of the Irish) could justly claim that history was proving it had been right, Fianna Fáil (Soldiers of Destiny) reaped most of the political rewards.

From the outset, Cosgrave's governing prospectus was Irishness at home and independence abroad. As the historian Roy Foster has put it, 'The dominant pre-occupation of the regime was self-definition against Britain.'[3] Teaching of the Irish language had been optional, and neglected. The new government put Gaelic front and centre as a pillar of the curriculum. Proficiency in the language became a precondition for senior roles in public service. The government's small-state conservatism – reinforced by the loss of the funding it had received from the Exchequer in London – gave the Catholic Church the space to extend its authority over education, health and public morals. The Censorship of Films Act was put into law during the first year of Cosgrave's government. The Committee on Evil Literature followed three years later. The publisher of James Joyce's *Ulysses* pre-empted the censor's frown by deciding against publication in Ireland of the seminal work of Irish literature. Some forty years later, the film censor banned public showings of the big-screen version of the novel as being 'subversive to public morality'. Filmgoers had to wait until 2000 to watch it in the country's public cinemas.

Independence meant international neutrality – the freedom not to join Britain's wars. The Irish battalions that had long served in the imperial army had gained a formidable reputation as a fighting force. Ireland would no longer fight for the Crown. Instead, it took its own place, and a calculatedly active role, in the new League of Nations, where it was self-consciously on the side of independence movements and other small nations seeking to slip the noose of great power dominance. It joined the League in 1923 and had soon established a permanent delegation at its headquarters in Geneva. Diplomatic missions were established in Washington, Berlin and Paris. To the extent that Dublin had an overarching foreign policy, it was the effort to set it apart from its former colonial master. In testing the limits of the treaty, Cosgrave benefited from the political tides flowing in the Commonwealth's other Dominion states. They too sought to loosen the bonds with London. At a series of imperial conferences, Canada led demands for a sharper definition of their sovereignty. The passage in 1931 of the Statute of Westminster marked a recasting of the relationship between the Crown and the Dominions that removed Britain's residual rights to intervene in the domestic affairs of its former possessions. Ireland had completed the first leg of Collins's journey.

In 1923 de Valera, in the guise of republican warrior, had been defiant. In the proclamation calling on the anti-Free State forces to dump their arms, he refused to admit the great fight was over: 'Military victory must be allowed to rest for the moment.' The new de Valera, the ambitious pragmatist seeking to lead his country, waited three years before abandoning the Sinn Féin policy of abstentionism – boycotting the Dáil – that it had adopted at the end of the civil war. The oath of allegiance to the king demanded from those taking a Dáil seat had been at the core of his rejection of the treaty. De Valera, however, was interested in power as well as ideology. In 1926 a second republican split saw him dismiss the oath as an 'empty formula' of no consequence as he took representatives of his newly formed Fianna Fáil into the Dáil. In 1932, holding the banner of anti-treaty republicanism that had belonged to Sinn Féin, Fianna Fáil won the election. De Valera's place in the new state's politics would span the next five decades, including three spells as Taoiseach and, from 1959, fourteen years as president. No one else would be able to claim such a decisive role in the shaping of the nation. True to the pathway that had been mapped by Collins, he began by dismantling the remaining symbols of British imperial rule. The oath of allegiance was scrapped. The role of the British governor general in Dublin was brutally downgraded. The Privy Council in London was all but stripped of its status as a court of last resort. Partition had figured only as a second-rank issue during the treaty debates. De Valera's alternative blueprint, the curiously named Document Number 2, had scarcely diverged from the treaty on the issue of arrangements for the north.[4] As Taoiseach he would nonetheless frame the commitment to end partition as the litmus test of republicanism.

The crisis in Britain provoked by the abdication of Edward VIII in 1936 presented de Valera with an opportunity to codify the separation with Britain. The Dublin government capitalised on the constitutional disarray in London with a new External Relations Act, further diluting Ireland's already thin allegiance to the Crown. The post of governor general and the role of the Privy Council were scrapped. All that was left for George VI, Edward's successor, was the right to sign off the credentials of the Free State's diplomats. As if to underline the rupture, when the Irish cabinet met to discuss the succession in February 1937 it solemnly declared that 'Wednesday 12 May 1937, the date of the coronation of King George VI, should not be appointed as a Bank Holiday or as a Public Holiday'.[5]

The same year, 1937, de Valera unveiled a new constitution. Sovereignty, it declared, was invested in the people. Command of the national defence forces belonged to a new, directly elected president, a largely ceremonial role that went in the first instance to the Gaelic League veteran Douglas Hyde. As Taoiseach, de Valera served as his own minister for external relations. The renamed Éire, or Ireland, claimed sovereignty over all thirty-two counties. 'The national territory consists of the whole island of Ireland, its islands and the territorial seas,' Article 2 of the constitution declared. The only concession, in Article 3, was that the exercise of this sovereignty in the north would be deferred until the border was removed:

> Pending the re-integration of the national territory, and without prejudice to the right of the parliament and government established by this constitution to exercise jurisdiction over the whole of that territory, the laws enacted by that parliament shall have the like area and extent of application as the laws of Saorstát Éireann [the Irish Free State] and the like extra-territorial effect.

Declaratory unity came at the price of further estrangement from the north. De Valera had set two ambitions. The first was to entrench the 'Irishness' of the Free State – in its language, Catholic faith, economic self-sufficiency, culture and separateness from the British. The second was to confront the calumny of partition and restore Irish unity. With the passage of the constitution and an agreement the following year for the return of the so-called treaty ports – naval facilities that had remained under the control of the British – he could justly claim significant advances towards the first of his goals. The price of this success, though, was to widen rather than narrow the distance between the Irelands of south and north. Seen from Belfast, the course de Valera had set in the south was proof of the new state's intention to crush Protestant unionism. For all that unionists were the majority in Northern Ireland, they never ceased to see themselves as a beleaguered minority in a nationalist Ireland. The answer was to build the sectarian wall still higher.

———

The British looked on de Valera's constitutional deliberations with consternation, exasperation and occasional fury. Cabinet papers written in the wake of his 1932 election victory are replete with less than complimentary descriptions of Ireland's leader. Lord Granard, who acted as an intermediary between London and Dublin during a dispute about trade relations, reported after meeting de Valera that he found him 'on the border line between genius and insanity'. Granard was well travelled. 'I have met men of many countries,' he noted, 'and have been governor of a lunatic asylum,' but 'I have never met anyone like the president of the executive council of the Irish Free State before.' The former Tory prime minister Stanley Baldwin described him as 'impossible', while others remarked on 'a lack of reason'.[6]

For all the frustrations, there was no appetite in London to reopen the Irish question. Some argued for a tough line, but the prevailing impulse was in favour of containment. De Valera, ministers noted, had held back from the declaration of a republic free of all ties with the Commonwealth. Britain had troubles enough in other parts of the empire, notably continued unrest in Egypt and India. Across the Channel, fascism was stirring in Europe. Hitler's Germany had remilitarised the Rhineland, was preparing for Anschluss with Austria and was threatening Czechoslovakia. Italy's Benito Mussolini had set off in search of an empire in Africa by annexing Abyssinia. The international clouds were gathering. Britain was unprepared for the looming fight with the Nazis. Assuming the premiership in 1937, Neville Chamberlain adopted a twin-track policy of rearmament and appeasement. This was not a moment, he judged, to reopen wounds with Britain's nearest neighbour. In calmer international waters, the government might have decided that the effect of the External Relations Act and the new constitution was to sever de facto, if not *de jure*, Ireland's ties with the Commonwealth – a unilateral abrogation of the Anglo-Irish Treaty. Instead, it decided to accept the fig leaf offered by a continued role for the Crown through Éire's new 'association' with the Commonwealth. To all intents and purposes de Valera had created a republic, British ministers privately concluded, but they would not force the issue. There were moments of tension, as when after the Italian invasion of Abyssinia the Irish government recognised the Italian king as emperor. Occasional public protests were matched by private acquiescence. De Valera seemed to understand the strategy. In September he reported to staff on a private conversation he had had with the emollient Malcolm MacDonald, the Dominions secretary in Chamberlain's government. The conclusion the Taoiseach had drawn from the discussion was that:

> At the time the constitution is about to come into effect the British will make some formal protest in regard to Articles 2 and 3. Their point seems to be that they do not want to appear to be acquiescing in our claim put forward in these Articles. I pointed out that we would have to reply fairly stiffly on that matter and there could of course be no question of any change.[7]

His judgement proved correct. The official British position, set out in a public statement at the end of 1937, was that the constitution did not mark a fundamental change in Éire's membership of the Commonwealth. On the question of partition, MacDonald refused to budge. Unity, de Valera reported him as saying, could come only 'by ourselves winning over the North'. All in all, Britain chose a relationship of choreographed private disagreement over public shouting matches with Dublin.

The same balm was applied by London to negotiations to unwind the tariffs and protectionist quotas applied by both sides since 1932. De Valera had marked his election victory by repudiating a clause in the 1921 treaty providing for the transfer from Dublin to London of income flowing from historic Irish land reforms. Britain retaliated by imposing tariffs and restrictions on imports of Irish agricultural produce, overwhelmingly the main source of the Free State's export earnings. Dublin's response, in the form of tariffs on imports of British manufactures, led to a six-year 'economic war'. This assertion of sovereignty carried a considerable cost for the Irish. The balance of pain was felt by its farmers. By 1937 Dublin was looking for a settlement. It was also seeking the return of the three strategically important harbours – Queenstown and Berehaven in County Cork and Lough Swilly in County Donegal – that had been left under British control by the treaty. For de Valera the British presence was an affront to Irish sovereignty. For the London government the harbours and naval installations had a strategic role as potential resupply points in the event of a war that spilled into the Atlantic and as a safeguard against any foreign (German) attempt to use Ireland as a base from which to attack the British mainland. Chamberlain faced both military and political opposition to the transfer. The admirals' fears that it would weaken British control of the Atlantic sea lanes won vocal support from Churchill. MacDonald sought to assuage the critics by seeking assurances from Dublin that the facilities would be handed back if war broke out. De Valera insisted that Irish public opinion would not accept such a dilution of neutrality. The most that he would offer was a commitment that the Irish government would 'defend the whole of their territory against external aggression whether the purpose of the aggression be a direct attack on the people of Éire ... or as a means for securing a base from which to attack the United Kingdom'.[8]

In April 1938 Chamberlain, backed by a cabinet committee, opted for compromise to reset the relationship with Dublin, persuaded that it was worth securing 'the essential goodwill' of the Irish Free State. The deal included the restoration of free trade, a one-off payment from Ireland in settlement of its outstanding financial liabilities and British withdrawal from the ports. It seemed to many that de Valera had got the better of the bargain. Churchill's critique in the House of Commons was searing:

> When I read this Agreement in the newspapers a week ago I was filled with surprise. On the face of it, it seemed to have given everything away and received nothing in return ... But then I supposed there was another side to the Agreement, and that we were to be granted some facilities and rights in Southern Ireland in time of war ... but soon Mr de Valera in the Dáil made it clear that he was under no obligations of any kind ... On the contrary, Mr de Valera has not even abandoned his claim for the incorporation of Ulster.[9]

Chamberlain, however, was a prime minister struggling to forestall the outbreak of war across the continent of Europe. He hoped the deal would send a wider signal that disputes between states could be settled peacefully by negotiation. Herr Hitler was not listening.

Frontiers between states conjure up images of lines drawn by the contours of the terrain, and of walls and wire, fixed crossing points and customs posts. Ireland was divided by a border of the mind.

A BORDER OF THE MIND

The 499-kilometre zigzag from Lough Foyle in the north-west to Carlingford Lough in the north-east that marked the line between the Irish Free State and the British province of Northern Ireland owed nothing to considered cartography. Based on the boundaries between Ireland's ancient local counties, it resembled rather a random walk between the Atlantic and Irish Sea. In the description of the historian Diarmaid Ferriter, the new border's physical manifestations were at once arbitrary and unenforceable.[10] The dividing line ran through towns, villages and occasionally individual dwellings. Its arbitrary nature meant that pockets of Protestant unionists and Catholic nationalists found themselves stranded on the wrong side. It was criss-crossed by some 180 roads. Sometimes the frontier ran down the middle of those roads. Drainage ditches meandered between north and south. Some residents found that their farms were now half Irish and half British. When the writer Colm Tóibín walked the length of the undemarcated frontier during the 1980s he came across a family whose house sat on both sides. The occupants could choose to spend their days in the Republic and sleep in Northern Ireland. Or vice versa. A border with so many unofficial crossing points was impossible to police. Smuggling was endemic almost from the moment that the Free State established its own tariff regime in the aftermath of partition. The free passage of bombers and gunmen to and fro during the campaign waged by the Provisional Irish Republican Army (PIRA) from the start of the 1970s led the army to blow up or block about 150 unofficial crossings. The impact was nugatory.[11]

The leaders of the Free State invested great hopes in the results of the boundary commission offered by Lloyd George's government in order to clinch the treaty compromise. At the very least, expectations ran, it would transfer swathes of the two Catholic-majority counties, Fermanagh and Armagh, from Northern Ireland to the south. At best it would so squeeze Northern Ireland's economic viability as to make reunification unavoidable. As it turned out, after years of deliberation the commission brought forward a mouse. Details of its conclusions were leaked in the autumn of 1925. They suggested the transfer to the Free State from the north of only 183,290 acres of land, affecting just 31,319 people. Some 49,242 acres, accounting for 7,594 people, would be moved from the south to Northern Ireland. In political terms this was trivial, far distant from the expectations of the Irish leaders who had signed the treaty. Fearing a backlash, Cosgrave's government felt it more prudent to abandon the project than seek to explain why it had gone so badly wrong. A deal was struck with London. The border would stay as it was and in return Britain would write off the sizeable financial contribution the Free State had promised to make towards Ireland's historic national debt. Just before his death in 1922, and even as the IRA waged an armed campaign in the north, Michael Collins had acknowledged that the north could not be coerced into the new Irish state. Cosgrave now admitted this reality. Ireland's border of the mind counted for more than passport controls and customs posts. The leaders of the Free State had not been alone in their hopes for unity. Churchill and others had expected economics and geography to exert a centripetal force. But matters of trade and employment were nothing against the centrifugal pull of competing religious and political identities. For all the apparent absurdities, the border marked out the territory of a Protestant redoubt in Catholic Ireland.

Inertia sided with the unionists. Britain would never have any great affection for Northern Ireland. Over time, it would be seen as a burdensome drain on financial resources. But all in all, its affairs were deemed best left to its parliament, installed from 1932 in an imposing new building in the grounds of Stormont Castle.

Dublin's rhetorical denunciation of partition was rarely accompanied by any significant support for nationalists in the north. 'The washing of southern hands could hardly have been more apparent,' as Diarmaid Ferriter observes.[12]

James Craig's government took full advantage. 'All I boast of is that we are a Protestant Parliament and a Protestant State,' he proclaimed in 1934. The shelving of the boundary commission report had removed the last potential threat to the Protestant grip on power. This is not to say Craig trusted Westminster to take Northern Ireland's side. It did not dispel the legacy of mistrust of the British government. During the furore over Home Rule in 1912 he had been ready to fight the British army in order to remain, well, British. Churchill fulminated against Craig's habit of demanding British arms while refusing to be bound by British decisions. But as Northern Ireland's first prime minister he was given the free hand he demanded. King George's plea at the opening of the new parliament in 1921 for it to serve as 'an instrument of happiness and good government for all parts of the community' went unheeded. Craig declared himself an 'Orangeman first and a member of parliament afterwards'. The goal was permanent Protestant hegemony.

Northern Ireland's electoral boundaries were redrawn – gerrymandered, more accurately – and proportional representation was scrapped to strengthen further the unionists' natural majority. The new RUC was buttressed by an all but exclusively Protestant part-time police force – some twenty thousand 'B Specials' – drawn in significant part from the viscerally anti-Catholic Ulster Volunteer Force. It was an army in all but name. The terms of devolution had specifically reserved to the Westminster parliament responsibility for the province's security, but Craig's arrangements effectively bypassed the agreement by reclassifying what was essentially a militia as a police service. Ministers in London knew what was happening. A paper prepared for the cabinet as early as March 1922 anticipated the strategy: 'It is difficult to avoid the conclusion that the Government of Northern Ireland has succeeded in assuming the military functions specifically reserved to the British government, simply by calling their forces "police". Our equivalent force of police in Great Britain would make at least... 800,000 men.' Nor were the authors of the report in any doubt as to Craig's intentions. The new forces were there as an insurance policy against unwelcome intervention from London, as well as any intrusions by the new state in the south. 'It is impossible to assume that the formidable forces now being organised under the guise of police are directed solely against the danger of invasion from the south,' the paper continued. 'The British Government has armed and is paying for forces which, it is told by the Government that controls them, will in certain eventualities, be turned against itself.'[13] Unionism had been prepared to fight the British state in 1912. It was ready to do so again. And the UK Treasury was picking up the bill.

With the security of the state belonging to Protestants, routine pogroms directed against Catholic communities went uninvestigated. Government departments operated an apartheid system, locking Catholics out of senior positions. The Belfast shipyards reserved the best jobs for Protestants, as did local authorities in the allocation of public housing. The discrimination was sometimes sharpened by nationalist boycotts. Unionist paranoia teetered on the absurd. One minister in Craig's all-Protestant cabinet announced that he would not put calls through the telephone switchboard at Stormont because one of the operators was said to be a Catholic. Sir Basil Brooke, later to become the province's prime minister, happily boasted that he had no Catholics in his employ.

The Free State was not immune from prejudice against a small population of Protestants. By accepting partition, Craig had effectively abandoned them in the south. A state in which the constitution declared Gaelic to be the official language and which all but anointed Catholicism as the official religion was a less than hospitable place for those of a different confessional persuasion. Accounting for less than 10 per cent of the Free State population, Protestants in rural areas in particular felt isolated. Many drifted away, some northwards, others to Britain. For all that, the absence of the institutionalised discrimination commonplace in the north assured Protestants in the south of a disproportionate number of senior positions in the professions and public administration – the law, medicine and civil service. Members of the old Anglo-Irish Ascendancy whose great houses had survived the depredations of the IRA during the revolutionary and civil wars had mostly sold off their agricultural land, but they stayed to hunt and fish on their estates. They were living now in a foreign country. By some estimates forty thousand Protestants left during the decade or so after partition.

Entrenched as they were, Northern Ireland's unionists were ever fearful. For Craig, the Free State's 1937 constitution was a gift. The territorial claim to the thirty-two counties could be held up as proof that the south wanted to coerce the north into a united Ireland – and worse, into a united Ireland that made no concessions to the Protestant faith or the British traditions of unionists. De Valera had codified the exalted place of the Catholic Church. Yet there was little beyond pro forma protests from Dublin about unionist discrimination against northern Catholics. A call from leaders of the northern nationalists for seats in the Dáil to be allocated to their elected representatives was refused. De Valera held firmly to the claim that partition was a problem created by the British that could only be undone by the British. In this mindset, the Free State's embrace of its Gaelic identity was irrelevant. There were some in Dublin who recognised the contradiction. In 1924 the poet-turned-senator William Butler Yeats had called for an Irish national culture that embraced all traditions:

> I have no chance of seeing a united Ireland in my time, or of seeing Ulster won in my time; but I believe it will be won in the end and not because we fight for it, but because we govern this country well. We can do that . . . by creating a system of culture which will represent the whole of the country.[14]

Others took a harsh view of Fianna Fáil's march into the past. In 1938 the northern-born Seán MacEntee, a member of de Valera's government, conveyed his frustrations directly to the Taoiseach. Partition could not be solved 'except with the consent of the majority of the Northern non-Catholic population. It certainly cannot be solved by their coercion.' Relying on Britain to wield a 'big stick' was doomed. Did the government believe, he asked, that the British could 'force the Northern non-Catholics to associate with us, when with our connivance every bigot and killjoy, ecclesiastical and lay is doing his damnedest here to keep them out'?[15] Here was the kernel of the post-partition paradox. From the outset, Craig's unionists had no doubt about their aim to deepen the divide with the Free State. In the decades after partition, a fair-minded observer would have concluded that Dublin had decided to aquiesce in their ambition.

'Now is your chance. Now or never. "A nation once again." Am very ready to meet you at any time.'[16] Winston Churchill's message was delivered during the early hours of 8 December 1941 to Éamon de Valera's Dublin residence. No matter the hour, Churchill had insisted that John Maffey, the head of the British mission in the Irish capital, hand it personally to the Taoiseach. De Valera recorded that he received it at 2.05 a.m. News had just reached Downing Street of the Japanese attack on the United States fleet in Pearl Harbor. America's entry into the war against the Axis powers was inevitable. A month earlier, the British leader had railed in the House of Commons against the Irish government's refusal to allow British forces to use the former treaty ports: 'It is a most grievous and heavy burden that we cannot use the south and west coast of Ireland to refuel our flotilla and aircraft.' Now, Churchill was saying to his Irish counterpart, America's entry into the war meant that Germany's defeat was assured. Ireland should seize the opportunity to join the Allies in the war against Hitler's Germany. The prospect of a united Ireland would be its reward.

De Valera was unimpressed by Maffey's pre-dawn call. The note he made of the encounter recalled that he interpreted the message as Churchill's way of saying that Dublin had a chance to take action 'which would ultimately lead to the unification of the country'. He recalled, however, that he had told Maffey that 'I saw no opportunity at the moment of securing unity, that our people were determined on their attitude of neutrality'. As for the suggestion of a meeting, de Valera declined. 'I pointed out that it was not because I did not wish to meet Mr Churchill . . . I was not in favour of it because I considered it unwise; that I didn't see any basis of agreement and that disagreement might leave conditions worse than before.'[17] Others in Dublin were more pointedly dismissive. Joseph Walshe, the director of the external relations department, recalled some years later: 'Our opinion was that Churchill had been imbibing heavily that night, after the news of Pearl Harbour had come over on the American radio at between 7 and 8 o'clock . . . and that his effusion flowed into the message.'[18]

The war was framed by de Valera as 'the Emergency'. The argument about neutrality was not a new one. It had been there since the foundation of the state. In the months preceding a formal declaration of war with Germany, de Valera's determination to stand aside had prompted contingency discussion in London on the possible seizure of Irish territory in the cause of Britain's national survival. As Hitler's forces marched westwards across Europe, it was evident that Britain's future would depend on the supply convoys bringing weapons, food and raw materials across the Atlantic from the United States. Without control of Irish ports in the south and west, the military chiefs feared, Britain would be unable to secure the sea lanes against the U-boats. The German navy could shelter in Irish waters. And how long, the chiefs asked, before the Berlin high command occupied the Irish Free State as a springboard to invasion of the British mainland?

Churchill, brought into the cabinet by Chamberlain as first lord of the Admiralty after the outbreak of war, was foremost among those demanding Britain recover use of the ports it had ceded in the deal struck with de Valera in 1938. He demanded that at the very least the military should take back Berehaven in County Cork to safeguard Britain's Atlantic flank. Chamberlain thought he had received an informal assurance allowing British use of the facilities in the event of war. In the event, the Dublin government insisted that such an arrangement would be a breach of its neutrality. Two months after the outbreak of war, in November 1939 Chamberlain lodged a formal request that the Royal Navy be given access to the ports. De Valera's answer was an abrupt no. Lest there be any doubt, the refusal was accompanied by a warning that Dublin was prepared to go to war to defend its national territory.

For a time, the Irish braced themselves for a British landing. Heading the British mission in Dublin, Maffey told Irish officials that he could not give an absolute guarantee against invasion. Walshe reported that he had been warned that they would 'take whatever measures here that might be necessary to save themselves'.[19] That seemed a faithful reflection of Churchill's view. The diplomatic crisis came to a head in June 1940, after British troops scrambled into small boats to return home in the extraordinary retreat from Dunkirk. Churchill had replaced the broken Chamberlain in Downing Street. In Dublin, a German victory now seemed inevitable. Writing to the Taoiseach on 21 June, external affairs director Walshe was certain. 'Britain's defeat has been placed beyond all doubt,' he briefed de Valera as Hitler's Wehrmacht swept aside Europe's last defences. 'France has capitulated. The entire coastline of Europe from the Arctic to the Pyrenees is in the hands of the strongest power in the world ... Neither time nor gold can beat Germany. It is frankly acknowledged in America that America must look to her own defences.' In a tone that seemed to betray personal satisfaction, Walshe continued that 'England has the most concentrated industry and system of ports of any great power in the world. Her power of production would be wiped out in a few weeks of intensified bombing and her ports put out of action ... The German air force is acknowledged to have had an immense superiority in numbers.'[20] Whatever Walshe's own feelings, such predictions of German victory scarcely encouraged any thought of joining the war.

In June the prime minister's emissary Malcolm MacDonald travelled to Dublin in the attempt to persuade de Valera that with German troops now sitting just across the Channel, Ireland as much as Britain was threatened by the Third Reich. Churchill's offer was explicit. MacDonald handed de Valera a note setting out the joint declaration to be made if Éire abandoned neutrality. The British government would accept the principle of a united Ireland and a working group would be established for Dublin and Belfast to work out the practical details of a 'Union of Ireland'. The two nations would establish a Joint Defence Council and Éire would enter the war against Hitler. 'This declaration to take the form of a solemn undertaking that union is to become at an early date an accomplished fact from which there will be no turning back.'[21]

De Valera again rejected the entreaties. His reasoning was expressed in a blunt briefing note from Walshe: 'There is not any guarantee that having accepted the very vague and half-baked proposal for a union of Ireland, the Northern government would be under any obligation to accept our view as to what that union should be.'[22] The Éire government would be prepared to accept a deal on partition that would see Belfast keep its own parliament, but only if 'an all-Ireland parliament' dominated by Dublin was 'free to decide all matters of domestic and foreign policy'. As for joining the Allies against the Axis powers, de Valera insisted the 'Unity of Ireland should be established on the basis of the whole country becoming neutral'. Britain, in other words, would lose military access to Northern Ireland without gaining anything in the south. Putting aside expectations that Britain faced defeat, the view in Dublin was that the proposed declaration lacked an essential guarantee that the British would if necessary force Craig's government in Belfast into a union. The result of the British proposal, Irish officials worried, could be the creation of a new Irish state with less independence than Éire. The plan, de Valera said in a letter of rejection, 'would involve our entry into the war ... Our people would be quite unprepared for it, and Dáil Éireann would certainly reject it.' As for Churchill's offer of eventual unity, 'It gives no guarantee that in the end we would have a united Ireland, unless indeed concessions were made to Lord Craigavon opposed to the sentiments and aspirations of the great majority of the Irish people.'[23]

Whatever the solidity or otherwise of the late-night telegram sent eighteen months later by Churchill after Pearl Harbor, the reality was that in de Valera's hierarchy of strategic goals, preserving neutrality counted for more than dismantling partition. He had said as much twenty years earlier, in a letter sent to Lloyd George on the eve of the treaty negotiations: 'The Irish people's belief is that the national destiny can best be realised in political detachment, free from imperialistic engagements which they feel will involve enterprises out of harmony with the national character, prove destructive of their ideals, and be fruitful only of foreign wars.'[24] To fight alongside Britain, in short, would be to acknowledge his country's subservience.

As for Hitler's intentions towards Ireland, the rebuff to Churchill was not without a whiff of cynicism. De Valera did not accept that, by standing aside, Ireland put itself in greater danger. What he would never say publicly was that he viewed Britain as Ireland's insurance policy against Hitler. Should the Germans mount an invasion of Ireland, he calculated, 'The British would in their own defence be compelled, if we did not do it, to make provision for the defence of our area.'[25]

That said, de Valera also spoke for the people. Tests of public opinion showed the Irish were overwhelmingly against the country's entry into the war. The IRA, outlawed in the Treason Act of 1939, had openly allied itself with Hitler's regime. In January 1939 it had formally declared a 'state of war' against Britain, launching a bombing campaign against power and water plants and railway stations in London and other big cities that continued until the late summer. Those aligning themselves so directly with Germany comprised only a few thousand Volunteers, but de Valera's claim to represent Irish republicanism would have been severely compromised had he entered the war on Britain's side. The same sensitivities were reflected in a warning from Dublin against the introduction of conscription in the north. John Dulanty, the Irish head of mission in London, told Churchill: 'It would surely be an outrage to seek to force the nationalists of the six counties to fight for a freedom they had never known.'[26]

Neutrality came in different shades. Much as de Valera insisted that Ireland had no part in the fight, its deep-seated ties with Britain could not be ignored. The tightrope that the Dublin government walked was set out in a briefing note prepared ahead of a meeting between the Taoiseach and Eduard Hempel, the diplomat who remained head of the German mission in Dublin throughout the war. De Valera should point out, it said, that Ireland's position as a member of the Commonwealth, its strategic geography and uniquely close political and economic ties meant that its relationship with Britain 'cannot have all the characteristics' applied by other neutral states. So while Ireland would not intend 'to participate in any active form in the war against Germany', it was to be hoped Berlin would accept that 'the continuance of the normal relations with Great Britain imposed upon us by historical and geographical considerations will not be regarded as a breach of neutrality on our part'.[27]

Ireland's 'benevolent neutrality', as it was sometimes described in conversations with the British, extended to passing secret intelligence to London. In October 1939 the war cabinet in London was told that the Irish government had helpfully banned the German mission in Dublin from sending cipher messages. Its communications with Berlin had instead to be routed through Washington – and the Irish were supplying copies to the British.[28] Nor did the absence of conscription in the north prevent young Irish men crossing from the south to join the British army. An estimated fifty thousand joined the fight, perhaps five thousand of them deserters from the Irish army. The British forces celebrated their Irish heroes, testimony to the interwoven nature of the two societies that defied differences of high policy between governments. The family of Wing

Commander Brendan (Paddy) Finucane had moved from Dublin to London during the 1930s. His father had been a member of the IRA, driven to leave home in order to find work during de Valera's economic war with the British. His skills and bravery as one of the most celebrated fighter pilots during and after the Battle of Britain counted him among the most celebrated and decorated of the RAF's wartime 'aces'. Some 2,500 people attended a memorial service after his Spitfire was lost in the Channel in 1942.

Neutrality saw senior Irish officials tell both sides what they wanted to hear. The Dublin government was assiduous in assuring the German government that it was doing nothing to break with neutrality. Walshe was particularly attentive to Berlin's sensibilities, signalling in the opening years of the war that the Irish diaspora in the United States could be a useful ally in persuading the Roosevelt administration not to join the war. To David Gray, the head of the American mission in Dublin, it seemed Walshe was conspiring with the Germans. Yet in May 1941 Walshe also drew up a 'Most Secret' memorandum headed 'Help given by Irish Government to the British in relation to the actual waging of the war'. To inform Dublin's discussions with the British, the list of thirteen specific areas of assistance included the passing of information on German aircraft and submarines, permission for the RAF to use Irish air space in certain areas, a 'constant stream' of intelligence information and the routing of German and Italian official communications through Britain.[29]

The principle, however, was non-negotiable, even when it forced an open rift with Washington. None had been as determined as de Valera to court the support of the Americans for the new Irish state. His fundraising among Irish Americans had made a big contribution to the republican effort in the Anglo-Irish War. After the treaty Washington was seen as a vital ally in efforts to put diplomatic pressure on Britain to end partition. Roosevelt's envoy Gray, however, was as determined as any British politician that Ireland should join the war. In the autumn of 1940, more than a year before America's entry, Gray pressed his hosts to allow British use of the treaty ports, to no avail. Gray reported back to Washington that the Irish government expected Hitler to win. A relative of Roosevelt's wife, he proved a constant thorn in the side of the Dublin government, accusing officials of colluding with the German foreign ministry and of encouraging the Irish diaspora in the United States to lobby against American entry into the war. For Gray, the conflict represented an existential contest between the forces of freedom and democracy and those of fascist authoritarianism. Once Washington had joined the Allies, the envoy pressed for sanctions to persuade Ireland to do likewise. For his part, de Valera protested at the stationing of American troops in Northern Ireland as an affront to the sovereignty over the territory claimed by Dublin. In the spring of 1944, at Gray's instigation, Roosevelt, in a démarche carefully choreographed with Churchill, demanded the closure of the German and Italian diplomatic missions in Dublin – viewed by American forces as dangerous sources of intelligence for the German military. De Valera's response was scolding. A note delivered to Washington remarked: 'The American government should have realised that the removal of the representatives of a foreign state on the demand of the government to which they are accredited is universally recognised as a first step towards war, and that the Irish government could not entertain the American proposal without a complete betrayal of their democratic trust.' Irish neutrality, it continued, 'represents the united will of people and parliament. It is the logical consequence of Irish history and of the forced partition of the national territory.'[30]

Defiant to the last and rarely shaken in his convictions, de Valera outraged even some of Ireland's best friends during the closing days of the war. Accompanied by Walshe, he called at the residence of the German minister Hempel to offer condolences on Hitler's death in his Berlin bunker. Frederick Boland, Walshe's deputy at the department of external affairs, had counselled strongly against the visit. It was hard to imagine a more provocative gesture of defiance towards Ireland's former colonial master. The predictable fury in London was accompanied by bemusement and anger in Washington. The editorials in the *New York Times*, the *Washington Post* and other leading newspapers were caustic. Technically, de Valera's action was in line with normal diplomatic protocol. But these were scarcely normal times. Staying out of the war had cost Ireland friends. Lamenting the suicide of the Nazi leader seemed positively perverse. In a telegram to Dublin, the Irish head of mission in Washington Robert Brennan noted: 'Radio Commentator announced item in bitter and caustic tone. Although similar action by Portugal is reported, Chief [de Valera] gets headlines in all papers seen. Particularly because of horror atrocity stories of German prison camps during past months. Anti-German feeling was never so bitter here as now.' De Valera was unrepentant, responding to Brennan that he had anticipated the furore but had merely been following the correct diplomatic courtesies. 'During the whole of the war Dr Hempel's conduct was irreproachable. He was always friendly and invariably correct ... I certainly was not going to add to his humiliation in the hour of defeat.' Staying away would have established a bad precedent. 'It is of considerable importance that the formal acts of courtesy paid on such occasions as the death of the head of a State should not have attached to them any further special significance, such as connoting approval or disapproval of the policies of the State in question or of its head.' In the circumstances, it would have been an 'unpardonable' discourtesy not to have called on Hempel. 'I am sure I acted correctly and I feel certain wisely.'[31]

Churchill's riposte came in his televised victory broadcast. Irish neutrality had put Britain in peril, he charged. 'Owing to the action of Mr de Valera, so much at variance with the temper and instinct of thousands of southern Irishmen, who hastened to the battlefronts to prove their ancient valour, the approaches which the southern Irish ports and airfields could so easily have guarded were closed by the hostile aircraft and U-boats.' It was a deadly moment in Britain's national life, he continued, but 'with a restraint and poise to which, I say, history will find few parallels, we never laid a violent hand upon them, which at times would have been quite easy and quite natural, and left the de Valera Government to frolic with the Germans and later with the Japanese representatives to their heart's content'. And lest the message to de Valera was insufficiently clear:

> When I think of these days I think also of other episodes and personalities. I do not forget Lieutenant-Commander Esmonde, VC, DSO, Lance-Corporal Keneally, VC, Captain Fegen, VC, and other Irish heroes that I could easily recite, and all bitterness by Britain for the Irish race dies in my heart. I can only pray that in years which I shall not see the shame will be forgotten and the glories will endure, and that the peoples of the British Isles and of the British Commonwealth of Nations will walk together in mutual comprehension and forgiveness.

The condescension was striking. Britain, Churchill was saying, deserved praise for its restraint in not invading its neighbour. Herein lay the enduring sense of proprietorship that shaped Britain's view of Ireland.

Churchill's great victory against Nazism was not rewarded by the voters. In July 1945 Clement Attlee's Labour Party was swept to power by an electorate still scarred by the Conservative government's response to the economic depression of the 1930s. Britain wanted a different peace. A briefing prepared for Attlee's cabinet by Maffey carried its own Churchillian tone. John Maffey, who had previously served as chief commissioner of India's North-West Frontier Province and as governor general of Sudan, looked at Ireland through the lens of empire. In the early months of the war he had shown some sympathy with the political constraints on de Valera. Now he told the new government that while the Taoiseach was no 'hater of England . . . Éire is more than ever a foreign country. It is so dominated by the National Catholic Church as to be almost a theocratic state. Gaelic is enforced in order to show that Éire is not one of the English-speaking nations.' Anti-British feeling, he continued, 'is fostered in school and by church and state by a system of "hereditary enemy" indoctrination'. De Valera's call on the German mission, he noted, had been calculated to emphasise Ireland's separateness. Far from causing dismay in Dublin, Churchill's subsequent riposte had been held up as proof of that independence. As to the national 'character' of the Irish people, Maffey offered a vivid insight into the imperial mindset:

> There still persist the dark Milesian strain, the tribal vendetta spirit, hatred and blarney, religious fanaticism, swift alternations between cruelty and laughter. A knowledge of the North-West frontier tribes of India is a good introduction to an understanding of the Irish. They are both very remarkable and in many ways attractive people with the same mental kinks. We were wise enough not to bring the Afridis under our direct rule.[32]

The breach over neutrality pointed the way forward: 'We can now talk to Éire on a cold, factual, horse-trading basis, knowing perfectly well that the cards are in our hands.'

Britain's intelligence services took a more sanguine view of de Valera's decision to stay out of the war. An analysis produced in

1946 and subsequently released from the archives of MI5 concluded that it would have been politically impossible for the Irish prime minister to join the war. It also raised the question of whether Ireland might have been more useful to the war effort as a neutral than a belligerent. The workers and military recruits crossing the Irish Sea during the early stages of the war had been critical to Britain's effort to halt Hitler's advance.

> Éire's 'unconscripted' nationals provided an invaluable reservoir of labour. So great was the need for this Irish labour before and during the Battle of Britain in 1940 that without it, the aerodromes, so desperately needed, couldn't have been built, and great as the need for Irish labour was then, it increased throughout the war as the calls on our own manpower became greater.[33]

At a conservative estimate some 37,440 (southern) Irishmen and 4,520 Irish women joined the British Army and Royal Air Force, and 3,000 Irish men joined the Royal Navy. Estimating that the Irish military would have been defeated within ten days in the event of a German invasion, the analysis noted the valuable intelligence that had been passed on by Dublin.

4 DE VALERA'S IRELAND

The early-evening train pulling out of London's Euston station en route to the North Wales port of Holyhead was full to overflowing. For the parents and young children squeezed with their cardboard suitcases and string-bound parcels into the second-class carriages this was an annual ritual during the 1950s and 1960s. At Holyhead the train connected with the night sailing across the Irish Sea. By the following dawn, good weather permitting, the ferry would dock in the port of Dún Laoghaire, just outside Dublin. Eight hours or so and three more trains would take us to the small station of Kiltimagh, a rural East Mayo outpost known best for its proximity to the Catholic shrine at Knock. Kiltimagh, I would later be told, had given the term 'Culchie' to the national lexicon. The precise etymology is disputed, but 'Culchie' became the pejorative commonly applied by Dubliners to those who hailed from Ireland's backwoods. It described, a good friend once told me, those who arrived in the Irish capital with 'the hay still in their hair'.

Britain's schools had broken for the summer. The Irish were heading home, swapping the noisy urban grime of London (and Liverpool, Birmingham and Manchester) for the open spaces of rural Ireland. Many, if not most, were heading to Ireland's west. In our case, we looked forward to six weeks exploring the mountains, boglands and the wild Atlantic coast of County Mayo, long Ireland's poorest county. For two young boys growing up on a London housing estate, Kiltimagh, a small town of a little more than a thousand people, was a wondrous place. The surrounding countryside offered hills to range across, rivers to swim in, peat bogs to get lost in. The fog and rain were part of the fun. Meals in my grandparents' house – potatoes, gammon, soda bread – were baked in a huge grate warmed by an ever-burning turf fire. Cows, pigs, carts and donkeys – scarcely a common sight in post-war London – made their way along the network of back alleys tucked behind the town's Main Street. Front doors were left unlocked, children set free to roam. The shops – draperies, ironmongers, newsagents, grocers and the rest – mostly boasted a small bar, or snug, in the back where farmers were found sipping Guinness as their carts were loaded. Children gathered at the open-air 'ball alley' – a large concrete handball court where the game was played with a ball so unforgivingly solid that it badly bruised the soft hands of visiting English boys.

Once a month the fair came to town. The streets were crowded with roaming livestock and ramshackle stalls stocked with farm produce and tools, pots and pans and all manner of gadgets and toys. Kiltimagh's only concession to modernity was the six-hundred-seat Savoy cinema, built in the art deco style and a magnet at weekends for farmers and townspeople alike. My grandparents' home had an iron tub in place of a bathroom. The privy was in the yard. A small mountain of cut turf was left to dry out in a large shed. Life was lived in the kitchen parlour, where my grandfather also cut the cloth for his small tailoring business. The smart front sitting room, home to the family china and a 'cold cabinet' that substituted for a refrigerator, was reserved for the frequent visits of the local parish priest. Kiltimagh was small, rural and reverential – above all, deeply Catholic. The large church filled to overflowing at each of the hourly celebrations of Mass on Sundays. The town was also, though I was only half aware of it at the time, very poor.

This was Éamon de Valera's Ireland, the pious rural idyll of the leader's political imagination. It was also the Ireland that the Irish were leaving behind. The people of Kiltimagh 'came home' every summer because so many had been forced to take flight from poverty and the absence of opportunity. My mother was one of eight children. All said goodbye as soon as they were old enough. One brother worked for the national railways in Dublin. The other siblings scattered – two priests and a nun to work in Catholic missions in Africa, and two sisters and another brother in the search for work in England. There was nothing remarkable in this. During the 1960s the journalist John Healy looked back at his departure from another small Mayo town, Charlestown. Tracking the subsequent lives of twenty-three classmates who had left school in 1944, he found that only three had remained. The majority had headed for North America and Britain. The rest settled in Dublin. Healy's work, which first appeared as a series of essays in the *Irish Times*, charted the hollowing-out of his home town. He found shops and businesses shut, the Eureka cinema up for sale. The scene, he recounted, evoked the words of Maurya, the mother in J. M. Synge's play *Riders to the Sea*: 'They're all gone now and there isn't anything more the sea can do to me.'[1] Twenty years later, in 1989, the *Irish Times* sent another journalist on a similar mission, this time to Kiltimagh. There had been only a brief economic bounce since Healy's time, the reporter wrote, before the economic slide had resumed. The town's hotel was sustained by farewell parties for departing emigrants and by the holiday visits of those who had long since left. Tom Higgins, the chair of the district community council, had a sign on his desk: 'The only difference between this place and the *Titanic* is that they had a band.'[2]

When de Valera moved into the Taoiseach's office in 1932, Ireland's population stood at 2.95 million. When he gave up the premiership for the presidency in 1959, after only two short spells out of power, it had fallen to 2.85 million. By way of comparison, just before the famine the population of the twenty-six counties had been more than twice those levels. Ireland's post-war birth rate was among the highest in Europe. So was the number of young emigrants. Small things such as the absence of economic growth or employment did not much trouble the celebrated leader. Austere in his own habits, de Valera saw virtue in hardship. 'The Irish genius', he said, 'has always stressed spiritual and intellectual rather than material values.'[3] During the many years my family visited Kiltimagh I do not recall politics being much discussed, but the songs in the town's bars carried a background hum of rebellion and spoke to an indelible memory of the Great Famine. Mayo was republican territory. Michael Collins, whose sister worked as a schoolteacher in nearby Bohola, would hide out in Kiltimagh during the war against the British, a guest of the relatively wealthy Jordan family. The town was part of the constituency of East Mayo – the seat won by de Valera when Sinn Féin swept the electoral board in 1918. The Chief was also an honoured visitor. Frank Hughes, a friend from school days who became the best man at de Valera's wedding, lived only a few hundred metres from Collins's hideout. Nowhere was de Valera more popular than in such towns. Yet somehow the irony – that the descendants of those who had been cast out of Ulster and sent west by Oliver Cromwell were now crossing the Irish Sea to raise their families in England – was lost to nostalgia.

De Valera set his mission as building Irish nationhood. He was that rare thing among Dublin's middle classes – an Irishman fluent in Irish. The 1937 constitution sought to embed in the national psyche de Valera's vision of an Irish Ireland. Éire was to be closed, conservative, Gaelic and Catholic. It would pay homage to Ireland's past as a rural, self-sufficient nation. Men would work the land, women would serve as the anchor of family life. Children would learn to speak and write Gaelic – the language was fixed in the national curriculum. History, long the property of the English occupiers, was reclaimed to celebrate a Gaelic past. The economy would be protected from overseas competition. Self-sufficiency counted for more than material progress. In crafting the constitution, de Valera had resisted calls from the Catholic hierarchy formally to declare Éire a Catholic state, but for all that, the church of Rome was anointed guardian of the faith and of the nation's public morals. The constitution, the preamble declared, was written 'in the name of the Most Holy Trinity, from Whom is all authority and to Whom, as our final end, all actions both of men and States must be referred'. Freedom of religion was guaranteed, but 'The State recognizes the special position of the Holy Catholic Apostolic and Roman Church as the guardian of the Faith professed by the great majority of the citizens.' Divorce was prohibited and the home rather than the workplace designated the most suitable place for women. 'Mothers', it said, 'shall not be obliged by economic necessity to engage in labour to the neglect of their duties in the home.'

Language and religion were the anchors of identity. These were the markers that also set Ireland apart from its former Protestant colonial master, and from the majority unionist community in the north. To be more Irish was to be less British. Yeats had celebrated Irish tradition in English poetry and prose. 'There is no use of talking of Irish nationality if you talk of it in terms of the English language,' de Valera declared in his speech to the Ard Fheis, or annual conference, of Fianna Fáil in 1937. His text had been previewed by his friend Douglas Hyde, when he laid out his stall in a speech to the Irish National Literary Society in 1892. If Ireland was to throw off the shackles of centuries of English rule, it had to break the 'constant running to England for our books, literature, music, games, fashions, and ideas'. By Anglicising, the Irish had thrown away 'the best claim which we have upon the world's recognition of us as a separate nationality'. Neglect of Gaelic was 'our greatest blow, and the sorest stroke that the rapid Anglicisation of Ireland has inflicted upon us. In order to de-Anglicise ourselves we must at once arrest the decay of the language. We must bring pressure upon our politicians not to snuff it out by their tacit discouragement merely because they do not happen themselves to understand it.' De Valera took him at his word. The constitution declared Gaelic to be the official language of the state. English was acceptable as a second language. 'We must get the people to recognise what the restoration of the language means for our nationality,' his Ard Fheis speech continued. 'The only way to hold our nation . . . is by securing our language as the language of the Irish people.'

De Valera echoed the same sentiments when the country's overseas diplomats gathered in Dublin in September 1945.[4] The challenges facing Ireland, he explained, had not passed with the end of the war. Most obviously, it faced the constraints imposed by partition – the occupation of a substantial part of its territory by a 'foreign power'. Beyond that lay an existential threat: 'the danger of losing our independence through losing our national distinctiveness'. Ireland's people, he explained, were increasingly exposed to 'the denationalising influences of Great Britain and, in a lesser but no means small, degree to those of the United States'. The nation's diplomats must maintain a 'special vigilance in maintaining and increasing all the elements and symbols of our national existence'. As for partition, 'no Irishman with a national tradition can be satisfied with the present situation, and it is a duty imposed on all of us to make that clear'. The speech left unanswered where a small, neutral state such as Ireland would sit in a world dividing between the communist Soviet empire – a dangerously unholy enterprise in the eyes of the Vatican – and a broad US-led alliance of the West. As for their 'denationalising' influences, the inconvenient facts of life were that Britain was a vital economic partner and the United States Ireland's best friend in the wider world.

Unabashed, de Valera instructed those leading Ireland's diplomatic posts in foreign capitals to educate their hosts in 'the partition of our country and the struggle to maintain and enhance our national distinctiveness as a necessary means of maintaining our separate and state life'. Diplomats should draw inspiration from the nineteenth-century Young Irelanders, nationalists who had 'nourished themselves on the story, the language and the literature of our country' when they rose against the British in the late 1840s. Catholicism was a vital instrument of foreign policy. For centuries, Irish Catholics had been forced to flee abroad to safeguard their faith. Now, shared religion promised important alliances in 'Latin Europe'. Joseph Walshe, heading the External Relations Department, called his diplomats 'apostles for the nation'. In 1946 he was appointed as ambassador to the Vatican. The posting was a promotion. De Valera ranked all this above partition: 'I would not tomorrow, for the sake of a united Ireland, give up the policy of trying to make this a really Irish Ireland,' he remarked in 1939. And yet, the same diplomats sent to promote this authentic, Gaelic Ireland abroad employed English as their working language.

Catholicism had a tighter grip than the language on the national consciousness, claiming the allegiance, often devout, of more than 90 per cent of the population. De Valera had found his religious confessor in John Charles McQuaid, from 1940 the archbishop of Dublin and until the year before his death in 1973 the most powerful prelate in the Republic. McQuaid, a member of the Holy Ghost order of missionaries, had previously headed the prestigious Blackrock College. The order was well known for its missionary work, and early in his vocation McQuaid had expressed hopes of joining his fellow priests in West Africa. Instead, he flourished as an administrator. Staunchly conservative, he saw the Church's role as reaching well beyond the spiritual well-being of its flock. Once installed as archbishop, he set himself as the counterweight to the intrusions of the state into Irish family life. Education, welfare and control of the written and spoken word all belonged to the Church. His biographer John Cooney saw in the autocratic McQuaid a Renaissance prelate, albeit operating with more modern methods.[5] The suffocating regime overseen by the Censorship of Publications Board and the Censorship of Films Appeals Board was controlled by McQuaid through a network of informants modelled on J. Edgar Hoover's FBI. McQuaid did not get everything he wanted. He had tried to persuade de Valera to stake out an even more commanding role for Catholicism in the constitution. He ensured, though, that education belonged to the Church, as did family morals. Unmarried pregnant women, deemed to have shamed themselves and their families, were effectively incarcerated in mother-and-baby homes. Their newborns were put up for forced adoption – many of them were sent across the Atlantic to be brought up as Americans. Orphans faced similarly harsh regimes in so-called industrial schools. The powerful religious orders, pious to the last in public, presided over institutions in which harsh discipline bled easily into cruelty and, as later official investigations would show, into widespread sexual abuse of the children in their care.

The archbishop's authority was briefly tested when in 1948, for the first time since 1932, de Valera lost an election. His Fianna Fáil government was replaced by a five-party coalition led by Fine Gael's John Costello. On the other side of the Irish Sea, Britain's government was building a comprehensive welfare service designed by the Liberal reformer William Beveridge. The assault on what Beveridge saw as the five great evils of Want, Disease, Ignorance, Squalor and Idleness extended to Northern Ireland. In the south state provision was rudimentary, with health still firmly in the hands of private doctors. Noel Browne, the health minister in the Fine Gael government, proposed a small step in the British direction. A new scheme would offer free health provision for mothers and children below the age of sixteen. Doctors protested it would cut their fees. McQuaid and the Catholic hierarchy led the real opposition. The scheme, they charged, marked an unwarranted intrusion by the state into family life. In truth, the argument was about politics and power. Socialised medicine, in the Church's eyes, marked a step in the direction of 'communism'. And the Church ran its own hospitals. State intervention would weaken its hold over its flock. Costello retreated, and Browne was obliged to resign.

All the while, Ireland's economic weakness was mirrored in the flight of its young people. Britain had its own troubles during the 1950s. The empire was unravelling. Independence for India and Pakistan was followed by the rise of nationalist movements across Asia and the Middle East. The fall of Singapore in 1942 had broken the spell of British power in the East. Now the empire faced insurgencies in Malaya and Burma. The enforced retreat from Suez in the face of Arab nationalism in 1956 read the rites over imperial rule in the Middle East. Cyprus was agitating for independence. Closer to home, industry was being challenged by post-war reconstruction across continental Europe. Industrial devastation in Germany, Italy and France had a silver lining for those nations – their new production facilities were the most modern available. All that said, free from the demands of war and underpinned by government-led construction projects, the British economy grew robustly. Labour shortages created strong demand for Commonwealth and Irish workers. Living standards rose along with industrial production. House building boomed. By the end of the decade Harold Macmillan could claim, albeit with self-serving hyperbole, that British voters had 'never had it so good'. It was another story on the other side of the Irish Sea. The economic pattern established during British rule was one in which Ireland exchanged basic agricultural produce, in large part live animals, for manufactured goods from Britain. Thirty years after the creation of the Free State, nothing much had changed. In the absence of government investment, of foreign capital and technological innovation, Ireland's economy stagnated. De Valera's quest for an illusory economic self-sufficiency militated against the growth of manufacturing and service businesses.

'Emigration is a great national problem. It is grievous to every one of us,' a report prepared for the Taoiseach by the External Relations Department had begun in December 1947, as the nation waited for the annual influx of emigrants returning home for the Christmas holiday. The majority of those leaving, it continued, came from rural Ireland, above all from the west. The arithmetic told the story. About half the population was employed in agriculture. The statisticians calculated that a little more than twenty thousand births were needed each year to hold the balance steady. But during the previous ten years the population had grown at an annual rate of between fifty-eight and sixty-six thousand. To make matters worse, employment in the agricultural sector had been declining. Industry and commerce could absorb some of the surplus, but the gap meant emigration was inevitable. Two-thirds of those leaving were young women, the report continued, and of those more than 70 per cent were under the age of twenty-five. Many of these women were heading to a life of domestic service in the homes of the affluent English. Those with a good school record, my own mother included, found secretarial jobs. Unskilled men were employed in small manufacturing and engineering companies, in construction, serving in public-house bars and in agriculture. The work was hard, the wages low, and housing conditions were atrocious. But emigration, as it had always been, was an escape from the grinding poverty of rural Ireland. As the historian Roy Foster recorded, by 1946 only 5 per cent of farm dwellings had an indoor lavatory and 80 per cent had no sanitary facilities at all. So much, as Foster put it, for the Ireland of 'cosy homesteads, athletic young men and comely maidens' that de Valera had evoked in a celebrated St Patrick's Day broadcast in 1943.[6]

The official report was careful not to challenge de Valera's ideal of an Ireland content with 'frugal comfort'. It focused on the facts and figures rather than policy options. The implicit conclusions, however, were inescapable. Ireland's farming sector could not absorb a growing population. Employment in manufacturing and services had been rising but a much faster expansion was needed to provide the jobs. The authors saw in the growth of the aviation industry an example of what might be done elsewhere. The Irish, they said, no longer lived in 'an island behind an island but have – or will soon have – our own direct travel communications not only to Europe but to the North American continent'.[7] Along the way, aviation had produced at least two thousand additional jobs for Irish workers. Whatever de Valera's dream, the hard truths of demographics and economics demanded industrialisation and urbanisation.

The flight across the Irish Sea underscored the message. As post-war reconstruction intensified Britain's labour shortages, Irish workers were offered special privileges. Under the 1948 Nationality Act, they were afforded the same employment rights and access to public services as their British-born counterparts. Uniquely, they were also given a vote in British elections. For several years after the war the Labour Ministry sought to direct the new arrivals into sectors facing particular shortages – engineering, agriculture and nursing, as well as construction. Between 1947 and 1949 more than ninety-five thousand workers were issued permits through its

Dublin office. During the decade leading up to the early 1960s an estimated half a million left Ireland to seek a better future abroad. The great majority chose to make the short journey across the Irish Sea to the home of the old colonial power.[8] Those leaving included a rising swell of professionals taking posts in teaching, the National Health Service and the law.[9]

Ireland's formal departure from the Commonwealth with the declaration of a republic in 1949 did not dent its special economic status in Britain. By the mid-1950s Conservative MPs at Westminster were raising concerns about the influx of overseas workers recruited from the Caribbean and other Commonwealth states to work in Britain's public services. A report prepared for the cabinet in 1955, however, drew a sharp distinction between what it saw as the potential social and economic dislocation caused by the arrival of 'coloured' workers and the minimal impact of Irish immigrants. For all the often bitter history, the report concluded, the Irish were not 'a different race from the ordinary inhabitants of Great Britain'. As for any strain on public services, including housing, the report noted, with characteristic Whitehall condescension, that living standards in Ireland were significantly inferior to those in Britain. The Irish would put up with conditions unacceptable to British workers. Much the same attitude prevailed in 1961, when the government legislated for restrictions on arrivals from the Commonwealth. No limits were applied to Irish workers. Crudely, Britain's policymakers saw Irish workers as a source of cheap labour who could be integrated without significant disruption or local complaint. Local communities did not always agree. Prejudice against 'Paddys' was commonplace. Conditions in factories were often appalling, and gruelling work on construction sites was available at the whim of local subcontractors. Calls for the Dublin government to help establish welfare projects for these workers went unanswered. The Irish ambassador in London reported the 'shocking' conditions faced by workers in Midlands engineering companies. Their lodgings were 'grossly overcrowded, ill-kept, dirty and cost-exorbitant'. The embassy considered itself in no position to help, though, reporting that 'the number of Irish citizens in this country is so large that the Embassy's discharge of this function [welfare provision] must be, even at the best, rather haphazard and inadequate'.[10]

While the nation's young people boarded the Holyhead ferry at Dún Laoghaire, the Dublin government's response was one of hand-wringing. A Commission on Emigration and Other Population Problems was established. It recognised the damaging consequences of a shrinking population. Those who left were overwhelmingly the young and most productive. The country was growing older as it was getting smaller. But suggestions of 'quotas' or other restrictions on those leaving soon dissolved into a resignation that there was nothing much that could be done. Tax allowances for those employing household workers in Ireland might discourage young women looking to England for jobs in domestic service, the experts mused, but overall the tide could not be turned unless the Republic created more employment in services and manufacturing. De Valera joined those complaining about the dire conditions faced by Irish workers in Britain.[11] It apparently did not occur to him to ask why they were prepared to endure the hardships.

Whatever the privations, the emigrants showed little inclination to return home. In January 1958 the Irish ambassador in London, Con Cremin, sent to Dublin a lengthy private assessment of the flight across the Irish Sea.[12] His dispatch, a fascinating sociological pen portrait of Britain's Irish community, challenged many of the familiar assumptions of unskilled, low-paid and exploited workers. It was true, Cremin noted, that a majority of the emigrants had unskilled jobs – the men with manual jobs in construction, manufacturing and, often enough, serving in pubs, and young women as waitresses or in domestic service. But there was also another story, he said – one of Irish office workers, teachers, nurses and doctors moving up the economic and social ladder. Though these professionals had yet to penetrate the inner sanctums of the 'English Establishment' represented by the gentlemen's clubs of St James's, the diaspora was increasingly visible among the country's middle classes. And they were welcomed. The Irish, he said, were not thought, as with the Germans or the French, to be 'foreign'. Rather, they were part of the family – 'no more alien to the English than the Welsh or Scots'. Their Catholic faith was rarely held against them. Though Britain was notionally a Protestant country, 'religious indifference is the predominant note of English life'. True, the 'old school tie' still counted for much in advancement within the highest social classes, excluding the Irish from some positions. But among sections of the upper middle classes, Catholicism actually carried a certain social cachet. There was respect too for Ireland's literary and theatrical traditions – for the works of William Butler Yeats and James Joyce, George Bernard Shaw, Seán O'Casey and John Millington Synge.

The immigrants certainly experienced prejudice. I caught a glimpse of it as a small boy while on holiday in a seaside town on England's south coast. 'No Blacks, No Irish' read the sign outside a boarding house we passed. 'What does that mean?' I asked my mother. 'Aren't we Irish?' She pulled me away quickly by the hand. 'Pay no attention, they are just silly people.' Only later did I understand how embarrassed she had been by this casual display of bigotry. For all that, Cremin's intriguing memorandum captured the gap between the generally easy relationship between the two peoples and the often fractious one between the governments.

While London and Dublin argued about partition, the prevailing sentiment was 'one of friendliness to the Irish as a people but indifference to Ireland as a power'. That was certainly the case on my family's London housing estate, where the overwhelmingly London-born residents seemed to judge the only 'outsider' to be a rather flamboyant lady from Austria. As for politics, insofar as they paid any attention to partition (and most did not) the English were content with the status quo, Cremin judged. Pressed on the subject, Brits would uphold the right of Northern Ireland to be part of the union. That was not to say northern unionists were particularly popular. 'To the contrary, the average Englishman probably prefers people from the 26 counties who fit the concept of their Irishness better.'

Some in Dublin thought the diaspora could be mobilised in the Irish cause. If Irish Americans could march under the nationalist standard and use their political punch to influence those they helped elect to Congress, why not those who had settled in Britain's great cities? It was a hope never realised, even if Harold Wilson, Labour prime minister during the 1960s, was said to have been attentive to the large Irish Catholic population in his Huyton, Liverpool, constituency.

The Irish-born population in Britain represented a bigger share of the electorate than in the United States, but the diaspora never made anything like the same impact as it did in Washington. Most voted for the Labour Party, known to be more sympathetic to the demands of Catholics in Northern Ireland for equal civil rights. But in Cremin's description, the support for Labour was largely 'class-based'. The Irish in Britain, the ambassador observed, 'vote with their interests as English residents rather than Irish nationalists'. Many of the more prosperous supported the Conservatives.

THESE DIVIDED ISLES

The Allied defeat of the Axis powers had left Ireland in search of a place in the world. As its young sought their fortunes elsewhere, the Ireland of the 1950s found itself all but isolated internationally. Soon after independence, the Free State's first external affairs minister, Desmond FitzGerald, had proudly declared that 'England is our most important external affair'. It was a sentiment that endured during the succeeding decades. But neutrality during the war, and the emerging confrontation between the United States and Soviet Union, carried the message that the new state could not absent itself entirely from the wider world.

De Valera was not blind to the common challenges facing Western nations. Yet everywhere he looked there were inevitable collisions between Irish vision and international realpolitik. Neutrality demanded Ireland stand aside from great power alliances, but in the mind of a conservative and devoutly Catholic nation Soviet communism posed a unique threat to 'Christian' civilisation. Dublin could not ignore the fact that its security and economic interests were shared with the United States and Britain. Bridges would have to be rebuilt with Washington in the wake of the recriminations about neutrality. The Americanisation of the West posed a cultural threat to 'Irishness', de Valera had told the country's diplomats, but the Irish American diaspora was a vital political ally in the campaign against partition. Nor were relations with the old enemy straightforward. Dublin's politicians could denounce Britain for dividing the country, but Ireland depended on it to take its exports of agricultural products and to absorb the workers for whom jobs were not available at home. Ireland also remained a member of the so-called 'sterling area', tying the value of its currency, the punt, to that of the pound. That left Dublin dependent on London for access to the dollars it needed for international trade.

For de Valera, the immutable goal was nation building. For Ireland to explain itself to the world, it had to be sure of its identity. The six counties counted as part of 'the national territory'. Britain was thus an occupying power. For as long as the border remained, Ireland could not be part of any alliance that included its neighbour. This was the case put to Washington when the United States gathered up its allies in the post-war North Atlantic Treaty Organisation (NATO) to counter the spread of Soviet influence. To those who denied the legitimacy of partition, the riposte was that Dublin could not be part of an alliance committed to defend, inter alia, a border that it did not recognise. Ireland could consider joining NATO, Harry Truman's administration was told, only if and when it exercised unchallenged sovereignty over all thirty-two counties. A few years later, Dublin took the argument further, refusing to sign the mutual assistance treaty that Washington demanded of its allies as a price for continued economic aid. The effect was to cut off Ireland from the American funding flowing to the rest of Western Europe. Better, it seemed, to be poorer than to be pulled into a nexus that identified Ireland's interests with those of Britain.

Nationalist theology in the cause of distance from Britain did not make life easy for those charged with steering foreign policy. A note written by the Department of External Affairs voiced exasperation with the constant search for distance from Britain:

> There is a class of people in this country who make a point, whenever we happen to be on the same side as Great Britain in any international discussion, of suggesting we are under the influence of the British. Some of them talk as if, simply because

Britain is on one side, we should automatically be on the other. People should have more sense.[13]

Sometimes, the sensitivities were trivial. In October 1946 John Dulanty, the head of the Irish mission in London, wrote to Sir Alan Lascelles, private secretary to King George VI. His concern was the occasional personal messages still sent by the monarch to Irish citizens to mark special occasions such as a hundredth birthday or a diamond wedding anniversary. Such messages, Dulanty said, threatened to become a cause of 'public controversy' in the Republic – presumably, though this was not spelled out, because they spoke to the age when the monarch's writ still ran. In any event, 'this is a practice which cannot now be continued'.[14] Some years later, on the eve of the coronation of Queen Elizabeth II in June 1953, ministers and officials were debarred from accepting invitations to any events marking the occasion.

The name of the state also proved a point of contention. The 1937 constitution had replaced 'Irish Free State' with 'Éire' or, as it noted, 'Ireland' in English. The British, though, saw in the English attribution a claim to sovereignty over the entire territory, including Northern Ireland. So British politicians and diplomats stuck to 'Éire', even when documents were drafted in English. For their part, Irish diplomats were instructed to insist on the use of 'Ireland' in international statements and agreements. After an embarrassing public spat between the two sides at a conference in Geneva, Dublin came up with a compromise. It would be content with 'Ireland/Éire' or 'Éire/Ireland'. Such quibbles scarcely concealed Ireland's self-isolation. As long as it was outside NATO it lacked a serious voice in Washington. An application to join the United Nations got caught up in the rapid cooling of East–West relations and was blocked for several years by the Soviet Union. De Valera was reluctant to concede the supposed loss of sovereignty involved in membership of the Bretton Woods institutions, the International Monetary Fund and World Bank.

Britain, it should be said, could indulge in its own diplomatic pettiness, but language and emblems loomed larger in Dublin: witness the formal declaration of a republic by John Costello's coalition government in 1948. De Valera's constitutional changes had given the new state full independence. He had demonstrated as much by breaking with Britain during the war. But seeking the return of the treaty ports and an economic deal with Britain, de Valera had opted in this instance for rhetorical pragmatism – to avoid souring completely the wider economic and political relationship with the United Kingdom. Continued membership of the Commonwealth acknowledged a titular role for the British monarch in the accreditation of diplomats. A decade later, Costello, claiming the banner of republicanism for Fine Gael, made the decisive break with the former colonial power. His external relations minister and coalition partner Seán MacBride, a former leader of the IRA and head of the fiercely nationalist Clann na Poblachta, pressed for the rupture. In September 1948, on the eve of a Commonwealth summit, the government declared the state's imminent departure from Britain's imperial family. Ireland had long before stopped attending Commonwealth meetings, so it could be said that the government was merely codifying rather than upturning the status quo. Clement Attlee's government in London was less indulgent. Why had Ireland sought to reopen the wounds?

The departure of Churchill from Downing Street in 1945 had raised hopes in Dublin of a softening in Britain's attitude towards partition. Lacking the imperial baggage of the Conservatives, Attlee's Labour Party had always been more sympathetic towards the nationalist position. Perhaps it could be persuaded if not to push the north into a united Ireland, then at least to indicate that this was a preferred outcome. In the event, the new administration took a hard-headed view. Its approach was set out in a report to the cabinet from Dominions secretary Viscount Addison just two months after the election victory. The war, this said, left Britain in a uniquely strong position vis-à-vis the Dublin government. De Valera's stubborn adherence to neutrality had led to its international isolation. Above all, it had soured Dublin's relations with the United States. The British were now on the side of the angels. 'Éire cannot hope, as in the past,' the report said, 'to embarrass us by counting on American sympathy in complaints against Britain.' In sum, 'Generally it can truly be said that never in our history have we been in such a strong position so far as Ireland is concerned and Éire's position has never been weaker.'[15]

The accompanying note from Sir John Maffey, the minister in Dublin, held out little hope of a warming of the relationship. To summarise Ireland's foreign policy he could do no better than to cite the Sinn Féin founder Arthur Griffith: 'On any international issue, find out where the British stand. Ireland will be found on the other side.' Attlee's government, however, had no interest in the disinterment of old enmities. And in spite of occasional squalls, Anglo-Irish relations seemed to improve with the conclusion in April 1948 of a new trade agreement. So Attlee was taken aback by Costello's announcement. The international context did not help. British power in the world was under challenge. In its own mind at least, Britain had 'won' the war, but along the way it had lost its great power status. Membership of what Churchill had called the 'Big Three' world powers was becoming a flimsy fiction. India and Pakistan had just left the empire, Britain was being forced out of Palestine and nationalist movements in Asia and Africa were weighing the opportunity of breaking with their colonial master.

This was not a good moment for Ireland unilaterally to tear up its relationship with the Commonwealth, an organisation that expressed Britain's continuing claim to significant global influence. So the initial impulse in London was to retaliate. Dublin was told that outside the Commonwealth, Ireland would be a 'foreign country'. It would lose both its trade access and the preferential rights of its citizens living in Britain. In the event, the crisis passed – in significant part because of the mediation of leaders of the other Dominion states, Canada, Australia and New Zealand. At talks convened at Chequers, the prime minister's official country residence, Attlee was urged by his Commonwealth partners to avoid a complete break with the Republic. By January 1949 the two governments had agreed on a mutual declaration of 'non-foreignness'. The trade and citizenship issues were finessed to preserve the special positions of the two states. For all that, Costello had misjudged the likely British response. The episode would carry a unionist sting in the tail.

De Valera had complained that Ireland had 'a long road to travel before we have put an end to the false ideas about the Irish people which have been disseminated all over the world in order to justify British treatment of this country'.[16] Costello's government, with MacBride in the lead, put the international campaign against partition at the heart of its prospectus. In January 1949 the external relations minister set out his plan. His 'Special Secret Memorandum to Government' recalled that 'the undoing of partition' was the issue 'placed foremost by every party and upon which there is complete unanimity'.[17] Drawing direct links with trade and future prosperity, it continued that securing Irish unity was of 'paramount importance to the welfare of the nation'. And yet, a trawl of government departments had revealed that of 32,171 civil servants in the employ of the state 'there is not one of them who is charged with any function in relation to partition'. The report drew a contrast with the 'Six County Government' which produced a stream of pro-union publicity, some of which 'has been very well done indeed'. Carefully prepared articles justifying partition appeared in American and British newspapers and magazines. MacBride's answer was a comprehensive propaganda campaign focusing on the United States, Britain, Canada, Australia and New Zealand, alongside the upgrading of diplomatic missions in Washington and elsewhere, and the dispatch to Belfast of a representative to gather economic and political intelligence. 'The real potential value of the Irish population in Britain', as MacBride saw it, 'lies in a small number of Irish people who hold key positions in the labour and trade union movements and in other political organisations, as well in the newspaper world.' For all the sound and fury, this was performance politics. Little was done to establish a serious relationship with the north or to analyse what a united Ireland might look like – nor to calculate the considerable economic costs that would fall on the south to fill the gap left by financial transfers from London.

MacBride was correct, however, about the adroitness of the unionists in Belfast in promoting their cause. His failure was to see how the northern government would turn his own policy to its advantage. The shift to republican status made little material difference to Anglo-Irish relations, but the Northern Ireland prime minister Sir Basil Brooke was quick to declare it a grievous threat to the province. Declaration of a republic was a prelude to a renewed push by Dublin to force reunification. 'We now have on our southern border a foreign nation,' Brooke declared.[18] Pressed by Brooke to provide stronger guarantees of the north's place in the United Kingdom, Attlee commissioned a report from his own officials. It seemed to confirm unionist fears. The Republic had left the Commonwealth family. Now that Éire would shortly cease to owe any allegiance to the Crown it had become a matter of 'first-class strategic importance' to hold on to the north. In spite of formal protests from Dublin – a note sent to London spoke of 'unnecessary provocation' and a 'gratuitous reassertion' of Britain's intervention in Irish affairs – the unionists got their guarantee. The 1949 Ireland Act passed at Westminster to provide legislative recognition of the Republic's new status also promised the unionists:

> It is hereby declared that Northern Ireland remains part of His Majesty's dominions and of the United Kingdom and it is hereby affirmed that in no event will Northern Ireland or any part thereof cease to be part of His Majesty's dominions and of the United Kingdom without the consent of the Parliament of Northern Ireland.

Dublin's protests were brushed aside. John Dulanty, the Irish ambassador in London, reported back on a conversation with Ernest Bevin, the foreign secretary. Bevin had remarked: 'It seemed to him that we felt free to throw a brick at their heads at any time we liked and be suddenly bitter by even a mild reply from them.'[19]

Within Attlee's government some questions were raised about handing a blank cheque to the Stormont parliament. The cabinet heard about doubts in the House of Commons regarding the wisdom of leaving the power of veto in the hands of a parliament dominated entirely by unionists. Some ministers thought the government should take steps to satisfy itself that the Belfast parliament fairly represented the views of voters. Prevarication prevailed. 'It was, however, the general view of ministers that the United Kingdom government would be ill-advised to appear to be interesting themselves in this matter, which fell wholly within the jurisdiction of the Northern Ireland Government.'[20] The idea of 'consent', in other words, would operate on terms decided by unionism. The outcome was that while the Dublin government had secured full sovereignty over its own affairs and retained its previous trade preferences and arrangements for ports and shipping, on the matter that it professed to care most about – the division of Ireland – it had taken a big step backwards. The inviolability of the unionist veto had been codified in British statute.

Costello's declaration also belied the Republic's continuing economic dependence on Britain – a dependence perpetuated by its protectionist trade and investment policies. In 1924 some 99 per cent of its exports went to Britain. A quarter of a century later, in 1950, the figure was still 93 per cent. As Maffey had put it some years earlier, Ireland was trapped in a sterling 'cage'. The receipts from its exports to Britain had to be spent on British-made goods.[21] Ireland, which had built up considerable credits during the war, was 'a prosperous customer eager to convert his bank balance into British manufactures and not able to look elsewhere for his requirements'. While the price of an 'Irish' Ireland was economic stagnation, Northern Ireland's experience told a contrasting story of industrialisation, rising prosperity and higher welfare standards. The war effort had delivered a boost to Belfast's traditional heavy industries. Now it was followed by the extension to the province of the generous public provision of Attlee's welfare state. Workers were assured of free health care and secondary education and, courtesy of British taxpayers, pensions and other social benefits. Economic growth in the Republic struggled during the 1950s to reach an annual 1 per cent. The growth rate in Northern Ireland averaged 3 per cent. The Belfast government ensured the greater part of these windfalls fell to the Protestant community, but northern nationalists shared in the prosperity. Ireland's politicians would privately admit that more had to be done to persuade citizens of the north that everyone would be better off in a united Ireland.

DE VALERA'S IRELAND

In 1955 the Soviet Union lifted its veto and Ireland took a seat at the United Nations. It was an important moment for the Republic. In the years immediately after partition it had sought to assert its identity as an independent nation by playing an active role at the League of Nations. Now it would do the same at the UN. The decision marked a path out of the decade of international isolation that had followed the end of the war. Sitting outside the American-led Western alliance, Ireland had been a bystander at world events. With a seat at New York's General Assembly it at least had a voice, albeit a modest one, in the cockpit of global relations. Unsurprisingly enough, it struck an independent, anti-colonial note, sticking firmly to its doctrine of neutrality and making friends with newly independent nations emerging from the break-up of empires. Irish troops joined UN peacekeepers in the Congo. Dublin's diplomats had a knack of making themselves useful as organisers and brokers at the Assembly. Over time, policy took on a more Western tilt. By the end of the 1950s the government had concluded (as had Britain) that Europe's Common Market was a serious project. For its part, the Soviet Union's march into Hungary dispelled any notion that Moscow was a reliable guarantor of the UN Charter.

The winds of modernity were also blowing closer to home. In 1956 a rising young civil servant, Thomas Whitaker, was appointed as director of the government's department of finance. During the following year the government took a step in the direction of openness by joining the IMF and World Bank, once scorned by de Valera as threats to sovereignty. Surveying an economy trapped in low growth and employment and drained of talent by migration, Whitaker drew up an ambitious plan. The First Programme for Economic Expansion was published in the autumn of 1958. De Valera, seeing out his last days as Taoiseach, gave it his blessing. Not that he admitted a change of course. To have done so would have been to admit his own failure. Instead, in the description of Irish historian and writer Fintan O'Toole, 'Rather brilliantly, he absorbed the shock of the new by pretending nothing new was happening.'[22]

Then, in June 1959, the seventy-six-year-old de Valera finally relaxed his grip on power, moving across from the Taoiseach's office to the less arduous, and more ceremonial, role of president. The Chief would remain in the president's office for another fourteen years, a ghostly presence in an Ireland struggling to banish many of its demons. His departure from the premiership, however, cleared the ideological cobwebs from Dublin's corridors of power. As a veteran of the Easter Rising his successor Seán Lemass had impeccable republican credentials. He was also keen to reconnect Ireland with the wider world. A first goal was to build economic relationships with continental Europe and attract overseas, especially American, businesses to set up in Ireland. He understood the importance of education, extending schooling beyond the age of fourteen. In place of autarky, Lemass proposed opening up the economy. The 1957 Treaty of Rome establishing the European Community had passed Ireland by. But as Harold Macmillan's government belatedly explored the possibility of British membership, Lemass saw the danger of being left behind – dependent on Britain as its main trading partner but cut off from wider European opportunities. In the summer of 1961 Dublin lodged its application to join – carefully timed to arrive in Brussels a month before Britain submitted its own request. The 1960s would see Ireland's economic tide begin to turn. It was too late to halt the flight of young people from Kiltimagh. The town inaugurated a 'Culchie Come Home' festival to encourage yet another generation of emigrants to keep up the tradition of the annual pilgrimage home. Ireland, though, had begun to say goodbye to de Valera's vision.

5 TRAPPED BY HISTORY

Out of sight and out of mind. In Whitehall's corridors of power, Northern Ireland, an integral part of the United Kingdom, was a place forgotten. The lodestar for government policy had been fixed by the conclusion of Clement Attlee's cabinet in 1949: the government would be 'ill-advised to appear to be interesting themselves in this matter'.[1] James Callaghan, a senior minister in Harold Wilson's government, discovered as much when he arrived at the Home Office in December 1967. Callaghan was a casualty of the latest in Britain's long procession of post-war sterling crises. The prime minister had assured voters that 'the pound in your pocket' would not be affected by the currency's devaluation against the dollar in November 1967. The duplicity was transparent. As chancellor, Callaghan paid the political penalty. The Home Office, and with it responsibility for Northern Ireland, was his consolation prize.

'Responsibility' was too strong a word. The red box ministerial briefings meticulously prepared for the new home secretary by his civil servants set out the agenda. The papers, he recalled, roamed from prisons policy to race relations, from the condition of state children's homes to the police, and from the operations of the fire service to reform of the House of Lords. And 'not a word about Northern Ireland'.[2] Oversight of affairs in the province was entrusted to what was called the Home Office's general department. It would have been better described as the department for odds and sods. The province took its place in bids for the attention of ministers alongside such grave issues as taxi regulation, the alcohol licensing regime and the protection of animals and birds.

Seven staff were allocated to these myriad tasks, only one of them of senior rank. The Home Office was not alone in its insouciant neglect. Ireland had left the Commonwealth in 1949. Such was the general Whitehall indifference to Britain's nearest neighbour that responsibility for relations with Dublin was not transferred from the Commonwealth Office to the Foreign Office before the two departments merged in 1968.

Northern Ireland fell outside the national consciousness. That, most politicians thought, was as it should be. Partition and the Anglo-Irish Treaty were fulfilling their original purpose. A handful of Conservatives still wore unionism on their sleeves. The mindset of most was rather closer to that of Reginald Maudling, who succeeded Callaghan at the Home Office after the 1970 Conservative election victory. Boarding a flight back to London after a trip to Belfast in 1972, Maudling would remark: 'For God's sake, bring me a large Scotch. What a bloody awful country.'[3] From time to time a handful of Labour MPs with nationalist sympathies would raise a protest in the House of Commons at the suppression of the rights of Catholics. They were brushed aside. For the British elite the Irish question had been answered. What happened in the north was the preserve of the one-party administration at Stormont. Custom and practice at Westminster had it that the affairs of Northern Ireland were not debated in the parliament of the United Kingdom of Great Britain and Northern Ireland. The structure designed by William Craig half a century earlier to lock out the province's Catholics had also been calculated to keep the British at a distance. For unionists to declare undying fealty to the Crown was one thing; to be told what to do by Her Majesty's ministers quite another. The unionist grip on power, Callaghan observed, was absolute. The Home Office afforded the province as much attention as it did the Isle of Man.

The same casual disregard ruled official relations with the Republic of Ireland, or the 'Irish Republic' as British ministers called it to avoid giving offence to Northern Ireland's unionists. Harold Macmillan spoke eloquently to the detachment. The Ireland story, he reflected in his prime ministerial diary in March 1963, had been one of centuries of bitter struggles followed by 'the complete surrender of the British'. Now there was peace, 'perfect peace'. It was not to be disturbed. Earlier that day he had met the Taoiseach Seán Lemass in Downing Street. Their talks had been uneventful. 'No-one ever cares or speaks about Ireland,' Macmillan's diary recorded. 'The Anglo-Irish gentry fish and hunt and play no role in the country.' Macmillan spoke from experience. Before long he would be embarking on an agreeable week of fishing on the Duke of Devonshire's Lismore Castle estate in County Waterford. Many of the 'big houses' of the Anglo-Irish Ascendancy had been razed during the wars of the early 1920s, but sufficient remained to provide rural recreation for the English ruling classes. As for the nationalists who had forced Britain out of the south, Macmillan observed that 'The Irish "rebels" now enjoy the most conservative, clericalist and reactionary government in Europe. The population has sunk to under three million.'[4] After playing host at Downing Street to the ageing de Valera, he noted that his guest could not understand why 'we are all so bored with Ireland'. The years had taken their toll, he remarked. De Valera was 'old and blind' and the revolutionary fire had gone. What he could not grasp was why Britain was 'so glad to be rid of her [Ireland] after all those weary centuries'. He 'kept trying to raise the issue of partition, but I would not allow him'.[5]

Such haughty condescension was unremarkable. For centuries the imbalance in the relationship, one of conqueror and conquered, had been described by the casual cruelty of the English. By the

1950s the ruling emotions were superiority and indifference. For the Republic, a long history of repression and the continuing grievance of partition were embedded in the nation's identity. Britain was the reference point, and the organising emotion, for Dublin's worldview. In London, the prime minister's days were filled with the Cold War struggle against the Soviet Union, the nuclear arms race and Britain's diminished standing in the world. The price of victory in the Second World War had been the loss of great power status. The question that preoccupied Downing Street was how to hold on to influence in a world where others were making the decisions. How could Britain position itself as a mediator between Washington and Moscow to avoid a third world war and how could the remains of a shrinking empire be held together? Churchill had done his best to keep up the pretence when he returned to the premiership in 1951. The hollowness had been revealed in 1956, when his successor Anthony Eden's vain – in both senses of the word – attempt to reassert a global role for Britain had ended in the Suez debacle. Macmillan was left to rebuild broken bridges with Washington (the Americans had not been told in advance of Eden's ill-fated misadventure in the desert) and then to clamber onto the Franco-German train that had set off from Rome with the creation of the European Economic Community. Anyway, the English had always talked down to the Irish.

France's veto in 1963 of the first application to join the Common Market spurred the signing of the Anglo-Irish Free Trade Agreement, cutting tariffs on Ireland's agricultural exports to the United Kingdom in return for the lifting by Dublin of tariffs on British exports of industrial goods. That in turn gave a boost to cross-border trade between the Republic and the north. From the British side there were small gestures of goodwill on the eve of the fiftieth anniversary of the Easter Rising. The remains of the executed republican Roger Casement – long requested by Dublin – were at last returned. And the Imperial War Museum was prevailed upon by Whitehall to send back the Irish flag that had flown over the General Post Office during the rebellion. For the most part, though, Ireland was a burden shed.

In 1970, just as the flames of sectarian violence were taking hold in Northern Ireland, the Foreign Office diplomat John Peck prepared for a posting as ambassador in Dublin. In his own mind, there was no other state with which Britain had had such an intimate relationship, a tapestry woven through centuries of shared ancestry and familial bonds, commerce, culture and history. But as he later recalled in his memoir, colleagues and friends proffering advice before his departure to Dublin felt it enough to warn him that the Irish were 'untrustworthy, idle and irresponsible ... They kept hens in the kitchen. Irish women never cleaned their jewellery.' The descendants of the old Anglo-Irish Ascendancy who had remained in the Republic 'did not mingle with the native Irish and generally conducted themselves as though independence had never happened'.[6] Such was the mix of ignorance and complacency with which Britain's governing elite greeted the tumult that was now engulfing Northern Ireland.

What would euphemistically become known as the 'Troubles' (the British would never admit they were fighting a war with the Provisional Irish Republican Army) began as a campaign for the basic civil rights that had been denied to the province's Catholic community from the moment of partition. As much as the grievances were particular to Northern Ireland, the wave of protests and marches on the streets of Belfast and Derry fitted the international mood. This was an age of upheaval. The status quo was under stress across Western democracies. The young were throwing off the shackles of deference. In the United States, the power structures and ruling assumptions of the post-war era faced angry challenges from civil rights campaigners and anti-Vietnam War demonstrations. Authority was challenged by students' and workers' strikes in France and by the anarchist Red Brigades in Italy and the Red Army Faction in Germany. It would have been strange had Northern Ireland's Catholics not seen an opportunity to break the chains of the past.

Sectarian tensions had never disappeared. The gerrymandering of political constituencies and the segregation of employment, housing and education, designed to underpin Protestant power, kept the two communities apart. While the rest of Britain enjoyed the 'swinging sixties', in Northern Ireland the Orange Order, the Apprentice Boys and other unionist fraternities still donned their ancient finery to mark their victory over the Catholics during the Williamite war three centuries earlier. The 'marching season', running from April to August, saw unionism celebrate its rule over nationalism in every corner of the province. On 12 July the Orangemen, with their sashes, elaborate floats and banners, flutes, fife and drum bands, marked the anniversary of the Battle of the Boyne. And each August, the Apprentice Boys of Derry recalled the Protestants' success in breaking the Jacobite siege of that city. Lest nationalists forget this history, the parades were habitually routed through Catholic areas. In 1966 northern nationalists joined island-wide commemorations of the 1916 Easter Rising. The response from working-class loyalists, the foot soldiers of militant unionism, was to revive the Ulster Volunteer Force established by Edward Carson to fight Home Rule. The first victim was claimed in May 1966, when John Scullion, a twenty-eight-year-old Catholic, was shot and mortally wounded outside his home in west Belfast.

The loyalist backlash against Catholic protests intensified with the emergence of the Northern Ireland Civil Rights Association, a mostly Catholic umbrella coalition of politicians, trade unionists and other nationalist groups modelled on the American civil rights movement. The Catholics' demands were straightforward: changes to the electoral laws that excluded poorer (and therefore mostly Catholic) voters from participation in local elections, redrawing of parliamentary boundaries to end the bias in favour of Protestants, equal access to employment, housing and education. The discrimination was indisputable. Partition, British officials privately recognised, had left Catholics in the north 'helpless spectators of a process whereby jobs, houses, electoral boundaries and local government could all be fiddled to their disadvantage'.[7] In the majority Catholic city of Derry, unionists accounted for a little under one-third of the electorate – and claimed the allegiance of three-fifths of the elected representatives.

By the standards of his antediluvian predecessors, the Ulster Unionist Party (UUP) prime minister Terence O'Neill was a moderniser. In an attempt to improve relations with the Republic O'Neill replaced his party's traditional triumphalist language with calls for reconciliation and collaboration between the two communities. He promoted a thaw in relations with Dublin. The old unionism was not listening. O'Neill's meetings with Lemass – the first such summits between a Northern Ireland prime minister and Taoiseach – brought charges of appeasement from within his own party. A fiery and charismatic Presbyterian prelate by the name of Ian Paisley raised the sectarian temperature. Paisley, later to lead the hardline Democratic Unionist Party (DUP), had greeted the death in 1963 of Pope John XXIII with the declaration that 'this Romish man of sin is now in Hell'. Three years later, after failing to secure a ban on events commemorating the Easter Rising, he was briefly jailed for unlawful assembly. By 1968 he had put himself at the head of angry loyalists determined to safeguard Protestant power. Attacks by the UVF and other paramilitaries on the civil rights protests, often with the collusion – sometimes open support – of the overwhelmingly Protestant RUC, put Catholic areas of Belfast and Derry under siege.

Britain's intelligence agencies were woefully unprepared for the upsurge in violence. When in the autumn of 1968 Callaghan asked for an assessment, the Security Service MI5 was forced to admit to itself (though not the home secretary) that it was completely reliant on the Protestant-dominated, and scarcely unbiased, RUC for its information. It did, though, have a sense of the threat. The long-dormant IRA, it accurately predicted, 'may well see in the Civil Rights Movement the broader base necessary for the achievement of its political aims', in turn creating a further backlash from loyalist extremists. 'In basic terms the security problem in Northern Ireland is simple. It springs from the antagonism of two communities with long memories and relatively short tempers.' The cultural and confessional collision between Protestants and Catholics had been amplified by the fears for the future of the former and the economic and social grievances of the latter. 'In this atmosphere attempts to improve relations, however genuine and well founded, only too often are greeted with suspicion by both groups.'[8]

The rest of Whitehall struggled to pay attention. The gulf between received wisdom in London and the realities of Irish politics was glaringly evident in an official report published in September 1969 on the civil unrest of the previous year. The conclusions of the Commission on the Disturbances, chaired by Lord Cameron, ran to more than 230 paragraphs. Only one made reference to relations with the Republic. Betraying the reflex bias against nationalism, it stated baldly that 'The fears and apprehensions felt widely among unionists have solid and substantial basis both in the past and even in the present. From the setting up of the constitution of Northern Ireland there has been an absence of full recognition by the Republic and the attitude of the Roman Catholic hierarchy in Northern Ireland has been ambiguous.' As for the role in the rioting of Protestant discrimination against Catholics, the latter had to share the blame. It was a pity that they had 'held themselves aloof from the community'. The facts on the ground told a different story. Touring Belfast, Callaghan noted that almost all of the destruction was concentrated in the Catholic districts.

In August 1969 Wilson's government ordered the army into the province to restore order. Callaghan's hope was that 'the mere presence of British troops would be enough to restrain both sides without the soldiers having to fire a shot'. Later, he would reflect that the immediate aftermath of the troops' arrival – at first they were greeted by the besieged Catholics as protectors – would mark the last moment the British were trusted in the province. Perhaps inevitably, the army would soon come to be seen as an agent of unionist power. During the following year, Callaghan's Conservative successor as home secretary, Reginald Maudling, would complain that 'the country is full of arms, legal and illegal'. And then, in a despairing report to cabinet colleagues: 'Sometimes it seems almost as if the peoples of Northern Ireland, or at any rate their political leaders (which in realistic terms includes the IRA), are possessed of a death wish.' Britain bore the opprobrium. 'Our whole position in the world is being seriously affected by Northern Ireland and, however hard we try, we will not get other countries to understand the reality.'9 It might have been Churchill speaking in 1921. Fifty years after partition, the Irish question, with all its violent intractability, had returned to haunt British politics. Little had changed. As Callaghan lamented, 'Most MPs know less about it [Northern Ireland] than we know about our distant colonies on the far side of the earth.'[10] It would be 2007 before the last soldiers left the province. And by then some 1,400 would have lost their lives.

In its way, the government in Dublin was as unprepared as its British counterpart for the approaching tumult. The unity rhetoric of politicians had never been matched by a serious effort from Dublin to monitor, let alone influence, events in the north. If Britain's intelligence agencies were absent, so too were those of the Republic. When the province tipped into violent disorder and Catholics fled across the border to the south, the Irish Taoiseach Jack Lynch's first response was to call for intervention from the United Nations. Detachments of Ireland's small army were sent to patrol the border and emergency aid facilities were marshalled lest the steady flow of refugees became a flood. Lynch's public statements recalled the old Fianna Fáil mantra. During talks in London with Harold Wilson in November 1969, he declared that the root cause of the upheavals was partition. The suppression of the rights of Catholics flowed directly from the artificial division of Ireland against the wishes of the majority. Responsibility lay with the British. The Republic's claim to the north was immutable. Yet for most in the Republic the north had become an afterthought. Voters had other preoccupations – employment, living standards, an education system that until recently had turned most children out of school at the age of fourteen and, of course, emigration. Some noticed that in spite of the discrimination many Catholics in the north seemed to have a better economic deal than citizens of the Republic. To be emotionally enraged at the treatment they received from unionists was not necessarily to direct energy towards righting the wrongs. In 1972 the Duke of Devonshire, a former minister with a particular interest in

Ireland, undertook a private fact-finding mission to Dublin, meeting the Taoiseach and Catholic leaders as well as officials and ministers. This was at the height of the violence and yet Devonshire's report back to ministers observed that 'no-one in the Irish government other than Lynch is deeply concerned with Northern Ireland; basically they consider it a nuisance that is interfering with their domestic and EEC [European Community] problems'.[11]

Sotto voce, politicians such as Lemass had begun a few years earlier to edge towards a recognition that there was more to partition than a British plot to remain in Ireland. Lemass quietly acknowledged that the Belfast government rested on the consent of a majority of the people. More radical voices admitted the Republic might also bear some responsibility in perpetuating division. As early as 1957 Donal Barrington, a liberal-minded barrister who would go on to be a supreme court judge, had offered politicians the unvarnished assessment they would now be forced to acknowledge. The border, he said, had been created by the conflicting demands of Irishmen. 'All the policies which the South had adopted in the past 35 years with a view to ending partition have, in fact, tended to strengthen and perpetuate it.'[12] The same sentiments were set out in eloquent terms in a memorandum drafted for Lynch a little over a decade later by Thomas Whitaker, the director of the nation's finance ministry and author of the 1958 economic plan. 'Long since', the lengthy note began, 'we abandoned force as a means of undoing Partition, and rightly so, because 1. The use of force to overcome Northern Unionists would accentuate rather than remove basic differences and 2. It would not be militarily possible in any event.'[13] The inference was clear. The only viable policy was one of seeking unity by agreement in Ireland between Irishmen. De facto, Dublin had recognised that Northern Ireland was part of the United Kingdom. The heart of the argument was that the allegiance of a majority in the north rested essentially on fear – 'fear of loss of power, property, privilege and even religious independence if they were subject to a Dublin parliament'. The task of the Republic was to ease those fears by promoting prosperity, openness and tolerance. That would take time, but:

> Nobody can read the history of the past century in these islands without some understanding of the deep, complex and powerful forces which went into the making of partition . . . The most forceful argument in favour of the patient good neighbour policy aimed at ultimate 'agreement in Ireland between Irishmen' is that no other policy has any prospect of success.[14]

The Dublin-based leadership of the IRA was also slow to respond to the rising violence in the north. During the closing years of the 1950s, the organisation had launched a series of attacks across the border, bombing RUC barracks, radio transmitters and courthouses. The campaign had failed to win broad nationalist support. By 1962 it had petered out. For its part, the IRA leadership, with a preponderance of southerners among the senior ranks, had shifted its energies away from Irish unity towards the Marxist goal of mobilising the working classes against the established political order in Dublin as much as Belfast. When British troops first arrived in August 1969, senior figures in the IRA were reassuring. They had no quarrel with soldiers on the streets of Northern Ireland, they said, as long as they were not deployed against Catholics. Mounting violence shifted the dynamics. Loyalist attacks on Catholic areas, the collusion of the RUC and the military's focus on rounding up republican paramilitaries created a state of siege in nationalist areas. The IRA's old guard in Dublin was pushed aside by a generation of young leaders in the north who assumed the role of defenders of Catholic communities. By the time the first British soldier was killed in February 1971, the organisation had split, with the military campaign largely in the hands of the new PIRA and its political wing, Sinn Féin. A smaller, still more radical group of republicans formed the Irish National Liberation Army (INLA). When during a brief ceasefire in 1972 the Northern Ireland secretary William Whitelaw invited the PIRA leadership to talks in London, the visiting delegation included the twenty-two-year-old Martin McGuinness.

The conflict was throwing up again the two truths that had permeated Anglo-Irish relations since partition. Britain could not wish away the Irish question. And the Republic could not blame everything on the British. It was too soon, though, for the politicians on either side to break free of the habits of history. Relations between London and Dublin remained a fog of misunderstanding. As the British ambassador Peck wrote:

> On the emotional, instinctive plane . . . there was a Conservative Party in power in Britain whose political ancestry was, to say the least, anti-Catholic, anti-Irish, and anti-Home Rule, and even more anti-Independence and anti-Republicanism . . . In Dublin there were leaders of both parties whose fathers had fought and died for Independence and on the issue of whether an independent Ireland should be entire or divided.[15]

The policy the Conservative prime minister Edward Heath had inherited in 1970 said that Northern Ireland was entirely a domestic issue, that it was part of the United Kingdom and there was no place for foreign (including Irish) interference in its affairs. For his counterpart Lynch, the border was an artifice. The Republic had an inherent right to speak for those who pledged their allegiance to Ireland rather than Britain.

The gulf between the two governments was on vivid display when Heath hosted Lynch for talks at Chequers in September 1971. A few weeks earlier, the two leaders had engaged in what Peck called a 'public brawl'. The proximate cause was Heath's decision to bow to unionist demands for the introduction of internment without trial of suspected republican terrorists. An overture to Dublin suggesting it adopt the same approach met with a flat rejection, and a warning from Lynch that nothing could be so calculated to strengthen the PIRA was ignored in London. The round-up in the north went ahead regardless, focusing entirely on republicans and leaving suspected loyalist paramilitaries untouched. Even on its own terms the operation was bungled. The intelligence was hopelessly out of date. In the days preceding the raids, advance rumours of a round-up were fuelled by advertisements in the Belfast press seeking to recruit prison officers. Armed republicans went into hiding, and the great majority of those interned were innocent of any crime. To Callaghan's mind, Heath had gone ahead with the policy because 'it was the only untried instrument the Protestants could think of'.[16] Lynch reacted angrily, calling for peaceful resistance to internment and the creation in Belfast of a new government that would share power with nationalists. The Taoiseach wanted four-party talks – including London and Dublin, as well as unionists and nationalists from the north. Heath's riposte was abrupt: 'I cannot accept that anyone outside the United Kingdom can participate in meetings designed to promote the political development of any part of the United Kingdom.'

The two leaders entered the same cul-de-sac during their private talks at Chequers. As the *New York Times* reported: '"Mr Heath said I did not have the right to be involved in discussions of constitutional change," Mr Lynch told a packed news conference at the Irish Embassy. "I insisted I had such a right and I maintain that right because I am the elected head of the Government of Ireland and I represent the mass opinion of the Irish people."' In truth, Lynch was navigating a narrow path. As the leader of the anti-Treaty Fianna

Fáil he would not compromise on the Republic's claim to the entire island. There were those in his own cabinet who wanted a still tougher line. In May 1970 Lynch had felt compelled to sack two of his ministers – Charles Haughey and Neil Blaney – amid allegations they had conspired to divert official funding to the PIRA's arms purchases. Both were subsequently acquitted of the charges by the courts, but the episode spoke to the intensity of nationalist emotions and growing sympathy for republicanism. For his part, much as he insisted on a united Ireland as the only long-term answer to conflict and took the British government to the European Court of Human Rights for the mistreatment of republican detainees, Lynch strongly denounced paramilitary violence. The killings went on.

The Taoiseach was right about internment. In locking up suspected republicans without judicial process, the Heath government was seen to have made a decisive choice in favour of unionism. A conflict with the PIRA had become an attack on the wider Catholic community. The outrage among nationalists was compounded by credible reports – only half refuted in a report commissioned by Heath's government – that the detainees were subject to brutal interrogation techniques that bordered on torture. Nor was there an answer to the obvious question as to why suspected loyalist gunmen had not been rounded up. The nationalist community now saw itself as the victim not just of Protestant sectarianism but also of British colonialism. PIRA recruitment rose sharply – as did attacks on British troops. During the four months before internment, four soldiers and four civilians were killed in Northern Ireland. In the explosion of violence during the four months after internment, thirty soldiers, eleven police officers and members of the Ulster Defence Regiment and seventy-three civilians died.

Within Whitehall, the search began for more radical solutions. In September 1971 Downing Street's Central Policy Review Staff presented Heath with three options. The first suggested the repartition of the province, dividing the six counties into Protestant and Catholic areas and allowing the latter to join the Republic if they so chose. The second was a power-sharing executive in Belfast in which Catholics were guaranteed representation. And the third was a new condominium status in which Britain would share sovereignty with the Republic. Options one and three were soon put to one side. Option two was the signpost.

Internment was an unforced error. The events of 30 January 1972 were every bit as damaging for already fading hopes of restoring peace. A civil rights march in the Catholic Bogside district of Derry was fired on by British paratroopers. Thirteen civilians were killed. Another later died of his wounds. None were armed. The image of a frantic priest waving a white handkerchief as a wounded youth was pulled out of the soldiers' firing line was emblazoned across newspaper front pages and television news bulletins across the world. Bloody Sunday, as it would be called, attracted international horror and outrage among nationalists on both sides of the Irish border. In Dublin, demonstrators burned down the British embassy. Peck would reflect that the killings had 'unleashed a wave of fury the like of which I had never encountered in my life, in Egypt, or Cyprus or anywhere else. Hatred of the British was intense.' Riots in the province became commonplace and water cannon and rubber bullets were routinely deployed against Catholic demonstrations. The damage done by the killings to Britain's international reputation was compounded by the seemingly pre-written conclusions of a subsequent investigation. A cursory report by Lord Widgery, the lord chief justice, largely accepted the British army's case that the soldiers had been returning fire on the PIRA. Nothing was said of the paratroopers' reputation for extreme violence. The shooting had 'bordered on the reckless', Widgery said, but responsibility for the deaths rested with the march's organisers for supposedly engineering a confrontation. A whitewash. It would be nearly forty years before a British government corrected the historical record. In June 2010 the newly elected prime minister David Cameron responded to an exhaustive inquiry by Lord Saville with a formal state apology. 'None of the firing by the Support Company [Paratroopers] was aimed at people posing a threat or causing death or serious injury,' Saville concluded. Speaking in the House of Commons, Cameron was straightforward: 'What happened on Bloody Sunday was both unjustified and unjustifiable. It was wrong ... on behalf of the government and indeed our country, I am deeply sorry.'

The killings and subsequent cover-up brought another surge in recruitment by the PIRA and another turn in the ratchet of unrestrained violence. Criticism among Catholics of the PIRA's brutal and often indiscriminate killings was diluted by anger at the British and unionists. The attacks spread to the British mainland – in February seven people were killed in a bombing at Aldershot barracks. Loyalist groups such as the Ulster Defence Association and Ulster Volunteer Force ratcheted up their killing of Catholics, claiming more than 120 lives during 1972. In 1969 the violence in Northern Ireland had seen a total of nineteen killings. In 1972 the number reached 498. In Peck's judgement, 'Everyone in close contact now knew that the security role and methods imposed upon the army in Northern Ireland were self-defeating.' Bloody Sunday and its aftermath merely proved the point. The army had been told its role was to preserve law and order. But without the political participation of nationalism, 'it was still to be Protestant Law and Orange Order'.[17]

Politicians in London belatedly acknowledged as much. The cabinet's decision in the aftermath of partition to cede policing authority to Stormont had left the British a pawn in the hands of unionism. In March 1972 the Northern Ireland government of Brian Faulkner resigned when Heath removed its responsibility for security in the province. Heath responded by suspending the Belfast parliament and imposing direct rule from London. Direct rule was unavoidable. It was also an expression of desperation. In advance of the announcement the home secretary Reginald Maudling told the cabinet as much. 'All possible courses of action, or inaction,' he reported, 'are fraught with danger. There are good grounds for arguing that the problem of Northern Ireland is insoluble and a violent confrontation between loyalist and republican is unavoidable.'[18] Better, though, for the government's actions to fail than to look on helplessly from the sidelines.

Whatever the reasoning, this was an important moment. Unionism's grip on power in the province had been broken for the first time since 1921. With Stormont shuttered, Heath's government could widen its political horizons. The prime minister acknowledged that Dublin could no longer be excluded. In November 1972 Whitelaw gave the assurance that Lynch had long demanded. The administration of Northern Ireland, a Green Paper on the future of the province acknowledged, was no longer the sole property of the British. Instead, 'it must take account of the Province's relationship with the Republic of Ireland'. The government's objective was to 'secure the acceptance, in both Northern Ireland and in the Republic of Ireland, of the present status of Northern Ireland, and of the possibility – which would have to be compatible with the principle of consent – of subsequent change in that status'. Lynch, of course, would have liked Whitelaw to give his backing to eventual unification. For all that, the Heath government had taken three important steps. It now formally recognised that any political settlement in the north needed to include the 'all-Ireland dimension' of collaboration with the south; it would not stand in the way of Northern Ireland's departure from the United Kingdom should the province's citizens so choose; and new political institutions in the province must 'seek a much wider consensus than has hitherto existed'. On this third point, the Green Paper added, the Catholic minority might best be given 'a share in the exercise of executive power'. Lynch's appreciative response came in the form of a new criminal justice bill that imposed tougher measures against the PIRA than those in force in Britain.

The depth of nationalist alienation was underscored the following spring. In advance of elections to a new assembly at Stormont, the Heath government called a referendum on the province's constitutional status. Calculated to give reassurance to moderate unionists and dispel a view widely held internationally that Britain was an 'occupying force' in the province, the border poll was boycotted by the moderate nationalists represented by the Social Democratic and Labour Party (SDLP), as well as by Sinn Féin. When the votes were counted, 591,820, or 98.9 per cent, backed the status quo. Just as striking was the scale of nationalist abstentions. Only 6,463 cast their ballots in favour of Irish unity. But an important precedent had been set. The 1949 Government of Ireland Act had left any decision on the constitutional status of the province in the hands of the unionist-dominated parliament. The referendum signalled that any future choice would belong instead to a direct vote by the people. Whitelaw's Green Paper also marked a broader political awakening. In December 1973 the British and Irish prime ministers and constitutional politicians in the province would hammer out a plan for a power-sharing executive in Belfast and a Council of Ireland to foster north–south cooperation.

The four days of negotiations, at a civil service training centre in Sunningdale, Berkshire, were overseen by Heath and Liam Cosgrave, a son of the Free State's first Taoiseach William

Cosgrave and the man who had replaced Lynch as Taoiseach. Garret FitzGerald, Ireland's foreign minister, noted that the conference of 120-odd politicians and officials was a unique occasion, the first time that the political leaders of the British and Irish states, as well as those of the two communities in Northern Ireland, had gathered in one place. Heath, who in 1972 had told the Irish government to keep out of the province's affairs, was now fully content to share the burden. Alongside the new power-sharing executive, the Sunningdale Agreement proposed a Council of Ireland, reprising the arrangements for cross-border ties first envisaged in the Government of Ireland Act of 1920 and subsequently scuppered by James Craig. Closer security collaboration between London and Dublin promised more concerted action against the PIRA. Some twenty-five years later, Seamus Mallon, the deputy leader of the nationalist SDLP, would lament the time and lives lost between the agreement and the Good Friday accord signed by Tony Blair and Bertie Ahern. The final peace deal, he said, was 'Sunningdale for slow learners'.

The accord did indeed set a course. Its three principal elements – shared power in Belfast, new institutions spanning north and south, and a formalised relationship between London and Dublin – supplied the architecture for future negotiations. But it was not yet a destination. Dublin was prepared to endorse the principle of Protestant consent for any change in the status of Northern Ireland, but not to surrender the territorial claim to the six counties embedded in the Republic's constitution. London would say that it would not stand in the way of Irish unity but insisted on a restatement of Northern Ireland's present position as an integral part of the United Kingdom.

The fatal challenge came from outside the conference room. Just as the institutional ties with Dublin proposed at partition were rejected by Craig's unionists, the opening months of 1974 saw an explosion of unionist opposition to their proposed reinstatement at Sunningdale. In February 1974 Heath called a general election – and lost to the former Labour prime minister Harold Wilson. The same election handed victory to the anti-Sunningdale unionists contesting seats in Northern Ireland. The UUP leader and chief minister in the prospective executive found himself abandoned by his own party. Loyalist workers' groups and paramilitaries – calling themselves the Ulster Workers' Council – called a province-wide strike. The action, enforced by violence and intimidation, effectively paralysed the north, cutting off fuel and other essential supplies. Unionists flirted with the idea of secession, and British army commanders betrayed their personal prejudices by refusing to break the blockades – an echo for some of the collusion of the generals during the revolt against Asquith's Home Rule legislation some sixty years earlier. The army's commanding officer Sir Frank King was entirely unapologetic. 'Dealing with intimidation was a police job,' he would say. 'The fact that the RUC didn't do too much about it was no concern of ours ... If [Northern Ireland secretary Merlyn] Rees had ordered us to move against the barricades we would have said, "With great respect this is a job for the police. We will assist them if you wish, but it's not terrorism."'[19]

Wilson retreated, scrapping Heath's accord. The prime minister used a televised statement to publicly lambast the loyalists manning the strike barricades as 'people who spend their lives sponging on Westminster and British democracy and then systematically assault democratic methods'.[20] Influenced no doubt by the large Catholic population of his Liverpool parliamentary constituency, Wilson's personal sympathies were with nationalists. In 1971, as leader of the opposition he had returned from a visit to Dublin and a series of secret meetings with leading republicans to tell the House of

Commons that Britain had to acknowledge the aspirations of those seeking a united Ireland. He frequently complained that while unionist leaders were forever marching under the Union flag and seeking larger financial subsidies from the rest of the United Kingdom, they scorned the views of the United Kingdom government. Privately, he asked whether Britain should set a time limit on its presence in the north. The prospective loss of subsidies from the Treasury might at least concentrate unionist minds. For all that, Wilson's capitulation in the face of the strike looked to Dublin like a loss of political nerve. The Wilson government, in the mind of Garret FitzGerald, had been too 'fearful of its own army'.[21]

The defeat was keenly felt in Downing Street. Never persuaded of the worth of the union, Wilson asked whether Northern Ireland was heading for uncontrolled chaos, followed by unionist secession and enforced British departure. Wilson was looking over his shoulder at the unresolved crisis in Rhodesia, where minority white settlers had scuppered the country's march to post-colonial statehood with a unilateral declaration of independence that excluded from power the majority Black community. In May 1974 the prime minister dispatched a secret memorandum to his private secretary, Robert Armstrong, asking for contingency planning to begin on what he called the 'Doomsday Scenario' in Northern Ireland. The strike, he said, had left the government in a position of responsibility without power: 'The traditional prerogative of something very unpleasant throughout the ages – I think a eunuch.' Loyalists could now hold the government to ransom: 'If we seek to take any action unacceptable to the UWC [Ulster Workers' Council] and their political associates . . . we are at their mercy again.' This, he said, could see Northern Ireland asserting, in effect, its independence. 'What I would envisage [is that] at the moment we considered that Doomsday was in sight, we should proceed to prepare a plan for Dominion status for Northern Ireland.'[22] British troops would withdraw, sovereignty would be transferred from Westminster and, over time, financial support would end. Bernard Donoughue, a close political aide in Downing Street, sensed the fear of senior civil servants that Wilson would act impetuously. 'The machine is preparing a counter offensive,' he wrote in his diary.[23] He was right.

The moment of crisis passed. But as the PIRA's campaign reached deep into mainland Britain and attempts to forge political agreements between the parties in Belfast foundered, Wilson returned to his theme in greater detail. His recurring fear was not so much of still further escalation of PIRA terrorist attacks but of the backlash from loyalist paramilitaries and the wider unionist community. The threat, as he articulated it, was one of unionism embracing the unilateral independence declared by the white settler population in Rhodesia in 1965. The government, Wilson wrote in another secret memorandum in January 1976, needed to consider 'the ultimate situation in respect of Northern Ireland if all present policies fail ... We have to face a situation where Northern Ireland becomes ungovernable.' Headed 'Apocalyptic Note for the Record' and distributed only to the cabinet secretary Sir John Hunt and a handful of officials in Number 10, it said that the danger was that the government would be unable to enforce law and order to ensure peaceful, democratic administration. In such circumstances, 'The only solution therefore would be one or other variety of withdrawal and abrogation of the responsibilities for the affairs of Northern Ireland.' Withdrawal would not be easy: 'It would mean surrendering the minority population, particularly the peaceable Catholic element, to anything that majority extremists may choose to inflict upon them.' Cities in Britain might face a period of 'Ulster-inspired terrorism'. But, Wilson concluded, the risks were such that 'urgent contingency planning' was needed.[24] On other occasions, the prime minister's frustration spilled over into calls for a drastic security crackdown. In January 1976 Donoughue recorded in his diary that the prime minister wanted 'a policy of letting the troops shoot on sight anybody they suspected of being armed'.[25]

Wilson was far from alone in his doubts. In 1972 Roy Jenkins, a former chancellor, had spoken to the sense of powerlessness. He had long regarded it a clear lesson of history, he said in a lecture delivered at Yale University, 'that the great British political genius, great though it may be in certain fields, does not extend to a peculiar talent to settling the affairs of Ireland'. When he returned as home secretary in Wilson's government two years later, Jenkins' view hardened. He worried about contagion. Donoughue reported Jenkins' contribution to a discussion among cabinet ministers: 'Everything he heard made him more convinced that Northern Ireland had nothing to do with the rest of the United Kingdom.' The discussion had been framed as 'how to impose the civilised standards of Britain on Northern Ireland'. To Jenkins' mind, 'the real prospect and danger was of the barbaric standards of Northern Ireland spreading to the rest of us'.[26] On the other side of the political aisle Alec Douglas-Home, Heath's foreign secretary, had been similarly despairing when he wrote to the then prime minister in March 1973. It would not be possible to secure peace, he judged, while Northern Ireland remained in the United Kingdom. It was time to start pushing it into a united Ireland.[27]

The response to this swirl of fears came in a lengthy Whitehall paper commissioned by the cabinet secretary Sir John Hunt to explore the implications were Britain to cut and run.[28] It began bleakly enough: 'The Irish problem is exceptionally deep-rooted. It goes back many centuries . . . for a significant part of the time a large part of the British army has been longer in Ireland than in Great Britain.' One thing, though, had changed. Britain had once feared that Ireland would be a launchpad for an attack on Britain by 'Catholic Europe'. More recently, Winston Churchill had feared that the Irish Free State could be a back door for Hitler's Nazis. But the geopolitical map had been redrawn by the Cold War. There was no longer a strategic imperative to keep Northern Ireland. The paper, drafted by Frank Brenchley, a senior diplomat seconded to the Cabinet Office, noted that the original intention of the 1920 Government of Ireland Act had been eventual reunification. Instead, partition, and subsequent Westminster neglect of Northern Ireland, had entrenched 'two traditions, two cultures, two religions'. Now, with the impartial diligence of a Whitehall civil servant, Brenchley set out a blueprint for a Northern Ireland carved out as a separate state. A new constitution would be needed, entrenching the rights of minorities. Dominion status would be an option, as would a new head of state. The government would operate its own foreign policy and diplomatic service, and might apply to join the European Community, the Commonwealth and the United Nations. A common trading area might be negotiated with Britain and the Republic alongside shared rights for British and Irish citizens. Less welcome would be the inevitable fall in living standards as the government in London withdrew its subsidies. At times, the author allowed himself flashes of optimism. On the departure of Northern Ireland MPs from Westminster: 'Few members of parliament would be other than glad to see them go.' More bravely still, 'The sharper and clearer the [constitutional] change, the more likely it is that in the course of time a natural relationship between the north and south and with Britain would develop.' Overall, such a constitutional settlement would command at Westminster 'fairly widespread bipartisan approval'.

For all its dispassionate analysis, the paper lacked one critical ingredient: the possible pathway from the violent antagonism between the two communities in Northern Ireland and the PIRA's war on the British to an independent state that would secure popular consent across the sectarian divide. Instead, rather lamely, the author acknowledged that republicans would probably see Britain's withdrawal as the halfway house to a united Ireland and step up their campaign as a consequence. Stability in the province might break down. If 'violence escalates into civil war Great Britain will certainly be blamed for abdicating its responsibilities'. Retreat, it seemed, would have to include a contingency plan for renewed military intervention.

The cabinet secretary's response was to bury the report. He warned of 'the severe damage' that could be caused if the proposals were judged an objective of the government rather than a piece of contingency planning. Only two copies of the document, marked with the highest classification, 'Top Secret UK Eyes A', were produced. The Northern Ireland Office – the department responsible for the governance of the province – was permitted to see only what Hunt called a 'sanitised' version. His own handwritten note accompanying the study was deeply sceptical that Britain could extricate itself: 'If (Northern Ireland) independent two sides would have to live together. Lot of dead before this happened . . . Govt of South horrified and might rush off to the UN either in political sense or to demand UN supervision and peace-keeping force.' The idea of 'managed independence', however, did not disappear from the corridors of Whitehall. Beyond Wilson it had support in the cabinet from senior figures such as Jenkins and Callaghan. The latter, who in the spring of 1976 replaced the retiring Wilson in Downing Street, continued to promote the idea of a pre-announced timetable for withdrawal in order to force the pace of an accommodation between unionists and nationalists. The reality was that there was no such escape route from history.

Ireland's nationalist politicians, for their part, were beginning to reinterpret the past. Lynch's Fianna Fáil administration was replaced in 1973 by Liam Cosgrave's Fine Gael-led coalition. According to FitzGerald, the lesson the new regime drew from the collapse of Sunningdale was stark: 'We had to face the fact that in the part of Ireland under British sovereignty a British government had been unwilling or unable to control events.' Nationalists had called since partition for Britain to leave. Now London's hurried abandonment of the north was Dublin's great fear. The Irish government understood the risk of civil war as well as the senior officials in London seeking to calm Wilson. Loyalist groups made no secret of the fact that, absent British rule, they would revive Carson's plan. Northern Ireland's Protestants would declare, and fight to defend, a new state independent of both Britain and the Republic.

The horrors of the conflict spoke for themselves. The attacks on civilians grabbed the headlines – the bombing by the UVF of a bar in Catholic north Belfast claiming fifteen lives, a wave of similarly indiscriminate PIRA bombs six months later killing eleven, the deaths in November 1974 of twenty-one people enjoying an evening out in two Birmingham pubs on the British mainland, the twelve lives lost to a fireball at the La Mon hotel restaurant outside Belfast from a PIRA incendiary device. Such outrages were the tip. Belfast came to resemble a war zone, with Protestant and Catholic areas separated by high, officially constructed walls. British armoured vehicles patrolled the streets. Soldiers with automatic rifles crouched on street corners. Along the border with the south, watch towers looked out over a border that was impossible to police, accessible to the troops only by helicopter. Nearly five hundred were killed at the peak of the violence in 1972. Though the numbers then fell – and 1975 saw a ceasefire lasting nearly a year – the death toll was still above three hundred in 1977. The Republic was not immune. PIRA gangs routinely raided banks in the south to raise funds for new weapons. In 1976 the newly arrived British ambassador to Dublin, Christopher Ewart-Biggs, and his assistant Judith Cook were killed when their car was blown up by a roadside bomb. The PIRA was challenging not just partition but also the legitimacy of the Irish state. On the other side of the Irish Sea, British citizens were forever alert to unexplained packages and bags lest they be packed with the Semtex explosive supplied to republican militants by the renegade Libyan leader Muammar Gaddafi.

'We all want to go to heaven,' Winston Churchill would sometimes remark, 'only not quite yet.' Such, despite the rhetorical denunciation at partition, was the Augustinian mood in Dublin about Irish unity. For leading politicians such as FitzGerald, as much as for the British, 'the importance of defeating the PIRA transcended all other considerations'.[29] The fall of the Fine Gael–Labour Party coalition in 1977 saw FitzGerald take the post of leader of the opposition. On the other side of the aisle, Fianna Fáil struggled to shake off its irredentist reflexes. The party's leader and newly elevated Taoiseach Charles Haughey could rarely resist the temptation to play to the republican gallery. It was bluster. FitzGerald shared the fears of those such as the finance ministry director Whitaker, who saw the attempt to coerce unionists as the route to violent upheaval across the island. FitzGerald's approach was twin-track. Dublin should press the case for full representation of nationalism in the political life of the north, but also make the Republic less threatening to unionists. The change in climate was noted by the British ambassador in Dublin Arthur Galsworthy, who reported back to London in June 1976 that unity was increasingly framed as 'a long-term national aspiration rather than something that can be realised in any foreseeable future'. It helped that the British were now willing to talk to Dublin.

Galsworthy reported that consultation between the two governments had become easy and established now that 'we no longer feel that discussing the affairs of Northern Ireland with Irish ministers or officials admits an unwarranted interference on their part in British domestic affairs'.[30]

FitzGerald was acutely conscious of the pull of the Catholic Church in the opposite direction. The number of Protestants living in the Republic, he noted, had halved since partition. A legal ban on contraception, a constitutional bar on divorce and strict implementation of papal rules on 'mixed marriages' (children were to be brought up as Catholics) made it an inhospitable place.

For its part, however, the Vatican itself felt under siege as its authority was eroded by a march towards secularism across much of the rest of Europe. Ireland was seen by Rome as a last redoubt. FitzGerald could expect no help from the Catholic hierarchy, as he learned when, as foreign minister in 1977, he was granted an audience with the pope. 'Ireland is a Catholic country,' he was told. 'Perhaps the only one left. It should stay that way.' The tragic situation in Northern Ireland 'could not be a reason to change any of the laws that kept us a Catholic state'.[31] Closer to home, he found the papal nuncio in Dublin, Monsignor Gaetano Alibrandi, still more implacable: 'He appeared to some of us at times to confuse Catholicism with extreme Republicanism.'

6 THE AMERICANS ARE BACK

Britain was Ireland's ancient enemy, America its most evident friend. They had both fought English imperialism in wars of independence. Millions of Americans traced their ancestry to Ireland. Yet the Ireland that emerged from the treaty of 1921 had long felt neglected by its more powerful comrade-in-arms. Emotion and familial ties pulled America in Ireland's direction. Realpolitik steered successive presidents in Washington into alliance with Britain.

This was about to change. At first glance, the statement issued by the White House late on a Friday afternoon at the end of August 1977 about the conflict in Northern Ireland scarcely looked like front-page news. Jimmy Carter had made little of his distant Irish heritage (great-great-grandparents from Antrim). In a concession to a diplomatic démarche lodged in advance by the British government, the presidential intervention was timed for just before Labor Day, while America was still enjoying its summer holiday. This was not a White House pitch calculated to lead the evening news. Yet Carter's reflections on events in the province marked a turning point. After decades in which the US had resolutely declared that Northern Ireland was a matter purely for the British, Washington was coming off the fence. More, in deference to Dublin it was throwing its weight behind power-sharing between unionists and nationalists.

Shared colonial history and the Irish diaspora made the United States a player in the Anglo-Irish relationship. Whenever they were fighting with the British, the Irish looked to their kith and kin in America for moral, practical and financial support. Britain, though, was also an important ally. And the PIRA's campaign of violence had dented Washington's natural sympathy for Irish nationalism. In deference to the oft-invoked special relationship with Britain, successive administrations had sat on the sidelines in the dispute about Northern Ireland. Woodrow Wilson's call for national self-determination at the end of the First World War had not included Ireland. The confrontation with the Soviet Union after the Second World War had led Wilson's successors similarly to prioritise British sensitivities. Now Carter had decided to shift the balance. Celebration of the presidential about-turn in Dublin was mirrored by consternation in London. Carter had set a precedent.

The connection between the two republics, rooted in the journey across the Atlantic made by millions of Irish emigrants, blended family connections with crude electoral calculation. Carter's successor Ronald Reagan expressed it during a visit in 1984 to what Irish Americans called the 'home country'. 'I'm proud to say the first embassy I visited as President was Ireland's,' he boasted after raising a glass of Guinness in his forebears' home town of Ballyporeen in Tipperary.

> And I'm proud that our administration is blessed by so many Cabinet members of Irish extraction . . . I had to fight them off Air Force One or there wouldn't be anyone tending the store while we're gone. And that's not to mention the number of Irish Americans who hold extremely important leadership posts today in the United States Congress.

The revolt against British rule by America's thirteen colonies supplied natural inspiration for Irish nationalism. The subsequent arrival of Ireland's huddled masses created an Irish American community steeped in memories of English cruelty. During the eighteenth century much of the emigration had been of Scottish Presbyterians and English Protestants from the plantation counties

ABOVE Royal reconciliation: Queen Elizabeth II lays a wreath in Dublin's Garden of Remembrance.

BELOW Signing the Treaty: seated (*from left*) Arthur Griffith, Eamonn Duggan, Michael Collins, Robert Barton; standing (*from left*) Robert Erskine Childers, George Gavan Duffy, John Chartres.

Declaring the Republic: the Easter Rising Proclamation of Ireland's independence. British retribution turned rebellion into revolution.

ABOVE A Protestant state: Northern Ireland's first prime minister James Craig greets army officers in Belfast.

RIGHT Searched at gunpoint: rough treatment of civilians by the notorious Black and Tans swelled the ranks of the IRA revolutionaries.

ABOVE The deal is done: David Lloyd George and Winston Churchill leaving 10 Downing Street.

BELOW Death sentence: Michael Collins leaving No. 10 during the treaty negotiations. The deal, he remarked prophetically, would cost him his life.

ABOVE From revolution to civil war: the Free State crushes the IRA forces at Dublin's Four Courts.

BELOW The price of freedom: the architect of the IRA's victory, Michael Collins, lies in state after his death at the hands of the anti-treaty forces.

ABOVE Kiltimagh, County Mayo, during the 1960s: rural, reverential and indisputably de Valera's Ireland. The price was the flight of its young.

OPPOSITE ABOVE Éamon de Valera, the leader who did most to shape the new Irish state: Catholic, austere and uncompromising in his Irishness, he would serve as Taoiseach and president.

OPPOSITE BELOW The second-most powerful man in Ireland: self-appointed guardian of Ireland's public and private morals Catholic Archbishop McQuaid (*centre*) with de Valera.

ABOVE The Reverend Ian Paisley, the firebrand Protestant leader who took to the streets in the unionist fight against 'popery'.

BELOW Gerry Adams and Martin McGuinness, leaders of the new Provisional IRA waging war on the British state.

ABOVE Harold Wilson. Officials had to talk the prime minister out of unilateral withdrawal from Northern Ireland.

BELOW Margaret Thatcher signs the Anglo-Irish Agreement with Garret FitzGerald. A self-declared unionist, it was Thatcher who read the rites over unionist hegemony.

LEFT Around every corner: British troops fight a war on the streets they cannot win.

BELOW Wars past and present: the British army could not win, but now, the PIRA discovered, republicans could not bomb them out of Northern Ireland.

ABOVE A bridge across the divide – Nobel prize-winners David Trimble and John Hume.

BELOW A declaration from Downing Street: John Major and Albert Reynolds open the door for peace talks.

ABOVE Leaving history behind: Bertie Ahern and Tony Blair.

BELOW Politics sometimes works: Martin McGuinness and Ian Paisley exchange violent enmity for partnership.

of Ulster. Their numbers were swamped by the exodus westwards of starving Catholic families fleeing the Great Famine. Estimates for the number of emigrants arriving on America's shores during the decade or so after 1845 range from 1.5 to 2 million. The great majority were Catholics from the south, and they carried with them the anti-colonial grievances of a generation. In the description of Conor Cruise O'Brien, 'the children of the famine emigrants grew up in America hating England'.[1] To their mind, the same people who had oppressed America were still oppressing Ireland. The ships kept on arriving. Between 1820 and 1860 the Irish constituted over one-third of all immigrants to the United States. As many as 4.5 million arrived between 1820 and 1930. The impact on American politics was keenly felt. Large numbers of the new arrivals settled in New England, while others pushed westwards to Delaware, Pennsylvania and Iowa. By the 1850s New York City boasted more Irish-born residents than Dublin. Irish Americans accounted for about a third of the city's voter population. They were quick to make their presence felt at Tammany Hall, the headquarters of the local Democratic Party. Power in the big cities was a springboard for national office – and conveyed a message to would-be members of Congress and presidential hopefuls that the Irish were a constituency to be courted. Their loyalty to their adopted country was not in doubt. While the British, mindful of their cotton trade interests in the southern states, offered tacit succour to the Confederacy, an estimated 150,000 Irish Americans fought in Abraham Lincoln's Union armies during the civil war. And the Irish in America stuck together. Even 150 years later, some 20 per cent of the populations of New Hampshire and Massachusetts and more than 15 per cent of those in Rhode Island, Vermont and Maine honoured Irish forebears. From Andrew Jackson in the 1830s to Joe Biden in 2020 some twenty-three American presidents would claim an ancestral bond with Ireland. In 2002 more than thirty million US citizens still identified as Irish Americans.

The emergence in Ireland of a clutch of new secret societies committed to the violent overthrow of British rule was mirrored during the second half of the nineteenth century by the appearance in America of the Fenian Brotherhood. None was more committed to the defeat of the colonial power. The Irish Republican Brotherhood, forerunner to the IRA, received a steady flow of money and guns from their American cousins. During the early 1870s the Fenians launched raids on British customs posts and military installations in Canada. The attacks fizzled out but the enthusiasm for Irish revolution tumbled down through the generations. By the 1970s, more than a hundred years later, Irish as well as British politicians were complaining that radical Irish Americans were sustaining the PIRA's campaign of violence. Much earlier, the diaspora tapped into the broader antipathy towards the British empire among America's political classes. The British, after all, had sacked the White House in 1814. During the American Civil War, though officially neutral, the government had allowed arms manufacturers to continue to ship weapons to the Confederacy in its attempt to break with the Union. By the turn of the twentieth century the United States, emerging as the world's biggest economic power, had its own global ambitions. Britain was an obstacle. Soon enough the American navy chased the British out of the Caribbean. When President Woodrow Wilson took the United States into the First World War in 1917, the objective was to defend American merchant ships crossing the Atlantic rather than to prop up the British Empire.

Few were more attentive to Ireland's unique influence than the New York-born Éamon de Valera. Following the sentences of execution passed on the commanders of the Easter Rising, friends of

THE AMERICANS ARE BACK

de Valera's wife petitioned the American consul in Dublin, Edward Adams, to intercede on his behalf. After the Rising Adams wrote to General Sir John Maxwell, commander of the British forces in Ireland, seeking information on the proceedings against 'Edward [*sic*] de Valera, American Citizen ... arrested in connection with the recent rebellion'. The reply came from Major I. H. Price of the General Staff:

> I am directed by the General Officer Commanding-in-Chief to inform you that this man was 'Adjutant' of the Dublin Brigade of Rebel forces, and was in command of a body of rebels which held the premises of Messrs Boland's, Ringsend, Dublin. He was tried by court martial and sentenced to death, but the sentence was commuted to Penal Servitude for life.

Whether the American intervention had had any bearing on the decision was left unsaid.[2]

While Michael Collins led the IRA to war against the British, in June 1919 de Valera embarked on his eighteen-month fundraising mission in the United States. A coast-to-coast speaking campaign, taking in New Orleans and San Francisco as well as the more familiar ground of Boston and Philadelphia, was calculated to turn public and political opinion against the British. As Wilson took up the cudgels on behalf of nations breaking free of declining empires, de Valera claimed to be waging exactly this fight. He spoke to packed audiences, filling New York's Madison Square Garden and attracting even larger crowds in Chicago. The launch of a Sinn Féin bond issue saw the New York mayor grant him the freedom of the city. At every stop de Valera drew historical parallels between America's break for freedom in its war of independence and the present Irish struggle. The *Kentucky Irish American* caught the flavour of the rallies. In its reckoning, Sinn Féin was 'the expression of a nation's soul just as the Declaration of Independence of the thirteen original colonies was the expression of the American soul'.[3] Elsewhere de Valera earned the soubriquet 'Ireland's George Washington'. All in all, de Valera was said to have raised an estimated $10 million during the trip to finance the new Provisional Government in Dublin and buy guns for Collins's military campaign. The stream of telegrams from the British embassy in Washington to the Foreign Office in London charting the progress of his tour worried at the damage being done by attempts to suppress the IRA insurgency. They warned of consequences for Britain's efforts to maintain its great power status in the international tumult that followed the end of the First World War. Seeking to reorder the world to forestall fresh conflicts, Wilson's administration wanted to rein in military competition. The Royal Navy was firmly in the sights of those in Washington seeking naval disarmament at a conference of great powers in the US capital. As Lloyd George's government called for a truce in the Anglo-Irish War, Harry Boland, Sinn Féin's representative in Washington, saw the connection, warning de Valera that if negotiations with the British broke down, it was essential that the blame was seen to lie with London.

That said, the limits to American idealism were also clear. In spite of Wilson's fine words about the right of nations to set their own destiny, Ireland's nationalists learned that the United States put its own national interests ahead of those of its friends. When world leaders gathered in Paris to negotiate the Versailles peace treaty, Sinn Féin lobbied hard for its new Provisional Government to be given a seat at the table alongside other aspirant nationalist groups. For all that he was prepared to press Britain to negotiate with Irish nationalists, Wilson did not take up the Sinn Féin case. He refused de Valera formal American recognition of Irish statehood. He disdained the British Empire, but the president had other ambitions for the conference and judged it inopportune to trigger an open breach with America's wartime ally. Realpolitik came before republican solidarity.

The rupture between Washington and Dublin about de Valera's insistence on staying out of the Second World War threw this tension between values and interests into sharper relief, presaging a turbulent period in the relationship. The American neutrality insisted on by Congress at the outset of the war did not alter Franklin Roosevelt's view that Ireland should put itself on the side of the world's democracies against Hitler and the Axis powers. The energetic campaign fought by David Gray, Roosevelt's minister in Dublin, for Ireland to join the war dispensed with the traditional bounds of diplomacy, openly backing Churchill's attempts to strike a deal that would see neutrality abandoned in return for British commitments to promote Irish unity. The Taoiseach's rebuff of Churchill's offer after America joined the war in December 1941 was followed a week later by an abrupt dismissal of Washington's overtures. 'The policy of the state remains unchanged,' de Valera said during a speech in County Cork. 'We can only be a friendly neutral.'

For his part, Gray charged senior Irish diplomats with conspiring with Berlin against the Allies, pressing Roosevelt to demand the removal from Dublin of the German and other Axis power diplomats. De Valera in turn protested against the arrival of American troops in Northern Ireland. Gray's views were widely shared in the State Department and prompted a sustained Irish campaign for his removal, organised by Robert Brennan, the senior Irish diplomat in Washington. In March 1946 Brennan reported to Dublin that he had broached the issue directly with President Harry Truman at the annual St Patrick's Day dinner in Washington. Told of Gray's allegedly subversive activities, Truman's initial response was apparently positive. 'Let's bring him back right away. We can't let that state of affairs go on.' Later the same evening, however, the president said that the issue could not be 'rushed' because of Gray's family connections with the Roosevelts. 'I imagine he had discussed the issue with someone during the interval,' Brennan ruefully concluded.[4] A few days later, Brennan was writing back to Dublin again, warning that he had received information that Gray was gathering potentially incriminating evidence about Ireland's cooperation with the Germans during the war. One document discovered in Germany's wartime files might prove 'very damaging' to the Chief and the government.[5] By the following month the Department of External Affairs had responded with an eight-point charge sheet against the American head of mission. Among the allegations was that he had made 'outrageously false and hostile statements against the Irish government'.[6] When Gray finally departed more than a year later in July 1947, emotions in Dublin were succinctly expressed in a letter from Frederick Boland, the director general of the External Relations department, to the Irish mission in Washington. 'David Gray left Ireland on the 28th June on the SS *America* sailing from Cobh. I needn't tell you that no tears were shed at his departure.'[7]

His return did not lift the chill between Washington and Dublin. De Valera's refusal to engage with the institutions – the International Monetary Fund, World Bank and NATO – at the heart of America's plans for the post-war order set it apart from the rest of Western Europe. The Taoiseach viewed this as an assertion of Ireland's neutrality. American policymakers considered Ireland was leaving a strategic gap in the common Western front against the expansionist ambitions of Soviet communism. Dublin's repeated attempts to buy American weapons were rebuffed, with one State Department diplomat reporting back to Washington that he had made it clear to his hosts that in the allocation of military supplies priority was given to those allies that had signed up to the fight against 'Commie aggression'. By 1950 a State Department review was concluding that Ireland's stance on neutrality was driven by 'isolationist and parochial' views. 'The fundamental problem of Ireland is the reconciliation of nationalist aspiration with strategic, economic and political realities.'[8] The following year, as he celebrated his return to power after the 1951 election, de Valera showed unusual self-awareness during a conversation with the head of the American mission in Dublin. 'I know that many people say that I am a dictator or that my government will be a dictatorship,' he admitted. 'But I am not a dictator – not at all. Far from it.'[9] But on the subject of neutrality nothing, not even Ireland's most important friend and ally, could move him. In 1952 Washington responded by cutting off the flow of economic aid.

The beginnings of a thaw came with John Costello's election as the head of a second Fine Gael-led coalition in 1954. Visiting Washington in the spring of 1956, Costello grasped that poor relations with the United States were costing Ireland both economic investment and the military equipment needed to modernise its armed forces. Reporting on his trip in a subsequent memorandum, the Taoiseach remarked on the immense potential that Ireland had in 'shaping the most important power in the modern world'. The St Patrick's Day parade in New York, 'an immense fillip to national self-confidence', offered a metaphor for Irish influence: 'For six hours, approximately a million Irish people watched one hundred and twenty thousand young people march through the streets of New York despite the weather, all conducted in the most perfect organisation with dignity and in a disciplined manner.' The Irish presence, however, was not matched by comparable diplomatic leverage. Admission to the United Nations provided a platform for Ireland to broaden its horizons, including 'changed policy with regard to America'. It was essential that 'we should not be merely anti-British or else we will come to be completely discounted'. Given the threat from communism, 'We must also recognise in our relations with America that America cannot have Irish friendship at the risk of division with Britain.'[10]

The rapprochement picked up pace with John F. Kennedy's triumphant procession across the nation during his state visit to the Republic in 1963. In terms of America's leadership, Irish American influence had never been higher. The presidency, the speakership of the House of Representatives and the majority leadership of the Senate were all in the hands of politicians of Irish heritage. The first Catholic president, the first serving occupant of the White House to visit Ireland (Ulysses S. Grant had left office when he visited eighty years earlier) and the first foreign head of state to address the Dáil, Kennedy spent four days on a tour of Dublin, Cork, Galway and his family's ancestral home in Wexford. With the creation two years earlier of Teilefís Éireann, Ireland had entered the television age. Kennedy, perhaps the world's most telegenic leader, was greeted with unabashed jubilation. His appearances brought glamour, glitz and excitement to a nation struggling to escape the backwardness bestowed by economic isolation. He was mobbed at the official reception offered by the Irish government. Photographs of the young president appeared alongside familiar images of the pope on mantels across Ireland.

Ireland's emergence from diplomatic isolation, however, was not enough to change American policy towards partition. As eloquent as he was in speaking about the shared history of the two nations and the critical role of Irish immigrants in building America, Kennedy paid deference to the State Department's strictures by saying nothing about the issue that most preoccupied his hosts. The Irish ambassador in Washington, Thomas Kiernan, was told in advance of the trip that the president did not want partition on the agenda of his talks in Dublin. Kennedy, who travelled to the Irish capital from Berlin, intended Europe's focus to remain on the Cold War confrontation with Moscow. So Northern Ireland's status as a British province went unspoken. Britain's claim of a unique relationship with Washington was often overstated by politicians in London. That said, the war had seen the creation of a dense network of collaboration established in areas such as defence, intelligence and, with occasional hiccups, nuclear technology. Britain was seen to hold a pivotal role in preserving Western Europe's common front against communism. So when American politicians representing constituencies with sizeable Irish communities pressed for the United States to be more sympathetic towards Dublin's case, they were slapped down by the 'realists' at the State Department. By the close of the 1960s the outbreak of violence in Northern Ireland had brought calls from the Taoiseach, Jack Lynch, for American diplomatic intervention. But the Nixon and Ford administrations stuck firmly to the traditional line. Britain was a vital ally in the US-led fight against communism. Northern Ireland was an integral part of the United Kingdom. It was not for the United States to speak out about what, in British terms, was a strictly domestic issue. In 1972, after repeated entreaties from Dublin, the Irish government was told it was not the position of the United States to 'judge, condemn, or advocate any particular solution or intervene in this tragic and complex situation'.[11]

Jimmy Carter's about-turn in the late summer of 1977 was no accident of history. Instead, it marked the culmination of an intense diplomatic campaign by the Irish government. Frustrated by Washington's determined silence, Dublin deployed some of its sharpest diplomats. Prominent among them were Michael Lillis, who would later have a leading part in negotiation of the

Anglo-Irish Agreement signed by Margaret Thatcher, and from 1978 the ambassador who would soon serenade Ronald Reagan, Sean Donlon. In Donlon's description: 'Official US policy since 1922 was not to get involved in Northern Ireland. The Americans slavishly followed the British line.'[12] Carter, the diplomats understood, was a newcomer to Washington politics, more reliant than most presidents on the support of big figures from his own party. They included the House speaker, Tip O'Neill, Edward Kennedy and Daniel Patrick Moynihan in the Senate and Governor Hugh Carey of New York. Later known as the 'Four Horsemen', they wielded formidable influence in the White House. O'Neill in particular could turn on or off congressional support for legislation sought by the president. Most importantly, they were all sympathetic to the Irish nationalist (as opposed to republican) cause. Dublin's objective was to secure support for a settlement that recognised a role for the Republic in bringing peace to Northern Ireland and guaranteed equal rights for the province's nationalists, while marginalising the PIRA. John Hume, soon to become leader of Northern Ireland's SDLP and fast emerging as the international spokesman for the Catholic population, was an important player. A frequent visitor to Washington, he worked with the Dublin government to nurture the alliance with the congressional leaders.

The diplomacy of the British embassy in Washington was directed at disarming the critics of British policy and persuading the United States to remain firmly on the sidelines. The work of the Irish embassy was to persuade the administration to press the British to do more to meet the demands of Northern Ireland's nationalist population. Dublin understood, however, that Irish American support was not without its risks. While politicians such as O'Neill and Moynihan were clear in their condemnation of PIRA violence, the republican paramilitaries had radical supporters among Irish Americans in the country's big cities. The Irish Northern Aid Committee, or Noraid, harked back to the traditions of nineteenth-century Fenians. It collected funds formally designated to help nationalist 'political prisoners' and families that had fallen victim to the violence in Northern Ireland. The open secret was that most if not all of the donations it received were directed to the PIRA to buy weapons. Noraid had friends in Congress, where the Ad Hoc Congressional Committee for Irish Affairs led by the congressman Mario Biaggi called for the immediate withdrawal of British troops. It was backed by the Irish National Caucus. Here, though the British were loath to admit it, the objectives of the two embassies aligned. The PIRA was seen as a threat to the political order in the Republic just as much as to that of Northern Ireland. Noraid and its friends had no harsher critic than Garret FitzGerald. On his appointment to the Washington embassy the then Taoiseach Jack Lynch told Donlon that his first priority as ambassador was to reduce US support for the PIRA.

In the event, Carter's statement struck a judicious balance. It denounced the violence and, in an implicit reference to Noraid and Biaggi's congressional caucus, called for an end to funding of the paramilitaries. Its backing for political negotiations and for human rights guarantees for all citizens of the province was carefully worded. Washington, it stressed, would not shift from its position of impartiality. But the simple fact of the statement marked an important diplomatic victory, and the first time since partition that the United States had taken a stance independent of Britain. The president also broke new ground by putting the US administration behind nationalist demands for a place in political decision-making in the province. The call for a form of government that would command the support of both communities set the template for the new approach. It also linked a promise to promote American investment in the province to the conclusion of a political agreement. The State Department, more comfortable with the strategy of sitting on the fence, had sided with the British in opposing the declaration. Once it was released, there was no going back. The United States had bestowed legitimacy on nationalist demands for power-sharing in Belfast and, by implication, on the Republic's call for a role in a settlement.

For Carter this was good domestic politics. The Irish vote had long belonged largely to the Democrats. This had begun to change during the 1960s and 1970s, reflecting a demographic shift of more affluent Irish Americans from the inner cities to the suburbs. Rising prosperity and a traditional Catholic conservatism uncomfortable with the more radical strands of Democratic Party policy created an opportunity for the Republicans. Reagan, bidding for the presidency in 1980, had set his sights on winning over a segment of the middle-class electorate soon to be called Reagan Democrats. Irish Americans would be prominent among them.

Privately dismayed, the British publicly made the best of Carter's initiative. The prime minister, James Callaghan, issued a statement pointing to the president's condemnation of paramilitary violence and his promise of investment in the north if the parties there reached an accommodation to share political power. London's fears of growing American interest in the affairs of the province, however, were realised two years later, when the Carter administration, under pressure from O'Neill, imposed a ban on arms sales to the RUC. The decision followed allegations of human rights abuses directed at the constabulary by international NGOs. Newly elected as prime minister, Margaret Thatcher reacted angrily to the withholding of export licences for the purchase of US-made handguns and semi-automatic rifles. She wanted it 'brought home to the Americans that for so long as they continued to finance terrorism, American lives as well as those of others would be lost'.[13] The new prime minister was equally sharp in her response to a request from another of the 'horsemen', Hugh Carey, for a meeting to discuss events in Northern Ireland. Carey should be reminded that Northern Ireland was part of the UK, and that 'she herself would not think of discussing with President Carter, for example, US policy towards their black population'. The anger spilled over into a letter sent directly to the president: 'It is an unhappy fact that perspectives on Ireland – and not only in the United States – are still apt to owe more to the 19th century than to the facts of the present-day world.'[14]

Thatcher renewed her protest when she met Carter during her first trip to Washington in December 1979. The president expressed himself privately sympathetic but said that he could not override the coalition in favour of the ban that O'Neill had assembled in Congress. In truth, Thatcher was out of date. In insisting that events in Northern Ireland were an issue only for the British government, she had missed the deeper shift in the political realities of the conflict. Edward Heath had adopted the same hardline position at the start of the 1970s, only to reverse himself when he signed the Sunningdale Agreement. The door opened to American engagement by Carter's statement could likewise not be closed. According to Nigel Sheinwald, who served in the Washington embassy as a young diplomat before later becoming the British ambassador: 'If you were representing Britain anywhere in the world, as I was in Washington during the 1980s, Northern Ireland was a millstone around your neck in reputational terms.'[15] The challenges were reflected in the so-called MacBride Principles adopted by about a dozen American states. Named after an Irish activist, Seán MacBride, they set out a code of conduct for American companies operating in the province to bolster the access to employment of Catholic workers. British criticism went unanswered. David Manning, Tony Blair's foreign policy adviser from 2001, observed that the images of British troops in Belfast had the unmistakable look for Americans of military occupation. 'I felt all the way through that Ireland was an open wound. It didn't really matter terribly whether you believed this was all very unfair. That wasn't the point. It was the perception.'[16]

Reagan's success in mobilising the support of conservative-minded blue-collar workers made him an obvious target for Irish diplomats. The president had fond memories of a visit to Ireland during the 1950s. Donlon set himself the task of researching if the president had Irish roots. The investigations turned up a family connection to Ballyporeen. Invited to the Irish embassy to celebrate St Patrick's Day, Reagan was presented with an illustrated family tree. The deal was sealed. Three years later, the president duly paid a state visit to the Republic. For Donlon's colleague Lillis, who had been instrumental in wooing the Americans, the effect was to 'even up' the imbalance between Britain and Ireland. Dublin could never match Britain's diplomatic weight in the world, but influence in Washington gave it leverage that the British could not ignore.

The relationship between Reagan and Margaret Thatcher was among the strongest between Western post-war leaders. They were kindred spirits in what they saw as an existential struggle against Soviet communism. The White House, however, no longer saw a bar to behind-the-scenes lobbying on behalf of Dublin. By Donlon's account, the change proved influential in encouraging Thatcher to sign the 1985 Anglo-Irish Agreement with FitzGerald. The impact of Reagan's prodding was certainly apparent when Thatcher was invited to address both houses of Congress during a visit to Washington in February 1985. Talks with FitzGerald had stalled as Thatcher insisted that a voice for Dublin in the province's affairs would infringe on British sovereignty. The message sent by Reagan was that she should be flexible. Thatcher's speech reflected the pressure, lauding FitzGerald and committing to working with him to secure a political settlement. She also prefigured the 'consent' principle that would become the key ingredient in the eventual peace. 'So long as the majority of people of Northern Ireland wish to remain part of the United Kingdom,' Thatcher said, 'their wishes will be respected.' But 'if ever there were to be a majority in favour of change, then I believe that our Parliament would respond accordingly, for that is the principle of consent enshrined in your constitution and in an essential part of ours'. If the people wanted Irish unity, Britain would not stand in the way. The conclusion of the agreement later the same autumn saw Reagan hold a press conference at the White House to offer America's blessing – and to redeem Carter's promise to encourage new private-sector investment in Ireland. Less than a decade later, another Democratic president from America's deep south would walk through the door opened by Carter when Bill Clinton ended the ban on Sinn Féin's president, Gerry Adams, visiting the United States.

7 THE LADY TURNS

It fell to the most avowedly pro-unionist prime minister since Andrew Bonar Law to read the last rites over the Protestant hegemony in Northern Ireland. Margaret Thatcher had arrived in Downing Street in 1979 believing the people of the province to be every bit as British as those in her North London parliamentary constituency of Finchley. The defeated James Callaghan had come to despair of any settlement in Ireland for as long as the British remained. Thatcher wore her commitment to the union on her sleeve. 'These people', she said of the unionist majority, 'shared many of my own attitudes, derived from my staunchly Methodist background.'[1] She had never been much troubled by the concentration of power in the hands of Northern Ireland's Protestants: 'I had always had a great deal of respect for the old Stormont system.' Nor did she have time for the aspirations of nationalists. Minorities were minorities, she would say, drawing comparison with Sikhs in India and Germans in inter-war Sudetenland. 'The Irish want more than we can give and always will.'[2] All in all there could be no more staunch defender of the indivisible sovereignty of the United Kingdom of Great Britain and Northern Ireland.

Conviction and temperament were to collide with the immoveable political and security realities that had vexed Thatcher's predecessors in Number 10. In signing the Anglo-Irish Agreement in November 1985, Thatcher became the first prime minister since partition to formally acknowledge the province's unique position within the United Kingdom and to cede a place for another state in decisions about the future of part of the United Kingdom. In one dimension this Northern Ireland exceptionalism was a statement of the obvious. The first allegiance of more than a third of the population of the province was to another state. The same could not be said of Scotland or Wales, or indeed of her constituents in Finchley. Yet Thatcher's (albeit reluctant) ratification of this reality marked the moment when the ground shifted irrevocably under the feet of Northern Irish unionism. Enoch Powell, the erstwhile Conservative MP and minister who had quit his party and become the UUP MP for South Down, denounced the agreement as 'treachery'. He was not alone.

Thatcher began her premiership persuaded that the conflict in Northern Ireland was a matter of domestic politics. The province was sovereign British territory. Members of the PIRA were criminals, not freedom fighters. There was no place for the Republic in decision-making in Belfast – nor, for that matter, for the American politicians in Washington who, to her mind, came perilously close to condoning terrorism. As she saw it, the real problem was one of security – and there much of the responsibility lay with a government in Dublin that stood idly by when terrorists moved freely between the north and the south. To the extent that the Republic had any claim to a role in the province, its responsibility was to tighten up border controls, end an effective judicial bar on the extradition of PIRA suspects to Britain and cooperate with the British military. The conviction was strongly felt, personal as well as political. On the eve of the election that swept her into Downing Street, her close friend and political adviser the MP Airey Neave was killed by a car bomb planted at the House of Commons by a republican splinter group, the INLA.

An early test of Thatcher's determination to 'face down' terrorism came with a series of hunger strikes by republican prisoners. Self-starvation had a long tradition in Irish nationalism, a powerful symbol of the sacrifice embedded in the struggle. In 1981 republican detainees demanded they be granted political status – treatment akin to that of prisoners of war – in the so-called H-Blocks of the sprawling Maze prison outside Belfast. They had been accorded the status in the early years of the conflict, but the concession had been withdrawn by the Labour Northern Ireland secretary Roy Mason in line with official insistence that they were terrorists rather than soldiers. A hunger strike in 1980 in protest at the regime change had ended without fatalities after republicans claimed to have made progress towards their goals. Within months they were accusing the British of reneging on the supposed deal. The protest that began in March 1981 when the PIRA's most senior prisoner, Bobby Sands, refused food was of a different order. Sands, and those who joined him over the following months, was determined to see it through to its mortal conclusion. The story was soon front-page news around the world. Thatcher's refusal to compromise provoked widespread anger in the Irish American community and deep unease in Washington. By the time the strike was called off in October 1981, ten prisoners had died. The PIRA and INLA had a new set of republican martyrs, and Britain's international reputation had suffered a serious blow. The government's dilemma had been set out in July in an informal discussion at cabinet. The record of the meeting noted 'increasingly disturbing signs of an erosion of international confidence in British policy in the light of the continuing hunger strike at the Maze'. The risk, ministers accepted, was that the government's refusal to bow to the prisoners' demands would be condemned as inflexible. On the other hand, 'Any gesture to reduce the appearance of inflexibility was likely to be interpreted both by the Protestant Community and the Irish Republican Army as a prelude to capitulation.'[3]

As it was, Thatcher could claim to have stood firm, even if intense mediation efforts by the Catholic Church among others had elicited from the government a quiet promise of some relaxation of the H-Block regime if and when the protest ended. The republicans, however, scored the propaganda victory. Through history the notion of a 'blood sacrifice' had served as a potent weapon in the struggle against the British. The peremptory execution by British military authorities of the leaders of the 1916 Easter Rising had done more than anything else to spur the transition from constitutional nationalism to armed insurrection. More recently, the shooting by British paratroopers of unarmed civilians on Bloody Sunday in 1972 had provided the platform for a dramatic escalation of violence. The names of Sands and his fellow hunger strikers were now added to the republicans' roll call of victims of British oppression. Thatcher's insistence that the government should not bow to terrorism was in tune with policy orthodoxy among democratic governments across the world. Indeed, it was publicly shared by the Irish government. But this approach was also supposed to leave room for quiet accommodation. Thatcher's unyielding defiance set her apart. Senior figures within the PIRA initially had their own doubts about the wisdom of the hunger strikes. In the event the republican leadership was soon declaring the protest to have been an unvarnished success. The deaths intensified feelings of estrangement and anger in the wider nationalist community and acted as a powerful recruiting tool for the PIRA. An estimated hundred thousand people turned out for Sands's funeral. Catholics mostly abhorred republican violence but many had sympathy for the cause.

The deaths marked a critical turning point in the PIRA's approach to the conflict. Republican theology had it that the movement should not field candidates in elections to the Westminster parliament lest they be accused of lending legitimacy to British rule. Five days after the start of Sands's fast, the death of the sitting MP foreshadowed a Westminster by-election in the Fermanagh and South Tyrone constituency. Sinn Féin broke with the past by nominating the imprisoned Sands as a candidate. His victory foreshadowed a new political strategy for republicanism – an attempt to combine PIRA violence with an electoral pitch to peaceful nationalism. The leading Sinn Féin official Danny Morrison spelled out the shift at the party's 1981 Ard Fheis, or party conference. 'Who here really believes that we can win the war through the ballot box? But will anyone here object if, with a ballot box in this hand and an Armalite in this, we take power in Ireland?'

Thatcher's assumption was that the relatively small number of active PIRA fighters – a few hundred – could over time be isolated and defeated. Sinn Féin's new electoral strategy pointed up the weakness of her approach. The great majority of Catholics in Northern Ireland abhorred the shootings and bombings. But a substantial proportion of them also held an emotional attachment to national unity and made little distinction between unionist and British rule. Loyalist attacks and the harsh tactics adopted by the British army in support of the Protestant-dominated RUC fed the ambivalence. PIRA paramilitaries assumed the role of protectors in Catholic communities. Now Sinn Féin canvassed for their votes. Gerry Adams, soon to be appointed president of Sinn Féin and fast becoming the public face of republicanism, was elected as the MP for Belfast West. Adams would always deny any role in the PIRA. British officials would insist that they had incontrovertible evidence that he was a member of the organisation's Army Council.

By the early 1980s the level of killings had fallen markedly since a peak a decade earlier, but the PIRA's military capacity was undiminished. Bombings and shootings on both sides, the constant presence on the streets of British troops and the barricades dividing the two communities sounded the drumbeat of a low-level civil war. A report on security submitted to Thatcher by the defence and Northern Ireland departments soon after she became prime minister underlined the disproportionate capacity of small numbers of paramilitaries to confound the security forces. Across Northern Ireland as a whole, the report noted, not more than five hundred active fighters were 'holding down' more than twenty thousand troops from the mainland and the Ulster Defence Regiment, along with more than ten thousand full- and part-time members of the RUC. A new 'cellular' structure introduced by PIRA commanders was thwarting the activities of the intelligence agencies by making it difficult to penetrate the organisation's senior ranks.[4] The report was delivered to Thatcher in August 1979. As if to prove the point, during that same month the PIRA assassinated the queen's cousin, Earl Mountbatten, exploding a bomb on his boat during a family holiday in the Republic's County Sligo. Just across the border eighteen British soldiers lost their lives when an army convoy was ambushed by republicans at Warrenpoint. Public opinion on the British mainland was shifting towards disengagement. Harold Wilson's private frustrations were becoming part of the national conversation: the Irish should be left to fight their own battles. A cabinet meeting in July 1981 was told of growing concern among ministers that Sands's by-election victory – 'the choice of an imprisoned terrorist hunger striker to represent a Northern Ireland constituency at Westminster' – was a watershed. Many in Britain now believed 'that a settlement of the complex problems of the area would be more easily reached by the Irish on their own and that continued British involvement could only mean the futile sacrifice of further British lives'. A change in the position of the Labour opposition, ministers concluded, would add to the government's difficulties. The former prime minister Callaghan, the note recorded, had been saying privately that the citizenship guarantee offered to Northern Ireland by the British government should apply to its individual inhabitants rather than to the territory itself. 'The whole context of the current British debate would be altered if the question he [Callaghan] addresses was not whether British policy was winning or losing in the struggle, but whether it was a struggle in which Britain ought any longer be involved at all.' Summing up the discussion, Thatcher was non-committal. But her closing remark that 'further thought would need to be given to all possible courses of action in regard to Northern Ireland, however difficult or unpalatable', signalled an emerging awareness that increased security would not alone provide an answer.[5]

What made the reopening of serious talks with the Republic possible was the arrival of a new Taoiseach in Dublin. November 1982 saw the creation of a Fine Gael–Labour coalition led by Garret FitzGerald. For most of the previous three years (FitzGerald briefly held power in 1981) Thatcher's counterpart had been Charles Haughey. After a brief honeymoon during 1980, when the two leaders pledged to upgrade the political dialogue between the two governments by creating an intergovernmental council, the relationship soured. Haughey, a showman with expensive personal tastes, played to his party's history. He carried himself as a torch-bearer for de Valera's uncompromising nationalism. Above all, though, Haughey was an opportunist. When it suited his political positioning he was happy to blur the line between peaceful nationalism and republican insurgency. His Ireland defined itself against the historic enemy. The relationship with Thatcher was never going to work. It began to break down when he overstated the remit of the proposed new council to suggest that Thatcher had given significant constitutional ground in their negotiations. It fractured completely during the Falklands War in 1982, when, after the sinking by a British submarine of the Argentine warship *Belgrano*, Haughey broke with Ireland's European Union partners to call for an end to sanctions against Argentina. Some in Dublin had long drawn a parallel between Argentina's claim to what it called Las Malvinas and the Republic's demand for the north. Siding with the Argentine generals after they had seized the Falklands by force went much further.

FitzGerald had an altogether more sober, and realistic, view of Irish aspirations. Thoughtful and mild-mannered, and lacking his predecessor's extravagant tastes, he did not share Haughey's compulsion always to stand centre-stage. From the early days of the PIRA campaign, he had recognised that republicanism was as dangerous for democracy in the south as in the north. The republican movement's aim, after all, was to overturn the political order in Dublin as much as in Belfast. FitzGerald judged that the importance of defeating the PIRA transcended all other considerations. The immediate threat was that Sinn Féin would replace the SDLP as the voice of mainstream nationalism in the north. As foreign affairs minister and then leader of the Fine Gael opposition, FitzGerald campaigned energetically in the United States to halt the flow of funds to the PIRA from the Irish American Noraid.

FitzGerald was a nationalist. He wanted a united Ireland and thought the British should declare that they would support such an outcome, but he carried little of the baggage that said that partition was nothing more than an exercise in British colonialism. Northern Ireland, he understood, could not be coerced. Over time, it might be persuaded. So FitzGerald's focus was directed at promoting reconciliation between north and south and between nationalism and unionism, and building cooperation between Dublin and London. That made him unusually (for an Irish minister) sensitive to the impact on Protestant opinion of the unrivalled power in the

Republic wielded by the Catholic Church. In 1981 he expressed his concerns publicly in a radio interview. Rather than building bridges across the border with Northern Ireland, the Republic had become 'a state imbued with the ethos of the majority in our part of the island. Initially partitioned by the British, our island had been further partitioned by constitutions and laws alien to the whole people of Ireland.' What he was seeking, he added in the BBC's 1982 Dimbleby Lecture, was a political structure that would safeguard the identities of the two traditions in Ireland. The goal of a united Ireland had not changed, but his call for a pluralist southern state to accommodate unionism broke with the nationalist tradition of presenting a binary choice between partition and a unitary, Catholic Irish state. Geoffrey Howe, Thatcher's foreign secretary, soon a leading actor in negotiations, spoke of FitzGerald's 'manifest sincerity' as a vital ingredient in persuading Thatcher to compromise.

The other side of the argument was that just as Irish nationalism needed to accommodate unionism, political institutions in the north had to offer the nationalist community a real stake in the governance of the province. 'Alienation' was a word that much irritated Thatcher, but it was an accurate description of what Catholics felt. At root, the problem was that nationalists did not recognise the legitimacy of the unionist regime. The reforms forced on unionism by British governments during the 1970s had removed much of the more blatant discrimination against Catholics – in voting rights, housing allocation and employment opportunities – embedded by half a century of Stormont rule. But the levers of power in Northern Ireland, whether in the senior ranks of the civil service, the judiciary or the police, remained overwhelmingly in the hands of Protestants. Thus, of the nine battalions of the Ulster Defence Regiment – six thousand men in 1985 – less than 3 per cent were Catholic. Protestants took 90 per cent of the jobs in the police and judiciary.

Peace, in FitzGerald's mind, required that Catholics identify with the institutions of Northern Ireland. Nationalism also demanded recognition of the legitimacy of its support for unity and its right to express allegiance to the Irish state. The Flags and Emblems Act barred any raising of the Irish flag in the province. There was no such prohibition against the flags of foreign states elsewhere in the United Kingdom. The FitzGerald government strengthened its contacts on the other side of the border. Northern Ireland's nationalists had been largely ignored by Dublin in the aftermath of partition. From the 1970s a cadre of diplomats, prominent among them senior figures such as Donlon and Dáithí Ó Ceallaigh, regularly visited the province in the effort to recast Irish nationalism as a peaceful enterprise. For her part, Thatcher often misread Irish attitudes towards the PIRA. It was true that the Republic's courts were inclined, perhaps over-inclined, to accept claims of 'political status' to avoid extraditing those accused by the British of alleged terrorist crimes, but FitzGerald's fears about the republican threat to the Irish state were no less real for that. If Thatcher thought his government 'soft' on terrorism, the irony was that one of the Taoiseach's abiding fears was that the British government might resume the secret negotiations with PIRA leaders it had held during the early years of the Troubles and thereby legitimise violent republicanism.

The possibility of a joint political initiative first came into view at a Downing Street dinner party during December 1982, the month FitzGerald took office. Thatcher had emerged victorious in the Falklands War, cementing her self-image as an implacable guardian of national sovereignty. Riding high in the opinion polls, she had begun to look ahead to a general election during the following year. David Goodall, a senior diplomat, would recall in his memoir that as the conversation across the dinner table turned to Northern Ireland, it seemed to some an 'often overlooked and scandalous fact that the only place in the world where British soldiers' lives were then being lost in anger was in the United Kingdom itself'. A guest at the dinner, Goodall was struck that for all her obvious distaste for Irish nationalism, Thatcher was seriously wrestling with the options for Northern Ireland. 'If we get back [into government] next time,' she remarked at the end of the conversation, 'I think I would like to do something about Ireland.'[6]

The next year, in September 1983, with Thatcher's landslide election victory behind her, two senior officials, one Irish and one British, took a walk alongside Dublin's Grand Canal. Michael Lillis, the seasoned Irish diplomat, had cut his teeth in Washington. He was joined by Goodall, who had been seconded to the Cabinet Office as a deputy to the cabinet secretary, Robert Armstrong. Between the canal's Leeson Street and Baggot Street bridges, Lillis, acting as FitzGerald's personal emissary, made a pitch. The alienation of Northern Ireland's Catholic community, Lillis argued, had created a vacuum now being filled by the PIRA and Sinn Féin. A transformative change was needed to end the sense of exclusion and regain nationalist trust. Dublin proposed a framework for negotiations calculated to reassure both sides in the conflict. The Republic was ready to address the insecurities of unionism by diluting or removing the territorial claim to the six counties enshrined in de Valera's constitution. In return Britain should offer nationalists an 'Irish dimension' in the governance of Northern Ireland by sharing authority with the Republic in sensitive areas such as security and the administration of justice. The overture was an informal one. Within months it had set in train a process that would begin to draw the map of Northern Ireland's path to peace.

The talks that followed during the next two years were an extraordinarily intense exercise in high-level diplomacy. Beyond Thatcher and FitzGerald the negotiations were led on the British side by Armstrong and Goodall. The Taoiseach's team was headed by Armstrong's opposite number, the secretary to the government Dermot Nally, and included Lillis and the Irish ambassador in London, Noel Dorr. The roles of Armstrong and Nally were particularly significant, putting the process directly in the hands of the two leaders and beyond the ingrained prejudices of parts of their own bureaucracies. The two nations' foreign ministers – Geoffrey Howe and Peter Barry – were pivotal players. All in all, between the autumn of 1983 and the signature of the Anglo-Irish Agreement at Hillsborough Castle in November 1985, representatives of the two sides would meet on dozens of occasions. Formal summits between the two leaders were interspersed with regular informal get-togethers in the margins of European summits in Brussels. According to Goodall, more attention was paid by senior British officials to the Irish question than at any time since the Anglo-Irish Treaty. On the Irish side, Lillis noted that this 'extraordinary exercise in diplomacy' saw the two negotiating teams meet every six weeks or so during 1984 and 1985, sometimes locked away in discreet country houses, sometimes in the quiet corners of gentlemen's clubs in St James's.

The process was not without stumbles. For Thatcher, the priority was always to improve security. This meant much greater cross-border cooperation between the British forces in the north and the Republic's police and military. She bridled at the claims of nationalist alienation and was infuriated by the refusal of the Republic's courts to extradite suspected terrorists. Her second refrain was that she would not accept any abrogation of British sovereignty. For his part, FitzGerald insisted that security had to be set in a political context. In 1984 the Taoiseach made a direct pitch for joint Anglo-Irish authority in the administration of the province. This, according to Goodall, 'stung her [Thatcher] into more than usually unguarded outbursts of irritation which, I noted in my diary, were the authentic echo of British ignorance, arrogance, contempt and dislike for Ireland down the ages'.[7] A few months later, when the Conservatives gathered in Brighton for their annual party conference, Thatcher was lucky to escape with her life after the PIRA planted a bomb in the town's Grand Hotel. Five people, including an MP, were killed in the explosion during the early hours of the morning. Thatcher's hotel suite barely escaped the full force of the blast. 'Today we were unlucky,' read the PIRA's chilling communiqué, 'but remember we only have to be lucky once.' Thatcher worried that the negotiations with Dublin might be misinterpreted in the aftermath of the bombing, noting privately that 'the events of Thursday night at Brighton mean that we must go very slow on these talks, if not stop them. It would look as if we were being bombed into making concessions to the Republic.'[8] To her credit, the pause was temporary.

At other moments, she cast around for alternative answers. One recurring theme was that the border between north and south could be changed. Britain would no longer have to pay benefits to nationalists who declared themselves Irish. Why could the government, she asked officials, 'not redraw the border to exclude predominantly Catholic areas and relieve ourselves of the expense of paying social security to people who did not want to belong to the United Kingdom'?[9] Much as she supported the union, like Harold Wilson she resented the subsidies paid to the province. A secret report produced for the cabinet in response poured cold water on the idea. 'The current population distribution in Northern Ireland is even more intermingled than at the time of partition. Even where the Catholics are a majority there tends to be a substantial Protestant minority . . . And around one third of the Catholic population live in Belfast, representing a quarter of the City's population.' The report concluded that it was 'tempting' to argue that 'people whose Republican views make it impossible for them to accept the Government of Northern Ireland should go and live in the Republic'. There was a snag. 'Whereas moving half a million people might be the obvious solution for a totalitarian regime, we face problems as regards the letter and spirit of human rights provision and international opinion.'[10] Thatcher would return to the issue in talks with FitzGerald. 'History shows that the Irish, whether the Scottish–Irish or the Irish–Irish, don't like to move,' she complained to the Taoiseach. 'However, they all seem to be terribly happy to move to Britain.'[11]

There were moments when the prime minister's outbursts threatened to derail the negotiations. In 1983 FitzGerald set up a public all-Ireland forum calculated to launch a debate among political parties on the constitutional future. It was boycotted by unionist parties, and its conclusions were predictably nationalist. It proposed straightforward unification, joint authority between London and Dublin over Northern Ireland or a new confederal structure in which both parts of Ireland would be self-governing except in the areas of monetary, security and foreign policy. More important for FitzGerald than precise recommendations was that the forum had reclaimed the government's ownership of the nationalist debate in the Republic. The simplistic mantra of 'Brits Out' was replaced by acknowledgement of the need for an accommodation with unionism. Thatcher did not see the subtlety. After a robust discussion with FitzGerald at a summit at Chequers in 1984, she was asked at a post-summit press conference for her views about the forum's proposed three scenarios. Her brusque response of 'out, out, out' was widely seen as a humiliation for FitzGerald.

Her mood, though, would change. She returned repeatedly to the cost of the Treasury's subsidies for the province. Net transfers continued to climb, from £1.2 billion when she came to power to more than twice that amount by the early 1990s. A decade earlier, Harold Wilson had talked of 'spongers'. When, in the wake of their agreement in 1985, FitzGerald suggested that the two governments should jointly seek more international funding for Northern Ireland, he was startled by Thatcher's response. 'More money for these people?' she retorted. 'Look at their schools, look at their roads. Why should they have more money? I need that money for my people in England who don't have anything like this.'[12] It seemed that unionists were destined to lose if the choice was between unionism and 'my people in England'.

Armstrong would later remark of Thatcher's mood swings that he had sometimes felt he was leading not one but two sets of negotiations: 'one with our Irish counterparts and another with the prime minister'.[13] Geoffrey Howe, at once emollient and dogged, did much to keep the process on an even keel. Thatcher often showed irritation with Howe's patient pursuit of diplomacy. In Goodall's estimation the foreign secretary 'displayed a statesman's breadth of vision and sense of history'. The prime minister never thanked him for it. Yet for all her misgivings – and in retirement Thatcher would offer a sour account of the negotiations – Armstrong concluded: 'I think she did want it. Though her instincts were unionist she had become disenchanted with the Northern Irish politicians.' Charles Powell, her long-time Downing Street policy adviser, offered a more shaded explanation. If there was a 'raw side' to Thatcher's views, reaching back to de Valera's closure of Irish ports to the British navy during the Second World War, it was also 'a tactic of hers to make outrageous statements and stake out maximalist positions as a warning to negotiators not to chance their arm . . . the art with her was to be able to distinguish theatre from reality'.[14] There were inevitable frustrations on the Irish side. By the summer of 1985 the even-tempered FitzGerald was telling British officials that he had lost faith in their government's trustworthiness. 'I know that British ministers think that their word is their bond. But if I were to give Mrs Thatcher a full-frontal view of what Irish nationalism thinks of a British minister's word she would be more shocked than if I gave her a full-frontal view of something else.'[15]

The agreement unveiled at Hillsborough on 15 November 1985 fell short of the boldest of the ambitions explored during the first canalside conversation between Lillis and Goodall. But it set the trajectory that would lead to peace. Thatcher's offer of a consultative role for the Republic in much of the governance of Northern Ireland didn't quite meet nationalist hopes of a decisive move to share responsibility. FitzGerald's government pulled back from calling a referendum on whether to remove the Republic's territorial claim from the constitution. But the bargain preserved the essential architecture of those initial discussions. From the Irish side came, if not revision of the constitution, then unequivocal recognition of the principle of unionist consent to any change in the status of the north. At Sunningdale in 1973 the two governments had issued separate interpretations as to what precisely was implied by 'consent'. The new agreement included a joint statement spelling out that constitutional change was possible only with the backing of a majority and that neither side would stand in the way of such a decision: 'If in the future a majority of the people of Northern Ireland clearly wish for and formally consent to the establishment of a united Ireland, they will introduce and support in the respective parliaments legislation to give effect to that wish.'

The Lady had turned. Thatcher's fears about a visible diminution of British sovereignty ruled out joint responsibility, but the deal accepted that the Republic had a legitimate voice in the affairs of the province. A new Anglo-Irish intergovernmental conference, enshrined in international treaty and with a permanent base – the Maryfield Secretariat in Belfast – would assure Dublin of a consultative role. The Republic had its foot in the north. This marked what Lillis would call an 'irrevocable change' in relationships within Northern Ireland and between London and Dublin.[16] Thatcher and FitzGerald had set the parameters for future political accords, including a dozen years later the Good Friday (or Belfast) Agreement. Crucially, they also removed the unionist veto over the province's future. Loyalists had been able to bring down Sunningdale because it depended on Protestant participation in new power-sharing structures. The Thatcher–FitzGerald bargain was struck between the governments in London and Dublin. The carrot for unionism came in the form of a provision that joint proposals from the new Anglo-Irish Conference would be limited to matters that fell outside 'the responsibility of a devolved administration in Northern Ireland'. The proviso assumed, of course, that such an administration would be established. And therein lay the warning for unionists: if they rejected power-sharing in Belfast, Britain and the Republic would press on regardless. The UUP leader David Trimble would grasp this a little more than a decade later when he signed up to a peace agreement with the PIRA. The choice for unionism was no longer between Protestant hegemony in Belfast and direct rule from London but between shared power with nationalists and ceding a role for the Republic in the affairs of the province. Only if unionists took the first course would the Republic, in Thatcher's words, be 'out'. The boast of Northern Ireland's first prime minister James Craig that partition created 'a Protestant parliament and a Protestant state' was robbed of meaning.

At Westminster the prime minister faced a small but noisy rebellion. For some Tory MPs, doing business with the Republic would always be beyond the pale. Richard Ryan, a diplomat at the Irish embassy in London tasked with liaising with the Conservatives, became inured to the prejudice. By way of compliment, the right-wing Wolverhampton MP Nicholas Budgen once told Ryan that 'as the representative of a marginal and residual race, you actually strike me as being at least three-quarters educated'. Ivor Stanbrook, the member for Orpington, was not so generous. Finding that Ryan was among a group travelling back by train to London from a funeral, Stanbrook announced that 'I will most certainly never fraternise with the fifth column agent of a hostile foreign power whose insidious purpose is to subvert the integrity of the United Kingdom'.[17]

The blend of prejudice and exasperated indifference towards Northern Ireland that described the attitude of most Tory politicians did have occasional exceptions. As the Earl of Kilmorey, Richard Needham hailed from the old Anglo-Irish Ascendancy. The ancestral stately home had been lost to his father's impecunious habits, but Needham, appointed by Thatcher as the minister responsible for the province's economic affairs, spent six years pushing the boulder uphill in the attempt to kick-start regeneration and draw in overseas investment and jobs. The PIRA's bombing of shops, hotels and businesses in Belfast was calculated to destroy any sense of normality. Needham had notable successes, including as the sponsor for a new shopping centre, Castle Court, in the heart of the city. Northern Ireland's politicians, nationalist and unionist, were surprised to discover a British minister seeking to make a difference. A more typically ignorant attitude was offered by the Tory MP who complained that some of the young workers at the new centre were being recruited from the staunchly nationalist west

Belfast. The government, this critic said, was 'giving in to terrorists by employing their children'.[18]

If Stanbrook and Budgen were far from alone in their bigotry, on the day of the vote on the treaty Thatcher's own unionist credentials won over many doubters on the Conservative back benches. Only twenty-one Tory MPs voted against the agreement. The overall tally was 473 in favour and 47 against. As Dáithí Ó Ceallaigh, one of the first Irish diplomats to join the new Maryfield Secretariat and later Dublin's ambassador in London, would say of the majority: 'This surely demonstrated to unionists that after 64 years of engagement in Westminster, they had in reality no parliamentary allies.'[19]

The realisation helped explain the din of angry protest from unionists. Enoch Powell's charge of betrayal echoed through the lodges of the Orange Order. Hundreds of thousands joined rallies and demonstrations in Belfast. Unionist MPs triggered fifteen House of Commons by-elections by resigning their seats. The UUP leader James Molyneaux charged that Thatcher had capitulated to the PIRA. FitzGerald too faced strong protests, but from the opposite side. Charles Haughey's Fianna Fáil voted against the agreement, charging that far from removing the Protestant veto, in recognising British rule in the north FitzGerald had undermined the claim to the entire territory of Ireland enshrined in the constitution. What wounded Thatcher, however, was the resignation from his middle-ranking post at the Treasury of her close friend and ally Ian Gow. In the description of Howe, Gow was the prime minister's 'unionist conscience'. For Gow, as for the unionists, Thatcher had struck a blow against British sovereignty. A few years later, in July 1990, he would be killed outside his house in Sussex by a PIRA car bomb.

The hurt of his resignation was reflected in Thatcher's own, later account of the negotiations. To Howe's mind, her head was persuaded, her heart was not. In her memoirs, she emphasised her own practical concerns with security, 'while the Irish indulged in gesture politics'. The agreement, she suggested, had done little to change things beyond relieving some of the international (American) pressure on her government. Lobbied by Dublin and mindful of his own Irish ancestry, her great ally Ronald Reagan had been a constant and, in Thatcher's eyes, troublesome advocate for a political agreement. She grasped only belatedly the constitutional significance of the agreement. Just as her signature on the Single European Act in 1986 would set the European Union off on an integrationist path that she would later disown, so, for all her protestations otherwise, the Anglo-Irish Agreement marked out a different road for Northern Ireland. The Republic had understood that its recital of the mantra of a united Ireland had for decades given Britain an excuse for inaction; Britain could no longer pretend that Northern Ireland was just another part of the United Kingdom. Belfast was not Finchley.

8 TALKING TO TERRORISTS

The importance of trust between political leaders is underestimated. The personal rapport that would see John Major and Albert Reynolds take the next step along the road to a political settlement in Ireland was first forged by chance at a meeting in Brussels of European finance ministers. In 1989 Thatcher handed Major the chancellor's job following the stormy resignation from her cabinet of Nigel Lawson, after a dispute about the management of sterling's exchange rate. Reynolds held the same position in the Irish government. The two men first met at Ecofin, the monthly gathering of finance ministers. Pressing a British initiative on his European colleagues, Major needed allies. Reynolds, a businessman-turned-politician with a liking for deal-making, offered him support in corralling other European colleagues into the British camp. Major got the help he needed and a useful political victory to take back to London. A bond had been forged. Four years later, as prime minister and Taoiseach respectively, they unveiled the Downing Street Declaration – a clarion call for Northern Ireland to surrender the Armalite in favour of the ballot box.

The European Union, as it was to become, had already staked a claim as an important agent in improving Anglo-Irish relations. Before the two countries joined in 1973, meetings between their respective leaders had usually focused on areas of disagreement. Mandatory exchanges on partition were a dialogue of the deaf. European debates changed over time the rhythm and texture of the relationship, not least because the two governments often found themselves on the same side in negotiations with their continental counterparts. The leaders met more frequently and their officials established networks of collaboration. The trust eventually forged between Thatcher and FitzGerald was in good part a product of their bilateral contacts in the margins of European summits. Brussels was the place where the two nations could get to know each other after the long estrangement of partition.

That said, there seemed little reason for Major to turn to peace-making in Northern Ireland. Brought up in modest circumstances in South London (his father had been a music hall performer before setting up a business selling garden ornaments), he had risen stealthily through the ministerial ranks. When Conservative MPs turned decisively against the Lady in the autumn of 1990, she named Major as her preferred successor. In truth, his political views were relatively obscure. Some saw him as the natural heir to Thatcher, others, more accurately, as a leader who would take the party back to the centre ground of One Nation conservatism. Ireland was a blank page. One official inadvertently teased out what proved to be an important clue to the search for peace that would follow. Jill Rutter, who served as a private secretary during Major's spell at the Treasury, once asked him what ministerial post he would like next. 'Northern Ireland secretary,' Major replied. Perhaps sensing her surprise (in terms of prestige the post sits at the bottom of the cabinet rankings), he said it was an affront that the United Kingdom should have its democracy scarred by such a conflict.[1] Here, unbeknown to colleagues, was the project he took into 10 Downing Street.

At first glance, it promised to be a thankless one. The Anglo-Irish Agreement had done little if anything to slow the tempo of violence in the province. Thatcher had grown to regret her signature on the accord. The return of Charles Haughey to the Taoiseach's office had cooled relations between Dublin and London. In November 1987 the PIRA provoked international outrage when eleven Protestants were killed at a Remembrance Day ceremony in Enniskillen. In September 1989 eleven military bandsmen died in Kent after republican bombers crossed to the mainland. In February 1991 the PIRA turned its mind again to assassinating a prime minister. An active service unit fired three mortar shells in the direction of 10 Downing Street from nearby Whitehall. Major was chairing a meeting of his war cabinet about the conflict in the Gulf following Iraq's invasion of Kuwait when one of the shells exploded in the garden. The windows of the cabinet room withstood the blast, but a handful of officials elsewhere suffered minor injuries. The PIRA's Army Council had originally planned the attack before Thatcher's departure a few months earlier. It decided to press ahead anyhow after Major replaced her. The prospects for peace looked dim. Republican attacks were matched by loyalist outrages. Elements of British intelligence and the military stepped out of the rule of law by colluding with loyalist paramilitaries in their fight against the PIRA. Special forces operated what later investigations would indicate was a de facto shoot-to-kill policy. In 2012 a subsequent prime minister, David Cameron, would admit in a Downing Street statement that there were 'shocking levels of state collusion' in the murder by loyalist paramilitaries of the prominent Belfast lawyer Pat Finucane in 1989.

The ground, though, was shifting. By the end of the 1980s it was evident to those British politicians who paid attention that they could neither defeat the PIRA nor simply withdraw and leave Northern Ireland to its own devices. Republicans were engaged in their own reassessment. British officials picked up signs that Gerry Adams and Martin McGuinness, both (though Adams always denied it) prominent figures on the PIRA Army Council, were reassessing republican options. In part this reflected the growing importance of the movement's political strategy. The years since the election of Bobby Sands to Westminster had seen Sinn Féin prosper at the ballot box. But the parallel commitment to the Armalite put a cap on its electoral support. Open conflict with the British state carried more visible costs. The aggressive targeting of republicans by loyalist groups reinforced a sense of military stalemate. And the PIRA's leaders were approaching middle age. The young men who had taken to the streets of Belfast and Derry during the early 1970s now had families. Did they want their children to inherit what seemed to be an unwinnable war?

In November 1990, the month of Thatcher's resignation, a group of slightly bemused business leaders from the British Association of Canned Food Importers and Distributors unexpectedly found itself the audience for a speech by Peter Brooke, the Northern Ireland secretary. Brooke, a mild-mannered English toff whose family history in the old Anglo-Irish Ascendancy had bestowed on him an unusual respect for Ireland and a determination to promote reconciliation, wanted to send a coded message to the leadership of the PIRA. He was reluctant, though, to speak in the sectarian glare of Belfast or Derry. His speech had been drafted, redrafted, checked and rechecked over several weeks before receiving Thatcher's approval. Now it needed a neutral venue and an audience. An enterprising official at the Northern Ireland office alighted on the food industry dinner scheduled at the Whitbread restaurant and conference centre in Brooke's Cities of London and Westminster constituency. The guests at the event had no clue they were witnesses to the beginnings of what would soon become known as the Northern Ireland peace process. Listening to a detailed, and rather dry, exposition of the government's position on the constitutional future of Northern Ireland, they must have been baffled as to why they were the chosen audience for Brooke's erudite exposition of the intricacies of partition. None could have guessed they were an unwitting channel for the opening of negotiations between the British state and violent republicanism.

The speech was part of a carefully choreographed strategy to test if the PIRA was ready to negotiate. The government in London knew it could never achieve a military victory. Republicans were reaching a similar conclusion. The British would not be bombed out of Ireland. Suffering heavy losses at the hands of loyalist paramilitaries, the Special Air Service and shadowy British units such as the Force Research Unit, the PIRA leadership, however, had not been shown an alternative path.

Much of what Brooke said was what Whitehall called 'boilerplate stuff', a repeat of oft-made statements. Northern Ireland was part of the United Kingdom. That status would change only with the consent of a majority of its people. Then came the crucial paragraph, a message crafted explicitly for Adams and McGuinness. While Britain would not shirk its obligations to the people of the province, Brooke said, 'The British Government has no selfish strategic or economic interest in Northern Ireland: our role is to help, enable and encourage. Britain's purpose ... is not to occupy, oppress or exploit but to ensure democratic debate and free democratic choice. Partition is an acknowledgement of reality, not an assertion of national self-interest.'

At another time a statement of neutrality as to Northern Ireland's future might have seemed unremarkable – an expression of views long held by British prime ministers. Hadn't the Labour leader Harold Wilson argued within his own cabinet that the province should be cut loose from the rest of the United Kingdom? Thatcher's government, though, was viewed by republicans as different. Every word mattered. She had held firm in the face of PIRA hunger strikes. She had barely escaped death at the hands of the PIRA's Brighton bombers. And only months before Brooke's speech, the PIRA had murdered her close political friend – and staunch unionist – Ian Gow. Now it seemed that for all her visceral loathing of 'terrorists', Thatcher was coming to terms with the reality of the military stalemate.

Soon after the speech, a high-ranking official with direct involvement in secret talks with republicans told me that the problem Brooke had been addressing was rooted in a Sinn Féin worldview that had been frozen in the past. The intelligence services judged that the PIRA was fixated on Northern Ireland's pivotal role in assuring the security of mainland Britain during the Second World War. Republicans knew that in the face of Irish neutrality, Northern Ireland's seaports had been critical to the British effort to keep open the Atlantic sea lanes to sustain the war effort against Germany. This strategic imperative, the PIRA concluded, meant that the London government would never relinquish control of the province. But now the Berlin Wall had fallen, and the Cold War had ended. 'We needed to give a public assurance that life had moved on,' the official said. 'The next world war would not be fought in the Atlantic.' This was not the first time the government had taken a neutral position as to Northern Ireland's future, but never had a minister been so explicit in its expression. If you want a united Ireland, Brooke was saying to republicans, we will not stop you, but you will have to win over unionists.

It had long been the public pose of democratic governments that they did not negotiate with 'terrorists'. In reality, political leaders had frequently decided that engagement with insurgents was the least worst option. British governments had held talks with the Mau

Mau forces waging a guerrilla campaign for independence in Kenya and with EOKA, the armed Greek Cypriot nationalist group seeking to end colonial rule in Cyprus. The most important thing for the politicians was that these contacts remained secret. So it was in Northern Ireland. By the early 1970s Frank Steele, an officer in the Secret Intelligence Service, had established the line of communication that led to the (secret) talks in London between senior PIRA figures and the then Northern Ireland secretary William Whitelaw. The task of maintaining the channel subsequently fell to another SIS officer, Michael Oatley. Officially, Britain had broken off all contact with the PIRA after the breakdown of the 1975 ceasefire. Officially. For nearly two decades Oatley kept open a line of communication to the new generation of republicans led by Gerry Adams and Martin McGuinness. He found an intermediary and partner in the Derry-based businessman Brendan Duddy, known to be firm in his republicanism but committed to a peaceful resolution of the conflict. The secret messaging ebbed and flowed with the levels of violence in the province. By the late 1980s Father Alec Reid, a Redemptorist priest based at the Clonard Monastery in Belfast, had emerged as another trusted contact point for both sides. Intermediaries made way for more direct – albeit deniable – discussions between intelligence officers and the republican leadership. It was a message from McGuinness channelled through Duddy and signalling the PIRA's willingness to open a dialogue that helped persuade Major's government that there was a credible opening for peace. Duddy, known even among those in Whitehall with the highest security clearances as 'the Contact', would later be described by Jonathan Powell, Tony Blair's chief of staff, as laying 'a claim to have been among the most persistent and effective of the unsung heroes of the peace process'.[2]

Brooke followed the speech with the launch of a new round of talks with the political parties in the province. Republicans were offered a seat at the table if they halted their military campaign. The Northern Ireland secretary also indicated that the government was ready to be 'imaginative' in response to a ceasefire. Brooke had understood that conflict resolution often meant talking to the 'enemy'.

John Hume, the energetic and sometimes combustible leader of the SDLP, was determined to move faster. From the start of the Troubles, Hume had been in the vanguard of nationalists campaigning for political reconciliation with unionism. He combined an unabashed belief in Irish unity with an abhorrence of violence and corresponding contempt for the PIRA. 'They are more Irish than the rest of us, they believe,' he once said of the PIRA leadership. They showed 'all the hallmarks of undiluted fascism'.[3] In Washington, where his tireless campaigning gave him considerable influence, he joined FitzGerald in seeking to steer Irish Americans away from the PIRA towards support for constitutional nationalism. Where he parted company with the Dublin and London governments was in his conviction that Sinn Féin and the PIRA had to be brought into the political process without preconditions. The search for a political settlement had hitherto rested on an assumption that the route to peace lay in an agreement among constitutional parties that over time would drive republican and loyalist paramilitaries to the margins. Hume changed the calculus, shifting the focus to pulling the PIRA into the process. So as Brooke gave the British intelligence services permission to open contacts with republicans, Hume began a series of direct meetings with Adams. The talks coincided with the fall of FitzGerald's government in 1987. Returning again to power, Haughey authorised direct contacts between his ruling Fianna Fáil party and the PIRA leadership.

As with the Anglo-Irish Agreement, the path to the Downing Street Declaration was replete with stumbles and disagreements.

For all that it had also opened a channel of communication with the gunmen, the Irish side complained bitterly when it discovered the British were operating their own secret contacts. Sometimes the cloak-and-dagger subterfuge misfired. In early 1993 Major was handed a message said to have been written by Martin McGuinness: 'The conflict is over but we need your help on how to bring it to a close,' it declared. 'We wish to have an unannounced ceasefire in order to hold a dialogue leading to peace. We cannot announce such a move as it will lead to confusion for the Volunteers because the press will interpret it as a surrender.' Major took the communication seriously, authorising a clandestine response that said that the government would be 'bold and imaginative' if the guns fell silent. The contacts intensified over several months until the process was blown up when they were disclosed by the media. Embarrassed by the charge that it was 'talking to terrorists' and facing pressure from Tory MPs, Major's government was forced to publish a detailed account of the communications. McGuinness for his part flatly denied sending the message. Much later, it seemed as if his intentions had been embellished by Denis Bradley, a former priest acting as an intermediary.[4] Amid the furore at Westminster, Patrick Mayhew, who had replaced Brooke as Northern Ireland secretary in a cabinet reshuffle, offered his resignation. He survived. But Major was shaken. All the while, the bombings and the shootings continued. Four women and two children were among the nine killed at a fish-and-chip shop in Belfast's Protestant Shankill Road when a bomb carried by a republican paramilitary detonated prematurely. Days later, Gerry Adams was pictured among those carrying the coffin of Thomas Begley, the bomber.

Major and Reynolds had their own shouting matches. In April 1993 Hume and Adams published a blueprint. It was far too 'green', or nationalist, for British tastes. Major worried that the political process was being hijacked by nationalism. During succeeding months the two governments struggled to agree on their own joint statement. Temperatures rose. At summit talks in Dublin Castle in early December 1993, Major and Reynolds let off steam. The former raged at the Irish government's unattributable briefings on the progress of talks. The latter countered that the British had broken trust by keeping secret their contacts with the PIRA. Roderic Lyne, Major's private secretary, described the exchanges: 'The chemistry between Major and Reynolds was very important and never more important than in the Dublin Castle meeting … that bloodletting sort of opened up the way to the final negotiations.' Reynolds offered a colourful description of the encounter: 'I raged and he raged. I chewed his bollocks off and he took lumps out of me.'[5]

It was a measure of their mutual trust that they pressed ahead. It was proof also of Major's political courage. More than once his officials warned him that he was wasting his time, that Northern Ireland was a source only of 'bad news'. Beyond perhaps the uncertain judgement of history, there was no political advantage for the prime minister in taking up the quest for a settlement. To the contrary, the process invited political pain. The 1992 general election had reduced to twenty-one the Conservative majority in the House of Commons. A rising revolt by Eurosceptic Tories against the further European integration that had been agreed by Major when he signed the Maastricht Treaty left the prime minister ever vulnerable to parliamentary defeat. At times the future of his government turned on a few votes. Margaret Thatcher, at once increasingly Eurosceptic and disenchanted with her own Anglo-Irish deal, stirred rebellion against her successor. The safe course for Major would have been to stall negotiations and hide behind the well-worn official position about the need to defeat terrorism.

Instead, the Downing Street Declaration unveiled on 15 December 1993, less than two weeks after the Dublin outbursts, saw the two governments take another important step towards the deal that would stand at the heart of an eventual end to the violence. 'We were on our way to peace in Northern Ireland,' Reynolds wrote in his memoir.[6] In the cabinet room, the two leaders looked out on the garden where fewer than three years earlier mortar shells had landed. For Kremlinologists who had followed the tortuous journey the two governments had taken since the abortive Sunningdale Agreement, the successful Anglo-Irish Agreement and the more recent clandestine talks with the PIRA, the text seemed to offer nothing startlingly new. But it captured an opportunity and it embedded, with hitherto unprecedented clarity, the principles on which the governments were now inviting the paramilitaries to embrace politics. On Major's part, the declaration said:

> The Prime Minister, on behalf of the British Government, reaffirms that they will uphold the democratic wish of a greater number of the people of Northern Ireland on the issue of whether they prefer to support the Union or a sovereign united Ireland. On this basis, he reiterates, on behalf of the British Government, that they have no selfish strategic or economic interest in Northern Ireland.

And from Reynolds:

> It would be wrong to attempt to impose a united Ireland, in the absence of the freely given consent of a majority of the people of Northern Ireland. He accepts, on behalf of the Irish Government, that the democratic right of self-determination by the people of Ireland as a whole must be achieved and exercised with and

subject to the agreement and consent of a majority of the people of Northern Ireland.

In summary:

It is for the people of the island of Ireland alone, by agreement with the two parts respectively, to exercise their right of self-determination on the basis of consent, freely and concurrently given, North and South, to bring about a United Ireland, if that is their wish.

The political shift is well described by Seán Ó hUiginn, an Irish diplomat viewed by the British as both infuriatingly nationalist and intellectually brilliant: 'The policy of uniting the moderates across the divide was sensible in every respect, with one exception. It had not worked in any of the forms that had been tried.'[7] The problem was that the moderates on both sides feared extremists on their own side more than they trusted moderates on the other side of the table: 'Invited to swing their political trapeze across the tribal divide, they had no confidence that they would be grasped by supporting arms in mid-air. Since peace had not been found through politics, it was time to try whether politics could be found through peace.'[8] The two governments had found their point of compromise; now it was time to see whether it was enough to pull in the paramilitaries.

The route out of the maze was a pathway between republican insistence that Ireland's right to self-determination applied to the whole of the island of Ireland (the last time the island had voted as one it had backed Sinn Féin in the 1918 general election) and unionist insistence on the north's right to opt out. In making a decision on the province's constitutional status, the new formula proposed, both parts of Ireland would vote concurrently (as in 1918), but the ballots would be counted separately, south and north. Republicans would get an all-Ireland act of self-determination; unionists would hold on to the safeguard of separate northern consent. The aim previously had been to marginalise the extremists. Now, in Reynolds's description, it was to bring them in.

The republican ceasefire that followed on 31 August 1994 – 'There will be a complete cessation of military operations,' the PIRA declared – followed a blizzard of contacts between republicans, the Irish, the British and, increasingly, the Americans. Many were clandestine – Reynolds remarked that his senior adviser Martin Mansergh was in 'constant contact' with Adams and McGuinness – others public. Progress was not even. In October 1994 President Bill Clinton lifted the long-standing visa ban barring Sinn Féin leaders from visiting the United States. Reynolds approached Clinton directly on this point. So too did the Irish American lobby on Capitol Hill. The British government sent Douglas Hurd, the foreign secretary, and Patrick Mayhew, the Northern Ireland secretary, to Washington to argue against it. The State Department was on the British side, maintaining its traditional concern not to disturb an otherwise good relationship with London. In a message to Clinton soon after he took office, the department had pointed up the range of areas where Britain was supportive of American policy, before adding:

> Few issues have more potential for creating problems in Anglo-American relations than Northern Ireland. The British regard it as an internal matter. They believe that the US tends to view it from the nationalist perspective. The extension of terrorist campaigns to England, innocent loss of life, and the targeting of Britain's political leadership have made HMG sensitive to advice from outside.[9]

Statements that Clinton had made on the campaign trail 'aroused hopes in the Catholic community and fears among the unionists that the USG would weigh in on the nationalist side'. The department cautioned against issuing a visa to Adams, pointing out that Sinn Féin had refused to abandon its support for PIRA violence.

The president rejected the advice as he did similar objections raised by the Justice Department and by the American ambassador in London, Raymond Seitz. Major wanted tangible evidence that the republicans were serious about peace. For London, Clinton's gesture, seen as an attempt to gather domestic political support for the White House among Irish Americans, had let the paramilitaries off the hook. Contacts between Downing Street and the White House were frozen. Clinton's aides countered that by taking the initiative, the president had gained leverage over Sinn Féin. Visas granted, they pointed out, could always be revoked. Clinton said later that the aim had been to test the PIRA: 'If Adams was in fact serious about peace, then it was worth supporting him. If he was not, granting him a visa and then having him fail to deliver a cease-fire would backfire and hurt his standing in America.'[10]

Clinton's interest in Northern Ireland pre-dated his presidency. As a student during the late 1960s he had been a Rhodes Scholar at Oxford and had watched the emergence of the civil rights movement in Northern Ireland. For a child of America's deep south, there was an obvious parallel with the campaigns for equality of African Americans in states of the old Confederacy. He had been particularly struck by the civil rights campaigns of Bernadette Devlin, one of the young nationalists who caught the imagination of onlookers well beyond Northern Ireland. Bidding for the Democratic nomination for the presidency more than twenty years later, Clinton promised a review of American policy. He told a meeting with the party's Irish American supporters in New York:

I think sometimes we are too reluctant to engage ourselves [in Northern Ireland] in a positive way because of our longstanding special relationship with Great Britain . . . But I have a very strong feeling that in the aftermath of the Cold War, we need a governing rationale for our engagement in the world, not just in Northern Ireland.[11]

This was the view he took into the White House. It was strongly shared by his key adviser on Irish affairs, Nancy Soderberg. Among British officials, Soderberg was viewed as a bête noire, blamed for leading astray an 'untutored' president from Arkansas. Like Clinton (and later Blair), however, she saw intuitively a moment of opportunity. Doubtless looking for the group's support in the nomination process, Clinton promised his audience in New York that if he were elected president, he would appoint a special envoy for Northern Ireland and would 'support a visa for Gerry Adams'. For their part John Major's Conservatives had made it easier for Clinton to break with traditional State Department policy. In the approach to Clinton's contest with George H. W. Bush in 1992, Major's party offered support for the Republican incumbent and access to Home Office files on Clinton relating to his stay in Oxford. Nothing came of a search of the files, but once it became known, Major could scarcely expect any favours from the Clinton White House. The subsequent PIRA ceasefire seemed to vindicate Clinton's visa decision. In response he announced an initiative to promote American trade and investment in Northern Ireland. The Democratic Party Senator George Mitchell, who would later assume a leading role in the political negotiations in Northern Ireland, was appointed as a presidential envoy charged with special responsibility for economic relations with Ireland.

Unionists took an altogether contrary view of the ceasefire. Peace put them under pressure to do what they had always resisted – to engage politically with nationalism. For the hard-liners, sitting down with republicans was synonymous with surrender. The DUP leader Ian Paisley thundered that the ceasefire represented 'the worst crisis in Ulster's history since the setting up of the state'. Unionists, he exploded, were being asked 'to become slaves in a country fit only for nuns' men and monks' women to live in. We cannot bow the knee to these traitors who tread the smoke-filled rooms of Whitehall.'[12] Molyneaux, the UUP leader, deployed slightly less incendiary language to make the same point. The ceasefire, he said, 'destabilised' the whole population in Northern Ireland. It was not an occasion for celebration – quite the opposite. Here, though the unionists were not yet prepared publicly to admit it, was the uncomfortable legacy of the Anglo-Irish Agreement. The Protestant state was gone. It was striking that the political leaders of the loyalist groups voiced a more pragmatic view than traditional unionist leaders. Led by fearsome characters such as Gusty Spence, David Ervine and Billy Hutchinson, these were the working-class Protestants who had been in the bloody vanguard of the bombings and shootings in the conflict with the PIRA. Their communities had carried the fight to republicanism, they would sometimes say, while middle-class leaders of the unionist old guard had slept safely and soundly in communities far distant from the inner-city battlegrounds. The loyalists were exhausted. Two months after the republicans stopped shooting, the loyalists did the same.

The British intelligence services have a reputation for being among the best in the world. They are not infallible. During the closing weeks of 1995 Stella Rimington, the head of MI5, invited a small group of journalists to spend an evening at the domestic security service's Thameside headquarters. For the guests (myself included) this was a rare invitation. None I spoke to had previously crossed the threshold of Britain's domestic security agency. The intelligence services were only slowly coming in from the cold after the collapse of the Soviet Union. Those accepting Rimington's invitation were told in advance that everything said was strictly 'off the record'. It was a strange event. Drinks and canapés were interspersed with briefings about MI5's operations against organised crime, domestic and international terrorism. I recall a cheerful MI5 officer introducing himself as the head of 'bugging and burglary' at the agency. A career that had started out with a routine job at the Home Office had seen this officer crawling through the lofts of terraced houses in republican districts of Belfast to plant listening devices, before his return to run the section in London. I was struck particularly by a presentation describing the surveillance operations mounted against individuals suspected of terrorism. Each operation pulled in immense human and technical resources. A couple of officers sitting in a car outside the target's house does not do the trick.

It took a while to grasp the purpose of this curious openness from spooks who had once so closely guarded their secrets. MI5 was engaged in a subtle public relations operation. It had concluded that the PIRA war was all but over. As welcome as that was for the nation, it left the agency exposed. How long before the Treasury began looking for cuts in the MI5 budget to match the diminished threat? Rimington's not-so-subliminal message was that this would be a huge mistake. Britain faced a clutch of new dangers. The service's unique expertise could now be usefully deployed in combating all the other threats to national security that reached beyond the competence of regular police operations. These included a rising tide of international drugs networks, money laundering and violent criminal gangs. It was all deftly done. The embarrassing flaw was revealed in February 1996, when the PIRA returned to its military campaign with the spectacular bombing of London's Canary Wharf financial district.

The fall in 1994 of Reynolds's Fianna Fáil administration saw it replaced by a new coalition led by John Bruton. The Fine Gael leader was no friend of republicanism. His politics were more closely rooted in the constitutional nationalism of the former Irish Parliamentary Party than in the revolutionary impulses of the PIRA. The habit of Fine Gael leaders had been to put a portrait of Michael Collins over their desks. Bruton preferred one of John Redmond, the Irish Parliamentary Party leader who had secured Home Rule in 1914. Like Reynolds, however, he backed the strategy of pulling the PIRA into the political process. In February 1995 Major and Bruton unveiled a new Framework Agreement, fleshing out the possible parameters of a political settlement. The three pillars of this accord – power-sharing in Northern Ireland to underpin mutual respect between unionism and nationalism, new arrangements for enhanced cooperation between the province and the Republic (north–south collaboration) and a fresh constitutional settlement between London and Dublin guaranteeing at once self-determination and the consent safeguard – formed the basis for the later Good Friday Agreement.

The challenge lay in starting a political process that brought the republican and loyalist paramilitaries to the negotiating table in a manner that was acceptable to Northern Ireland's mainstream politicians and did not appear to reward violence. Unsurprisingly, the Major government (and more so unionists) wanted assurance that Sinn Féin would not be negotiating with PIRA guns held under the table. It was being asked to take on faith two radical assumptions: the first that Adams and McGuinness were genuinely committed to a peaceful outcome; the second that, if they were, they had sufficient authority within the senior ranks of the PIRA to bring the movement with them. Republican history was littered with splits between those willing to compromise with the British and those wanting to continue the fight. The government's answer, set out in a speech in Washington by Sir Patrick Mayhew, was to insist that the PIRA commit to the decommissioning of its weapons and, as a token of intent, destroy some of them immediately, before joining other parties at the negotiating table. The disarmament process would be handed over to an international and independent body. In November George Mitchell, Clinton's economic envoy, was chosen to oversee it.

This approach was at once entirely explicable and a strategic error. Taken at face value it seemed reasonable that those who for decades had waged war in Northern Ireland should offer some proof of their change of heart. It also reflected the intense political pressures on Major. A sizeable number of Tory MPs grumbled that the prime minister had already gone too far in seeking to draw in the republicans. His majority at Westminster had all but disappeared under the weight of rebellions against his European policy. Yet framed in the broader context, as Bruton and Bill Clinton argued in their discussions with Major, setting disarmament as the precondition risked derailing the process. By hallowed tradition, the PIRA had never surrendered its weapons. De Valera's forces had 'dumped' rather than given up their arms at the end of the Civil War in 1923. To destroy arms at the command of the British would be tantamount to surrender. To the extent that Adams and McGuinness were willing to contemplate peace, this was something that would happen at the very end of negotiations. Even then, there were figures on the Army Council who would always be deeply unhappy at the idea of blowing up the arms dumps. The Brits could not be trusted, the argument ran. Disarmament would be followed by betrayal. The stumbling block became one of sequencing. Who would jump first? The republicans gave their answer with the Canary Wharf bombing. The next move would await the British general election due in 1997. But the sequencing question – who jumps first – would not go away.

9 THE END OF HISTORY

New Labour, New Britain. Tony Blair swept to power in May 1997 with brash immodesty. New Labour's young prime minister would change everything. A month later, Bertie Ahern was elected Taoiseach. Ahern's was a quieter pledge: to put people before politics. Both leaders, though, spoke for a rising generation – Blair was forty-three, Ahern two years older – who were impatient of the weight of the past. Ahern's Fianna Fáil may have lacked New Labour's chutzpah, but it had a head start. Blair was promising modernity. Ireland had already embraced it.

Autarky had made way for openness. De Valera's isolated backwater was fast becoming an economic powerhouse. Europe's Celtic Tiger, it was called. The clue lay in the job advertisements appearing in Britain's big cities. Ireland, a nation defined since the Great Famine by high unemployment, mass emigration and a shrinking population, now needed foreign workers. The Irish economy was booming. During the decade from 1990 the Republic's national income grew by nearly 8 per cent a year. For the first time since the state's creation, there were more jobs than workers. At home, growing numbers of women were joining the labour market. Emigrants were returning. Workers were also travelling south from the north, with the number of residents born in Northern Ireland rising from thirty-six thousand to fifty thousand. Businesses looked to Britain and beyond to fill the remaining gap. Almost absurdly – at least, that is how it seemed at the time – Ireland was recruiting British bricklayers. The 1991 census recorded 126,000 British-born residents in the Republic. By 2002 that number had jumped to 183,000. There were increases in the, albeit small, communities of French, Spanish and Germans. Ireland's population increased from 3.5 million to 3.9 million. The new arrivals would soon be joined by workers from the post-communist nations of Central and Eastern Europe and, further afield, India, Brazil and China.

The seeds of this transformation had been planted more than thirty years earlier by Seán Lemass, de Valera's successor as Taoiseach and a pathfinder for modernity, open both to market economics and to building a better relationship with the north. During the 1960s restrictions on foreign investment were lifted, and free education was extended to over-fourteen-year-olds. These domestic reforms were followed, critically, by the competitive jolt to the economy from Ireland's accession to the European Community in 1973. It now had no choice but to join the international economy. The transition would take time. Ireland during the 1970s and 1980s remained prone to bouts of inflation and recession. But the essential framework was in place. A closed society had become an open economy. Generous funding from Brussels to modernise the nation's infrastructure (roads in the rural south were soon much better than those in the industrialised north), low taxes on corporate profits, higher education standards and good industrial relations made a compelling pitch to international (above all American) companies, casting around for a base from which to sell into the rest of Europe. Intel, Dell, Microsoft, Cisco and Apple were among the roll-call of technology companies setting up or expanding operations. Pfizer, SmithKline and Johnson & Johnson formed a phalanx of global pharmaceutical companies joining them in what Charles Haughey called America's economic bridgehead. Unemployment, as high as 17 per cent at its peak during the mid-1980s, fell to 4 per cent at the turn of the century. Participation in Europe had triggered a step back from economic dependence on

THE END OF HISTORY

Britain. The Irish currency, the punt, was tied after partition to parity with sterling. The nation's monetary policy was set, in effect, by the Bank of England, and British banknotes and coins circulated freely in the Republic. The link was broken in 1979 when the Republic joined the European Monetary System's exchange rate mechanism. Britain stood aside from the currency system, leaving the value of the pound and the punt to diverge. The symbolism mattered. Twenty years later, the Republic would swap the punt for the European Union's single currency, the euro, while Britain stuck with the pound. British Eurosceptics saw the euro as an encroachment on national sovereignty. For Ireland, joining the euro was proof of its economic independence.

Economic and social change marched in step. The progressive policies that swept through Europe during the 1960s and 1970s reached Ireland's shores. The Republic remained a Catholic country, but the triumphal visit to the Republic of Pope John Paul II in 1979 turned out to mark the summit of the Church's influence over Irish politics and society. A younger, better-educated and less deferential generation shed the old habit of obedience. Women, all but consigned to the home by the 1937 constitution, demanded greater equality. The psychological spell woven by de Valera in the decades after partition was broken. The Church found itself under scrutiny as the nation began to look hard at the dark, unspoken side of the untrammelled power exercised by the Catholic hierarchy. John Charles McQuaid had set the Church as the guardian of the nation's morality. Now it emerged that the bishops had been condoning and covering up the sins of priests and nuns – and some of them were hiding their own mistresses. The Church's authority unravelled as successive investigations uncovered damning evidence of the widespread sexual abuse of children and the brutal treatment of young, unmarried mothers in so-called 'mother-and-baby homes' run by religious orders. The hallmark of these supposed refuges, it turned out, had been cruelty rather than compassion. The numbers of young people following religious vocations fell precipitately. During the 1950s and 1960s Catholic families would see a great honour in a son or daughter choosing service in the Church. In 1966 the seminaries had accepted more than 1,400 young men to train for the priesthood. Thirty years later, the number had fallen to 111.[1] The repeal of laws barring contraception, divorce and homosexuality spoke to the weakening of the Church's grip on the nation's morals. Many still attended Sunday Mass. But Irish society had stepped out of the Catholic straitjacket. Before long, Ireland would be in the vanguard of nations giving official blessing to same-sex marriage.

Economic opportunity and new European relationships and interests took Ireland out of the centuries-long shadow of British rule. The Republic had defined itself by its anti-Englishness. Irishness had been Gaelic, Catholic, inward-looking and consumed by grievance. The Ireland emerging through the 1990s had a different sense of self – modern, secular, economically successful, internationalist. Geography and history meant that Britain would always loom large in Ireland's affairs. So too would the Irish diaspora in the United States. But the Republic was reviving the continental connections which under British rule had seen the Catholic middle class forced to cross the seas to study at colleges in France, Spain, Belgium and beyond. With the European Union came myriad new friendships, different demands on diplomacy and, as immigration replaced emigration, the emergence of an ethnically diverse society. The change reached deep even into de Valera's rural Ireland. Kiltimagh, I noticed on one of my visits, now had a Chinese restaurant.

Northern Ireland's fortunes were moving in another direction. The global shift to Asia of traditional manufacturing industries had been turbo-charged by the Thatcherite economic policies of the 1980s. The industries that had sustained Belfast's prosperity – heavy engineering, shipbuilding – were among the worst affected. Attempts to build new industries, notably a new car production plant owned by the American auto manufacturer DeLorean, foundered in expensive failure. The sectarian division and violence of the Troubles weighed heavily against international investment. For the American technology and pharmaceutical companies looking for platforms for their European businesses, setting up in bomb-scarred Belfast or besieged Derry seemed a less than enticing prospect. While the Republic loosened the bonds of Catholicism, the conflict sharpened the confessional clash in the six counties. Northern Ireland held tightly to its cultural conservatism. The centrist Alliance Party led by John Alderdice sought to take religion out of politics, appealing to middle-class voters and young professionals across the divide, but its supporters represented only a small segment of the electorate. Protestants still went to Protestant and Catholics to Catholic schools. So-called peace walls, covered in the graffiti of republican and loyalist paramilitary groups, separated the two communities in the big cities. Politics was a zero-sum game. Now in the shadow of an economically vibrant republic, Northern Ireland was ignored in a Britain ever more mystified by its apparent obsession with battles fought three centuries earlier.

Blair understood that modernisation in the south and stasis in the north changed the political context. In his later reflection:

> It was no longer the backward old South that was looked down upon, but the North. The South was sprinting down the track towards the future, while the people of Northern Ireland were hanging around the starting blocks arguing about Protestants and Catholics . . . For the Republic this was no longer a dispute to be

clung to as a unifying symbol of Irish identity, but a painful and unwelcome reminder of Ireland's past. For decades, also, unionists could point to Irish economic backwardness and their cultural and religious differences as making a fit between the two impossible. Now these elements were either fading or being reversed.[2]

Blair and Ahern were leading their nations during an era of global tumult. The formerly communist states of Eastern and Central Europe were queuing to join the European Union and NATO. Nelson Mandela led a new post-apartheid South Africa. Israel and the Palestinians had signed the Oslo Accords. A visit to Northern Ireland did nothing but bring to mind Winston Churchill's reflection on 'the dreary steeples of Fermanagh and Tyrone'.

Blair had personal insight into the bigotry. His mother had emigrated to Britain from Donegal in the Republic. During his childhood the family joined the annual summer pilgrimage 'home'. They returned to the small community of Protestants who had remained in the south after partition. The familial devotion was to unionism. His grandfather, Blair recalled, had been a grand master of an Orange Lodge. His grandmother, though a kind woman, warned him that whatever other choices he made, he must 'never marry a Catholic'. It was advice he had discarded when he exchanged vows with the Catholic Cherie Booth. As he embarked on the push for peace, Blair said of the conflict: 'I thought the whole thing had become . . . ridiculously old-fashioned . . . and out of touch with the times in which the island of Ireland lived.'[3]

There was another reason to find a settlement. Blair's ambitions reached beyond Ireland. Untroubled by self-doubt, he wanted to dance on the international stage, to restore Britain's prestige and influence in overseas capitals. Major had been besieged by his party's Eurosceptics. After nearly a decade of fights about Europe, the Conservatives had left Britain on the margins of the continent. Blair counted himself a European. He had plans for a military partnership with France, to take Britain back into the mainstream of the European Union and, perhaps, to join the soon-to-be-minted euro. Looking across the Atlantic, he wanted to capitalise on a warm relationship with Bill Clinton to revive the so-called special relationship with the United States. Blair was the first prime minister since Britain had signed the Treaty of Rome to see the value of leveraging the nation's twin relationships with Brussels and Washington. There was no need to choose. To be stronger in one was to be more influential in the other.

The conflict in Northern Ireland, a scar on the country's international reputation, stood in the way of such vaulting ambition. A swingeing majority of 179 in the House of Commons and a Tory Party broken by arguments about Europe gave him the political space to take risks. How could the United Kingdom, as Blair proposed, serve as a global beacon of democracy and progress, while it was obliged to put troops on the streets of its own cities? For their part, the message of his majority to unionists and republicans alike was that there was little purpose holding on in the hope of a better deal from another government. Blair would likely be there for ten years. Many in the United States and beyond saw the conflict through the prism of British colonialism. Jonathan Powell, Blair's chief of staff, was struck by the prime minister's unshakeable faith in himself:

> Tony has often been criticised for his messianic belief in other contexts. But for Northern Ireland that belief was essential . . . If republicans had ever become convinced we had lost interest in Ireland, as so many British prime ministers had before, the chance of success would have been lost. It was our interest and

involvement they wanted above all else. Paying attention was nine-tenths of the battle.[4]

One of Blair's important decisions in the aftermath of the 1997 election was to choose Belfast for his first official trip outside London. In a place where symbolism matters, it sent a powerful signal.

Alongside Blair's self-belief sat Ahern's willingness to recast Ireland's historic claim to the north. The son of an anti-treaty Volunteer in the civil war, Ahern was a staunch nationalist. Charles Haughey had been his mentor during his rise within Fianna Fáil. He also had a reputation as a fixer and dealmaker. In Haughey's description, Ahern combined political skill with considerable cunning. Like his British counterpart, though, he had decided it was time to move on. And as a dealmaker he understood the art of compromise. In Blair's description: 'He was heroic throughout the whole process, smart, cunning in the best sense, strong and, above all, free of the shackles of history.' Ahern's family had fought the British, 'but he had that elemental quality that defines great politicians: he was a student of history not its prisoner'.[5] He would never abjure the goal of a united Ireland, but he was ready to compromise on the route.

Among the other actors, none was as persistent as John Hume. Driven, sometimes overly emotional, he had made reconciliation with unionism his life's work. On the unionist side stood the decidedly unemotional David Trimble, the leader of the UUP. It was evident that Ian Paisley's DUP would boycott any political process that included Sinn Féin. Trimble might have done likewise. After all, the UUP leader had flirted during the 1970s with Vanguard, a hardline unionist party with close ties to loyalist paramilitaries. He was elected to parliament in 1990 as a UUP candidate and his route to the leadership had seen him champion the Orange Order's angry confrontations with police over the routing of its annual, triumphalist march from the church of Drumcree through a Catholic area of the town of Portadown. Abrupt, often angry, Trimble hailed from the 'no surrender' unionism sworn against compromise with nationalists. He was also, however, among those who grasped the significance of the Anglo-Irish Agreement. Doing nothing, he would remark, was not an option because 'the status quo post the Anglo-Irish Agreement was the status quo where unionism was weak and marginalised, where the system was being run for the benefit of nationalism and the long-term effect of that was going to be disastrous from the point of view of the union with Britain'.[6] It was about peace, yes, but also realpolitik.

Demographics pointed unionism in the same direction. When the boundary was drawn in 1920, two-thirds of the population in Northern Ireland were Protestants. In every subsequent decade this 'natural' unionist majority was further eroded by the higher birth rate among Catholics. The crossover point was coming into view. By the late 1990s a little under 40 per cent of those who identified as Christians were Catholics, while for Protestants and Presbyterians the figure was about 45 per cent. The underlying trend said that within a couple of decades a majority would count themselves Catholic. The shift was already visible in local elections. In 1997 unionist parties lost control of Belfast City Council. The implication was evident. Maintaining a majority for the union with the United Kingdom would soon enough require the recruitment of Catholics to the cause. Trimble, and some time later Ian Paisley, understood this when they made a grudging peace with nationalism.

Marjorie (Mo) Mowlam, Blair's choice as Northern Ireland secretary, brought an ebullient, unconventional energy to the cast of peacemakers. Plain-spoken, careless of diplomatic niceties – at one point she turned up at the Maze prison to speak directly to leaders of loyalist paramilitary groups – Mowlam appealed over the heads of mainstream politicians to the working-class communities that had borne the brunt of sectarian violence. She was an inspiration for the increasingly vocal and influential women's movements on both sides of the sectarian divide pressing for an end to violence. Unionists were ever suspicious as to where her sympathies lay, but Mowlam's breezy honesty won her the trust of republican leaders and the respect of loyalist paramilitary leaders such as David Ervine, Gary McMichael and Gusty Spence. The urbane George Mitchell, enlisted by John Major to wrestle with the problem of decommissioning PIRA weapons and now persuaded by Blair to act as an independent chair of peace negotiations, brought calm and sobriety to the process. Close to Clinton, Mitchell showed infinite patience as he navigated the dense undergrowth of grievances, suspicions and hatreds. 'People here are nice and friendly,' he would remark. 'They're just not friendly to each other. Centuries of conflict have generated hatreds that make it virtually impossible for the two communities to trust each other.' What Mitchell shared with Mowlam was a transparency that helped rebuild trust. He would say of Mowlam that she was 'blunt and outspoken and she swears a lot'. She was also intelligent, daring and unpretentious. 'People love her, though many politicians in Northern Ireland do not.'[7]

US President Bill Clinton slipped through the door that had been opened twenty years earlier by Jimmy Carter. Offstage but always close to a telephone, he deployed the White House's formidable authority as a mediator. Clinton claimed distant Irish ancestry, though the diligent Dublin diplomats who were expert in drawing the family trees of American presidents did not find it. No matter. He would make three trips to Belfast during his time in the White House. Whatever his motives – and an eye on the Irish American vote would certainly have been among them – the

THE END OF HISTORY

president's engagement would prove invaluable. As the Irish diplomat Michael Lillis put it: 'Without the American dimension, I don't think there would have been a successful peace process.' The president was sometimes accused privately even by his own diplomats of playing to the Irish American gallery. He stayed the course, deploying the leverage this gave him over republicanism and building bridges with unionism. Unionists, he understood, also enjoyed appearing under the television lights in Washington. Here was something to trade. Trimble and his colleagues received invitations to meet the president. Politicians who through their careers had been hardly known, or noticed, outside Northern Ireland became addicted to the glittering photocalls at the White House.

Behind the scenes, Jonathan Powell pursued a strategy of 'never letting the talking stop'. An ever-present go-between in the talks, when he was not drawing up position papers in Downing Street, Powell was meeting secretly with senior PIRA figures in obscure 'safe houses' in the province. A dogged optimist, Powell gave form and structure to the prime minister's unshakeable confidence in his own persuasive talents. As Blair's private secretary, John Holmes, quiet, unassuming and deeply experienced, added knowledge and expertise to the mix. Holmes had been at the centre of John Major's outreach to republicanism. He stayed on to work for Blair in the same role. Holmes was one of those diplomats with stamina – though during the last lap of the peace talks, Powell found the exhausted official fully dressed, asleep on a table in the delegation's office at Castle Buildings. Irish officials described him as tough but also 'one of those people you could never shout at'.

Holmes had made a personal, albeit inadvertent, contribution to the peace process when in the weeks after Blair's 1997 election an Irish group organising a commemoration of the 150th anniversary of the Great Famine wrote to the new prime minister. They were staging an event in County Cork and wondered if Blair had a message for the audience. The prime ministerial response, read out by an actor at the commemoration, came as a pleasant surprise to the organisers. 'The famine was a defining event in the history of Ireland and Britain. It has left deep scars,' Blair's statement began.

> That one million people should have died in what was then part of the richest and most powerful nation in the world is something that still causes pain as we reflect on it today. Those who governed in London at the time failed their people through standing by while a crop failure turned into a massive human tragedy.

In formal terms, this was not quite an official apology, but was widely interpreted in the Republic as such. No previous prime minister had recognised so clearly British complicity in the tragedy. The statement made front-page news in Ireland and drew a warm response from the Dublin government. Unbeknown to the wider world, Blair had neither written nor approved the words. Holmes had sent the text to the prime minister with a half-apologetic note explaining that because he had been unable to contact him in sufficient time for the commemoration, he had approved it 'off my own bat'. He added that he hoped the decision did not cause Blair 'any problems'. The prime minister was content. It was precisely what was needed to signal a new beginning in the relationship.

Blair's choice of Belfast for his first trip after the election was carefully calculated to reassure the other side. The aim was to convince unionism that the Labour Party had shed its traditional bias towards Irish nationalism. The Royal Ulster Agricultural Show at the city's Balmoral show grounds – as strong a bastion of Protestantism as could be found – was chosen as the venue. At the core of his speech was a solemn commitment that the British would never be bombed out of Northern Ireland. The province's destiny rested with the wishes of its people. Blair went further, beyond anything he could ever control. 'None of us in this hall today, even the youngest, is likely to see Northern Ireland as anything but a part of the United Kingdom.' Holmes, who had drafted the speech, saw Blair as a 'natural unionist'.[8] He wanted a 'bigger' rather than 'smaller' Britain. Few things during his early months in office discomfited him more than attending the handover to China of the former colony of Hong Kong.

Blair's pitch to republicanism was framed as a challenge. He was opening the door to political engagement. But only if they eschewed violence. A few months later, he would be back in Belfast, this time to shake hands with Gerry Adams and Martin McGuinness, the first prime minister since partition to meet the leaders of the republican movement. Unionists protesting outside the meeting accused Blair of betrayal, shouting the now familiar 'Traitor' when the prime minister emerged. But the PIRA had called a ceasefire and Sinn Féin had duly been invited to join all-party talks. Trimble, for all his anger, decided that the UUP had more to lose from boycotting negotiations than from sitting down with republicans. Later, Adams and McGuinness would meet Blair in London, the only republicans to cross the threshold of 10 Downing Street since Arthur Griffith and Michael Collins had signed the treaty. As so often in the long story of British decolonisation, talking to terrorists had merged into mainstream politics.

The pressing question for Blair was whether the Sinn Féin and PIRA leadership really had grown weary of its military campaign. Getting an answer required the government to maintain an uncomfortable pretext. The leaders of Sinn Féin and the paramilitaries of the PIRA were mostly indistinguishable. Not every Sinn Féin activist had carried an Armalite for the Volunteers, but the senior leadership of republicanism was indivisible. McGuinness's rise through the ranks of the Derry brigade was well documented by the British intelligence services. Adams, despite his denials, had long been identified, like McGuinness, as a member of the ruling PIRA Army Council. The PIRA, however, was legally proscribed, so to negotiate with Sinn Féin the British were obliged to go along with the flimsy fiction that it was not tied to the PIRA.

A second uncertainty was whether, even if Adams and McGuinness were genuine in their intent, the rest of the PIRA leadership could be persuaded to go along. On Ahern's side there was considerable confidence that republicanism was ready for peace. Blair was unsure. 'If you ask me if the republicans have definitely decided to give up violence the answer is probably no,' Blair privately admitted soon after entering Downing Street. 'But I do think that the more they are drawn into the political process the harder it gets for them to return to violence.' And if the effort failed? 'It is essential to show – to the United States, to the Irish government, and to the nationalists in Northern Ireland – that if the IRA remains wedded to violence, it is their decision: that they have rejected the opportunity for peace.'[9] British officials in the intelligence community were inclined to accept that Adams and McGuinness were genuine. They were far less sure that they would carry with them more militant republican commanders. The republican message was less than straightforward. Holmes would recall that sometimes the movement's leaders seemed to be saying: 'We want to give up violence but if you don't give us what we want we will return to violence.'[10] Other officials questioned whether 'hardliners' such as Martin Ferris and Gerry Kelly could be brought around. They had more confidence in McGuinness. Unlike Adams, McGuinness never disavowed his prominent role on the front line of the PIRA's military campaign. For some on the British side the fact that he had actually 'pulled the trigger' made him the more credible interlocutor. 'McGuinness was the one who convinced us they were serious,' one of the spooks involved in the early contacts remarked. 'You have the sense that you can take him at his word.'[11] For all his PIRA record, Holmes found him 'straightforward'. The Americans took the same view. Bill Clinton would later say of McGuinness that he saw someone who would choose as his epitaph 'I fought, I made peace, I made politics'.[12] Many years later, as the province marked the twenty-fifth anniversary of the peace accord, Ahern would recount that McGuinness would voice his own frustrations about the PIRA's hard men. 'Listen, I'm the one who has to go into the caves and talk to these guys,' he would say.[13]

The PIRA was well supplied with guns and explosives. Its arms stores had emerged as the roadblock to progress during Major's premiership. Many of its weapons had been supplied by the Libyan dictator Gaddafi. Others had been bought using funds provided by supporters in the United States. Major had set the decommissioning of some part of the arsenal as the price of entry. Republicans had refused to pay. As chair of the talks process Mitchell produced an ingenious detour: what became known as the Mitchell Principles, applicable to paramilitary groups on both sides. The first of these demanded a public commitment to exclusively peaceful means, the second that all weapons would eventually be destroyed and a third that there would be independent verification of this. The fourth required renunciation of the use of force and the fifth rejection of the threat of force as a negotiating tactic. The final condition was an end to punishment beatings and killings. The key was that the conditions envisaged the removal of guns and bombs from Northern Ireland as part of, rather than as a precursor to, settlement negotiations. Mitchell's aim was to keep the process moving forward by pushing the weapons issue into the future. The corollary, however, was intensified unionist mistrust. There were many in Trimble's party who agreed with Ian Paisley that they could not strike deals while the PIRA kept their guns.

The parameters of an eventual political settlement had been drawn by the Anglo-Irish Agreement, by the Downing Street Declaration and subsequently by the Framework Agreement drawn up by John Major and John Bruton in 1995. The latter reflected Dublin's demand that the Republic be given a role in the affairs of the north through the establishment of institutions to promote cross-border partnerships. Parity of esteem for nationalism required in turn that republicans agreed that Ireland could be reunited only with the consent of a majority in Northern Ireland. For their part, unionists had to accept genuine power-sharing in a Stormont executive, fundamental reform of the police and criminal justice system, and structured cross-border partnerships. The price for the Republic would be acceptance that Northern Ireland would remain part of the United Kingdom for as long as its people wished.

The problem, even if all sides were honest in their intent, remained one of sequencing. Why should unionists sit down in government with republicans who had not yet surrendered their weapons? Likewise, how could the PIRA's demand for the release of its prisoners be met until their arms had been put beyond use? And beyond that, how could Adams and McGuinness persuade republican militants to give up violence until they secured a guarantee of a place in government? What assurance did they have that once the weapons dumps were destroyed, unionists would not disavow a settlement? And behind all these specific problems, how to reconcile permanently republican insistence that the future of Ireland must be decided by the people of all thirty-two counties, with the promise to unionism of a separate vote for the six counties of Northern Ireland? Political leaders on both sides were negotiating not just with each other but with their own constituencies. Adams and

THE END OF HISTORY

McGuinness had to bring with them those in the PIRA set on continuing the armed struggle. Trimble had taken on board the essential truth of the Anglo-Irish Agreement, but there were many in his party and still more among Paisley's DUP unprepared to admit the end of Protestant supremacy. The prize offered to unionism by Ahern was the long-demanded removal of the constitutional claim to the six counties as an integral part of the Republic's national territory. Unsurprisingly, the months between the opening of talks in the autumn of 1997 and the Easter 1998 deadline set by Blair for their completion were punctuated by walkouts, roadblocks and swerves. Blair's answer to the collisions and contradictions included a series of ingenious, sometimes dubious ambiguities. Some choices were deliberately blurred, others deferred. From time to time, as with an eleventh-hour promise to Trimble linking Sinn Féin's participation in a future Northern Ireland executive to the decommissioning of PIRA weapons, the prime minister made promises he could not keep. But the basic principle was that all sides would 'jump together'. As Powell would say, the game was to keep the show on the road.

The bargain finally struck on Good Friday, 10 April 1998, followed four days and nights of intensive negotiations. Three months earlier, in another gesture of reconciliation with Irish nationalism, Blair had announced a new, entirely independent inquiry into the killing of Catholic civilians by British troops on Bloody Sunday in 1972. Unionists were to be reassured they would not be 'sold out', nationalists and republicans that the British government was open-minded about the future of the north. There was no guarantee of success. The talks took place at Castle Buildings, a nondescript 1960s office block whose shabby condition and poor facilities belied its name. Powell would describe it as a 'sick building' stinking of sweat and stale food. But there was a now-or-never quality to the gathering. On his arrival Blair told the media that this was too grave a moment to indulge in political soundbites. In the next sentence he declared that the 'hand of history' lay on the shoulders of the participants. He was gently mocked. What was true was that this was the first occasion since partition when all the actors in Ireland's tragic drama sat down with each other in the same room. Ahern, supported by a team of Irish officials long steeped in the intricacies of Anglo-Irish affairs, understood the significance of the moment. His mother had just died. No one could have complained had he delayed his arrival. Instead, he travelled back to the Republic for her funeral before rejoining the negotiations. Clinton, three thousand miles away, was never far from a telephone, nudging the republicans or reassuring the unionists at critical moments. The architecture of the Agreement was entirely familiar to old hands such as Ahern's adviser Martin Mansergh, but there had never been anything as comprehensive or as carefully calibrated. The package combined agreements on the three sets of critical relationships: between unionism and nationalism in Northern Ireland, between the province and the Republic, and between London and Dublin. The critical decision taken by Ahern was to agree to the removal from de Valera's 1937 constitution of the territorial claim to Northern Ireland.

Jack Lynch and Garret FitzGerald among previous Taoiseachs had considered revision of the clauses in the context of the Sunningdale and Anglo-Irish agreements but had ultimately concluded that the British had not gone far enough in terms of recognising the legitimacy of nationalist aspirations. Ahern's roots were in Fianna Fáil nationalism but he saw in the Good Friday Agreement the moment to give indisputable substance to the Republic's respect of the consent principle. In its revised form the constitution would simply give everyone living on the island of

Ireland the right to belong to the 'Irish nation'. In parallel, the deal would put in place at last the cross-border collaboration between north and south envisaged in the Council of Ireland proposed some eight decades earlier by David Lloyd George. Above all, though, republicans and loyalist paramilitaries agreed to put down the gun.

The following, difficult years would show that it was easier to set down such changes on paper than to implement them. It would be a decade before the new Stormont Assembly and executive were properly operational. For Blair and Ahern, unwinding the fudges and ambiguities that were needed to secure a settlement would be anything but easy. During one of many subsequent crises, Bill Clinton would liken unionists and republicans to a pair of drunks leaving a bar for the last time after promising to dry out: 'When they reach the swinging door they turn right round and go back in and say, "I just can't quite get there."' The president later apologised for the remark, but his frustration was widely shared. After some particularly bruising encounters, Blair told Labour MPs of his exasperation with unionists: 'There is nothing more irritating than sitting in a room with someone who claims to be British but who treats you as though you are nothing to do with Britain even though you are the prime minister.'[14]

The agreement was ratified in simultaneous referendums north and south of the border. The referendum in the Republic produced a vote of 94.4 per cent in favour of the accord. In Northern Ireland Paisley's DUP campaigned against the agreement as a surrender to the paramilitaries but overall it secured 71.1 per cent of the votes. Among unionists, the figure was estimated as somewhat below 55 per cent, with support among Catholics at more than 90 per cent. Then, in August 1998, it seemed for an instant that politics might yet count for naught. A bomb planted in the centre of the town of Omagh by the republican splinter group the

Real IRA killed twenty-nine people and injured more than two hundred. It was perhaps the worst atrocity of the Troubles, claiming the largest loss of life. The victims included Protestants and Catholics, women and children, teenagers and overseas tourists. The aim of the bombers had been to destabilise the peace before it took hold. As it turned out, the horror and revulsion in Ireland, Britain and internationally generated the opposite reaction. What more vivid expression than all these innocent deaths could there have been of the terrible futility of violence? There were plenty of subsequent frustrations as the two governments sought to translate a political agreement into a functioning administration in Belfast, but the accommodations made between nationalism and unionism on Good Friday had robbed violence of its rationale. Like communism in Eastern Europe and apartheid in South Africa, Irish terrorism was indeed out of date. The two parallel referendums marked the first time Ireland had spoken as a nation since 1918, when Sinn Féin swept to power. The outcome eighty years later was to embed across Ireland the need for consent.

A few months after the Omagh bombing Blair became the first British prime minister to address the Dáil. 'It is all about belonging,' he told Ireland's parliamentarians. 'The wish of unionists is to belong to the United Kingdom. The wish of nationalists is to belong to Ireland. Both traditions are reasonable. There are no absolutes. The beginning of understanding is to realise that.' Peace was possible because enough unionists and republicans had come to recognise the twin misjudgements that flowed from partition. The PIRA finally accepted that the Protestant, overwhelmingly unionist majority in the six counties was the main obstacle to a united Ireland. And unionists acknowledged they could not safeguard their British identity by denying civil and political rights to the Catholic, mostly nationalist minority.

THE END OF HISTORY

The benefits were felt in the south as well as the north. The strong support in the Republic for the Good Friday Agreement, the historian Roy Foster wrote, was its chance to shed its 'negative' definition of national identity. This had set Irishness as the exclusive property of those who were Catholic, Gaelic or nationalist. 'For many years refuge has been taken ... in wishful thinking about the supposedly temporary and deluded nature of unionism in the North, while little effort was made to present the Republic as somewhere positively worth joining.'[15] The Republic could now retrieve the expansive view of Irishness, with its respect for Protestant Ireland's traditions, that W. B. Yeats had promoted in the wake of partition. It was for the people to decide whether Ireland might be united at some point in the future. And if they did so choose, the agreement declared, unionists would be afforded the same guarantees of their rights in the new state as were now afforded to nationalists in Northern Ireland.

There was a small but symbolically important codicil. For more than fifty years the two countries could not agree on what to call each other. Refusing to acknowledge the legitimacy of partition, Dublin had declined in formal diplomatic exchanges to refer to 'the United Kingdom' because of the inclusion of Northern Ireland. It opted instead for 'Great Britain'. For their part, governments in London would refer only to 'the Republic of Ireland', excluding the province, rather than to the official 'Ireland', lest they seemed to be undermining the north. From 1999, the Irish representative in London was designated the ambassador to the United Kingdom, and their British counterpart in Dublin as ambassador to Ireland.

When George V had travelled to Belfast in June 1921 he had done so in the spirit of conciliation and hope. Crossing the Irish Sea in 2011, Queen Elizabeth II carried the same hopes for the future. State visits are about froth and flummery. Rarely do they bend the arc of history. The queen's visit, however, spoke to a deep change in mindset. For the first time since partition Ireland's nationalists and unionists had recognised the legitimacy of each other's traditions. Britain no longer saw the Republic as a backward former colony. Nationalist Ireland had stopped seething about the wrongs of history. The guest of Irish President Mary McAleese, the queen followed a carefully chosen itinerary. At the Garden of Remembrance in Dublin she honoured the memory of fallen republican Volunteers; at Croke Park, that of the civilians killed by rampaging British forces. Her speech at a grand banquet at Dublin Castle acknowledged fault on all sides. Consciously or unconsciously, her words reached back to those of her grandfather: 'What were once only hopes for the future have now come to pass.' Sinn Féin politicians raised a token protest at the visit. They did not have their heart in it. A year after the visit, Martin McGuinness, by now serving as deputy first minister in a new power-sharing executive at Stormont, shook hands with the monarch when she arrived in Belfast.

Yet the journey from the deal struck in the dank conference rooms at Castle Buildings to the queen's arrival at Farmleigh, the Republic's state guest house in Phoenix Park, had not been an easy one. The compromises made on Good Friday may have robbed violence of its logic but they did not extinguish the resentments, hurt, grievances and hatreds nurtured through nearly three decades of sectarian conflict. The military infrastructure of the Troubles was dismantled. The troops went home. Reconstruction funds flowed in from the European Union. Visitors to Belfast's Europa Hotel, the headquarters during the Troubles of visiting international journalists, no longer worried they would be woken from their sleep by another bomb. Yet separate communities of Protestants and Catholics still resembled mini-fortresses. Their children went to different schools. Many paramilitary groups had reinvented themselves as criminal gangs. The gulf was psychological as well as physical. It seemed everyone had lost a relative or friend to the Troubles. Forgiveness would not come easily. Nor did an agreement to stop fighting conjure up the fabric of trust on which well-functioning democracies depend. The default suspicion was that the other side would renege. An agreement that had been built on constructive ambiguities – no one, it was often said, left a meeting with Blair unconvinced that he was anything but fully on their side – bequeathed a plethora of loose ends. Putting the deal into effect required uncomfortable clarities as promises collided with prejudices. The ends had to be tied. Complex power-sharing arrangements carried their own problems, sometimes as a brake on decision-making, actually entrenching the divide by discouraging cross-community agreement.

For unionism, the agreement above all meant formally surrendering its monopoly control of state institutions. The doors to political and civil administration, the judiciary and, most sensitively, the police had to be opened fully to Catholics. Chris Patten, who had served as a minister in Northern Ireland before joining the cabinets of Thatcher and Major, and more recently had been the last governor of Hong Kong, headed an independent commission to overhaul policing in the province. The brief was clear enough: 'a new beginning to policing in Northern Ireland with a police service capable of attracting and sustaining support from the community as a whole'. This could only mean dismantling the RUC – long seen by unionism as a vital protector, but by nationalism as an instrument of oppression. The statistics told the story. In spite of reforms during previous decades, some 88 per cent of the RUC regular and reserve force counted itself Protestant. The figure for Catholics was 8 per cent. Measured against such an imbalance, Patten's recommendations for a fundamental reshaping of training, recruitment and political oversight in a new Police Service of Northern Ireland were measured and careful. They aimed to double the proportion of Catholics within four years and quadruple it within a decade. But there would be no wholesale redundancies among existing officers. Patten handled his task skilfully. For many in Trimble's party, however, this was about more than numbers. The old name, the Royal Ulster Constabulary, spoke to the force's place as a guardian of the union with Britain. The cap badge – historical emblems remained at the heart of Northern Ireland politics long after they had ceased to have relevance elsewhere – carried the same message. Both were lost to Patten's reforms. The reaction of Paisley's DUP was predictable. It had opposed the Good Friday Agreement from the outset as a surrender to republicanism. In Paisley's description the RUC had become 'a final sacrificial lamb, to appease the Roman Catholic Republican murderers and their nationalist fellow travellers'. In Britain, Patten's Catholic faith had gone largely unnoticed during a distinguished political career as a Tory MP and cabinet minister. Not so in Northern Ireland.

If Paisley's views could be discounted, the disquiet in the UUP could not. Trimble had struggled to carry his party into the agreement, with nearly a third of its ruling council voting against it. Implementation presented a higher hurdle. In June 1998 Northern Ireland elected its first power-sharing assembly. Under the complicated terms of the Good Friday accord, Trimble and Seamus Mallon, the deputy leader of the SDLP, were chosen respectively as first minister and deputy first minister designate. And then the process ran into a series of roadblocks. There were myriad points of friction destined to create stresses within unionism. Beyond reform of policing, Trimble had signed up to the release of paramilitary prisoners. Loyalists as well as republicans were to be set free within two years. For many unionists, this did not make the return to the streets of convicted PIRA killers any more palatable. Hardline unionists refused to give up their triumphalist marches through Catholic areas in places such as Drumcree. The truly neuralgic issue, though, remained decommissioning of paramilitary weapons. The PIRA had refused during the Good Friday negotiations to give a specific pledge covering the nature and timing of disarmament. Blair had given Trimble an assurance that Sinn Féin would not be allowed to join the new executive until it had given up some weapons. Clinton had weighed in to personally assure the unionist leader that he would hold the PIRA's feet to the fire. The ambiguity was essential to get the accord 'over the line'. But it deferred rather than solved the problem. The accord signed, Adams and McGuinness said that arms would be put aside but refused to accept the conditionality insisted on by Trimble. John de Chastelain, the retired Canadian general chosen by Blair to lead an independent, international commission overseeing decommissioning, was left to unravel the knot. In the autumn of 2001 the PIRA said the process of disarmament had begun, confirmed by de Chastelain as a first 'significant act of decommissioning'. It was not enough to persuade unionism.

In spite of its declaration of 'a complete cessation of military operations', the PIRA's paramilitary apparatus remained in place. Decommissioning took place, but in fits and starts. The discovery of a PIRA spying operation at the Stormont parliament, once the bastion of unionism and now the seat of the new assembly, alongside continuing, albeit low-level, violence and criminal operations fuelled unionist suspicions of republican intentions. The multi-party executive was eventually established at the end of 1999, only to collapse a few months later. Loyalist paramilitaries were likewise reluctant to surrender the weapons that had provided them with a place in the politics of the province. By 2002 both the assembly and executive had been indefinitely suspended, with power reverting to Westminster. Paramilitary groups were slow to disband. In 2004 senior figures in the PIRA were heavily implicated in a £25 million robbery at the Northern Bank in Belfast. The war was over, but the absence of sectarian violence could not properly be called peace. Martti Ahtisaari, the former president of Finland, and Cyril Ramaphosa from Nelson Mandela's African National Congress were called in to certify that the PIRA had put its weapons permanently beyond use. But the PIRA's insistence that it would never publicly surrender its arms collided with unionist suspicions that unless disarmament was verified, republicans would hold some back. Hume, exhausted by more than two decades of peace-making, retired in 2001. Four years later, Trimble resigned as UUP leader after his party was heavily defeated by the DUP in the British general election.

The assumption of the Good Friday Agreement had been that a political settlement belonged to Northern Ireland's mainstream parties, the UUP, the SDLP and the non-sectarian Alliance party. The political dynamics proved otherwise. In the years following the signature of the accord, power shifted from the centre towards the extremes. As unionism had second thoughts about the agreement, Trimble found himself under pressure both from doubters within the UUP and from rising support among Protestant voters for Paisley's DUP. For their part, Hume's nationalists found themselves overshadowed by the rapid political rise of Sinn Féin, now a growing force in the politics of the Republic as well as Northern Ireland. In 1998 Trimble and Hume were jointly awarded the

THE END OF HISTORY

Nobel Peace Prize in recognition of their role in the Good Friday Agreement. Trimble used his acceptance speech to offer a candid acknowledgement of unionism's role in sectarian divisions. 'Ulster unionists, fearful of being isolated on the island, built a solid house, but it was a cold house for Catholics. And northern nationalists, although they had a roof over their heads, seemed to us as if they meant to burn the house down.' On the ground, however, Adams and Paisley emerged as the political beneficiaries of peace-making. Elections for the Stormont assembly in November 2003 saw the DUP and Sinn Féin emerge as the biggest players on each side. In the words of Powell, 'All our hopes of building agreement out from the centre in Northern Ireland were dashed.'[16]

The constant during these years was the refusal of Blair and Ahern to admit failure. An ever-turning roundabout of talks took the participants to what Blair later called a 'roll-call of stately homes' – among them Hillsborough, Weston Park, Leeds Castle and St Andrews. The prime minister's frustration showed in a speech in Belfast in October 2002 which demanded 'acts of completion' from republicans and unionists alike. In Powell's judgement, 'The ambiguity that had made the Good Friday Agreement possible in the first place had ceased to be constructive and had become a hindrance.' Unionists needed to be sure that republicans would not return to violence. Republicans needed to know that unionism would not renege on the commitment to share power.[17] Each setback was followed by another round of negotiations. London and Dublin frequently disagreed about tactics but the strategic ambition had been set. Bill Clinton, the now former president, was ever on hand to reassure and cajole. International experts provided neutral oversight in tricky negotiations on such issues as prisoner releases. Clinton's successor, George W. Bush – another president with Irish ancestry – joined the peace cast, travelling to Belfast to add his voice for an irrevocable break with paramilitarism.

'That was yesterday, this is today and tomorrow will be tomorrow... From the depths of my heart I can say to you today that I believe Northern Ireland has come to a time of peace. A time when hate will no longer rule.' Ian Paisley's speech to the newly elected Stormont Assembly in May 2007 marked an extraordinary conversion. Damascene seemed an understatement. Blair and Ahern had travelled to Belfast to listen to the DUP leader take the oath of office as Northern Ireland's first minister. The champion for decades of the ugly sectarianism that had inflicted such pain on Northern Ireland, and a Presbyterian prelate who saw the hand of the pope in every act of evil, had been reborn as a conciliator. Leaving behind his trademark bigotry and bombast, Paisley was preparing to govern with Martin McGuinness as his deputy. Here was a republican, according to British intelligence officers, who had blood on his hands. Two years earlier, the PIRA had formally declared the war to be over and destroyed the last of its weapons. No one had imagined Paisley and McGuinness sharing jokes with each other as they were in the new power-sharing executive. Looking on, Jonathan Powell would reflect, 'You would never have thought that they had been blood enemies leading two warring communities for three decades.'[18] Two days after the parliament's opening Blair stood down as prime minister to make way for Gordon Brown. The gaudy sectarian murals scarring the streets of Belfast still pointed to an imperfect peace, but something had truly changed.

The judgement of British officials who had long been engaged in the process was that Adams and McGuinness had been serious

THE END OF HISTORY

from the outset in looking for a way out from the PIRA's war, but the decision of the Army Council was uncertain until the end. So a deal was never inevitable. Adams and McGuinness might well have fought on rather than risk splitting the republican movement. Paisley's about-turn was not so easily explained. Some said that, like Trimble before him, Paisley had come to see the dangers inherent in unionist wrecking tactics. If they did not share power with nationalism, Northern Ireland would over time come to be ruled jointly by London and Dublin. Others, including Blair, thought a bout of serious ill-health and advancing age the most likely causes of the about-turn. A brush with mortality, Powell judged, had changed his mindset. The former Northern Ireland minister Richard Needham caught a glimpse of realism in the decision. As long as the PIRA was waging war, Paisley had a ready ally in radicalising unionism. When the guns fell silent, it was that much harder to energise his brand of fire and brimstone sectarianism.[19] Whatever the reason, Paisley had decided the time had come to make his peace with the past.

It is tempting to conclude that some sort of peace was inevitable. The question was one of timing. All sides were exhausted by a war that had reached stalemate. An estimated 3,600 people had died, the majority innocent civilians. The British had come to understand they could not win a military victory, and the PIRA likewise. Unionism, and paramilitary loyalism, realised it could not turn the tide of demographics. Rhetorical nationalism had been robbed of its illusions. A less determinist view credits the principal players. None of it would have been possible without the leadership of Blair and Ahern, the unshakeable conviction of Hume, the realism of Trimble, the risk-taking of Adams and McGuinness and the intervention of Clinton. In truth, circumstance and leadership both played their parts. For all that, the images of Ian Paisley sharing the leadership of Northern Ireland with Martin McGuinness were extraordinary beyond all prediction. That the fiery Presbyterian unionist whose political life had been defined by implacable hostility to Catholic nationalism would govern in partnership with a former military commander of the PIRA showed the impossible to be possible. It could never again be said that politics does not work. In the words of the Irish diplomat Seán Ó hUiginn, the Good Friday Agreement was 'first and foremost a vindication of the much maligned art of politics'.[20]

10 A CHOICE OF UNIONS

The royal visit to Dublin and a successful return trip to London by Irish President Michael Higgins promised to see the Irish question return to the margins of politics in the two capitals. Anglo-Irish relations were as cordial as they had ever been. Northern Ireland had a functioning government with the potential to give expression to the ambitions and anxieties of unionism and nationalism alike. Politics in the province still travelled in fits and starts and the new institutions at Stormont did not always run smoothly. The legacy of grievance and mistrust would dissipate only slowly. But the war was over. A rising generation of Protestants and Catholics, unionists and nationalists had no personal memory of sectarian violence. Power-sharing seemed to be putting down roots. As for a united Ireland, well, it might happen one day, but it was scarcely front of mind for a majority, north or south. Political leaders in London and Dublin had more pressing matters to concern them. The long economic upturn that began in the 1990s ended in 2008 with the global financial crash. The banking meltdown was followed in turn by a slide into economic recession as the two governments battled with exploding budgetary deficits. For a time the crisis seemed to threaten Ireland's membership of the euro. Banks were nationalised and Ireland's property boom turned to calamitous bust. In Britain a new Conservative-led government introduced deep cuts in public spending. Austerity ruled on both sides of the Irish Sea. No one could have guessed that the new prime minister, David Cameron, would soon throw everything into the air by gambling on a referendum to decide whether Britain should remain a member of the European Union.

Cameron's political career had been one of effortless advancement. His life experience – Eton, Oxford and a safe Tory seat in the English home counties – spoke to the entitlement of the English ruling classes. Leading from 2010 a coalition government with the Liberal Democrats, he had no great plans for his premiership. Rather, it was enough that he held the keys to Downing Street. He knew he could play the part of prime minister and never bothered to ask if this was the same as being a good prime minister. Beyond the need to restore the nation's battered finances – a task largely delegated to his chancellor George Osborne – Cameron faced one stubborn political challenge. Since becoming leader in 2005 he had tried to shake his party out of the infighting about Britain's place in Europe that had doomed John Major's government. But he faced a rising swell of anti-Europeanism on the Tory back benches. Though Britain had stood aside from the European single currency when Ireland swapped the punt for the euro, a sizeable segment of the Conservative Party had not come to terms with the political ambitions for the European Union implicit in the Maastricht Treaty. The constant sniping from his own side was amplified by the emergence as a serious political force of Nigel Farage's United Kingdom Independence Party (UKIP). Farage, a politician lacking principle and policies alike but one with a considerable political presence, had harnessed concerns among voters about high levels of immigration to his party's unabashed anti-Europeanism. He looked unlikely to break through into Westminster politics. Cameron's fear rather was that UKIP's unabashed populism would win enough votes on the political right to severely damage the Conservatives in their contests with Labour.

The prime minister's answer was to throw the dice, to call a referendum to settle the issue of British membership of the European Union, as the Labour prime minister Harold Wilson had done in

1975. His assumption, as on most things, was that, like Wilson, he would win the vote to stay in. Politics would return to normal and his premiership to serene success. Ireland, and more directly the impact on Northern Ireland should the vote go against the government, played no part in any of these calculations. Cameron paid lip service to Conservative unionism, but he was not at all interested in the province. In any event, he was confident of winning, so why trouble himself about a theoretical risk to the fragile political peace that had been negotiated in 1998? A hard look at the possible consequences would have told him that a vote to leave one union would risk seriously destabilising the other. Quitting the European Union would loosen the constitutional bonds of the United Kingdom and, quite possibly, put in question the new-found peace and political stability in Northern Ireland. A cursory glance at the Good Friday Agreement would have told him that it rested on the assumption of British and Irish membership of the European Union and on the open-border economic relations that flowed from it. Cameron would have none of this. Whitehall departments, including the Northern Ireland Office, were given firm instructions not even to prepare contingency plans for a Leave vote. Veterans of Harold Wilson's referendum offered informal advice about tactics. They were brushed aside. The prime minister knew he would win.

The vote to leave the European Union by a narrow margin of 52 to 48 per cent in June 2016 spoke to the nation's discontent. In many respects it was a last blast of Britain's imperial trumpet. A fair number who voted Leave were long-standing opponents of engagement with the nation's continental partners. On the far right stood self-styled defenders of a purist interpretation of national sovereignty; on the far left those who had always viewed Brussels as the agent of a global capitalist conspiracy. Woven into the anti-Europe campaign were nostalgia, self-deception and a hankering for past glory. Others wanted simply to kick the government. Amid the harsh austerity measures introduced in the wake of the financial crash, the 'left-behind' voters in the Midlands and north of England who gave the pro-Brexit camp its majority had been stranded by falling living standards, job insecurity and indifferent political leaders. Public disquiet in many poorer regions about an upsurge in immigration from the former communist states, and now European Union members, of Central and Eastern Europe was channelled by the populist Farage into a campaign against the 'globalists' of Brussels. The Tory Brexit campaign, effectively led by Boris Johnson and Michael Gove, proclaimed a distinctly English nationalism – and warned, mendaciously, that if Britain remained in the European Union, it would soon be overrun by Turkish migrants. Unshackled from Europe, the argument ran, the nation could rediscover itself as 'Global Britain'. The ingredients – the global reach, the indivisible sovereignty of parliament, the nation's great victory in the war – were little different from those that had been widely rehearsed sixty years earlier, when Britain had initially scorned the Franco-German project to build a European Common Market. Sovereignty returned to Westminster, the Brexit pitch ran, would restore the fortunes of an English working class that had been stripped of its economic security by a European Union in cahoots with international bankers and big business.

All this was fantasy, as the nation's poor economic performance in succeeding years would show, but truth and facts were of little concern to the leaders of the campaign. There was more than an undercurrent of racism in much of the campaigning, and of the economic populism that a few months later would propel Donald Trump into the White House. Taking his cue from Trump's embrace of 'alternative facts', Gove scorned warnings from national and international organisations about the likely damage to national prosperity. The voters, he boasted, had had enough of 'experts'. He was putting his trust in 'the British people'.

The Anglo-Irish relationship and the constitutional stability of Northern Ireland were collateral damage. Scotland, Wales and Northern Ireland had at best walk-on parts in what was essentially an English enterprise. None had been consulted about the referendum by Cameron, even though there were plentiful warnings that departure from the European Union would throw Britain's constitutional settlement into doubt. His goal was personal – to shore up his own authority by taming the Eurosceptics in his own party. Two years previously he had won a referendum against the Scottish National Party's call for independence. Hubris told him he would repeat the trick. When the votes were counted, Cameron simply walked away, leaving it to his Downing Street successor Theresa May to make sense of the chaos.

The cheerleaders for Brexit recalled the worst of the lofty condescension and ignorance long shown by Conservatives towards Ireland. Without careful handling, Brexit threatened at best a rupture in an Anglo-Irish relationship, at worst a serious danger to the peace itself. The reaction among leading Brexiters spoke to indifference and irritation. Johnson, foreign secretary in May's new government, was dismissive of Irish concerns. In subsequent battles with Brussels about the terms of Brexit, Johnson would seek political advantage from aligning himself with the DUP. But he had neither respect for nor an interest in the affairs of the province. Northern Ireland, Foreign Office officials would hear him remark, was nothing more than 'a sink into which the English are obliged to pour their money'.[1]

Gove, as co-leader of the Leave campaign, echoed the nativist sentiments once promoted by Enoch Powell. Powell combined visceral Euroscepticism and fierce opposition to immigration with strong support for the unionist cause. Gove, a political journalist at the time of the Good Friday peace deal, had joined Ian Paisley in condemning the agreement, accusing Tony Blair of 'selling out' to the PIRA. For most senior Conservatives, however, Northern Ireland was a foreign country of which they knew little and cared less. Typical was the cabinet minister Karen Bradley, who was given the Northern Ireland portfolio in May's administration. She had been surprised, Bradley volunteered, at the sharpness of the sectarian divide in the province: 'I didn't understand things like when elections are fought, for example, in Northern Ireland – people who are nationalists don't vote for unionist parties and vice versa.'[2] Such glaring ignorance of the history and politics of the province for which she was responsible was at once shocking and far from exceptional.

One immediate consequence of Brexit was to transform the all but invisible border between Northern Ireland and the Republic into the United Kingdom's only land frontier with the European Union. This in turn threatened to upend the all-Ireland economic ecosystem created by the Good Friday Agreement. The bargain at the heart of the accord was recognition of the legitimacy of nationalist calls for a united Ireland alongside the guarantee for unionism provided by the consent principle. This assumed frictionless trade and investment flows across an 'all-Ireland' economy. British departure from the European Union turned an open border into an international frontier. Enforcing the panoply of regulations needed to protect the integrity of the European single market would require a 'hard' border – with all the requisite passport, regulatory and customs controls. An open border underpinned the mutual respect for the competing identities of the two communities in the north. The absence of frontier checks and controls permitted nationalists to embrace their Irishness, while the consent principle safeguarded the interests of those pledging allegiance to the United Kingdom. In the sombre description of the senior European Commission official Stefaan De Rynck, 'Brexit was the proverbial bull in a china shop. It destroyed a fragile political equilibrium.'[3] John Major and Tony Blair had warned as much during a symbolic joint visit to Derry two weeks before the referendum vote. With a majority of voters in Scotland backing continued membership of the European Union, Major saw an existential threat to the United Kingdom. The Scottish National Party had been defeated in the 2014 referendum, but Brexit reopened the question of separation. Scotland was now confronted with a new choice. It could be British or European, but no longer both. As for Northern Ireland, in Major's words, 'All the pieces of the peace process jigsaw would be thrown into the air and no one knows where those pieces would land.' Jeopardising the peace would be 'unforgivably irresponsible', Blair said. Heedless of anything but their anti-Europeanism, Johnson and Gove dismissed the warnings.

They showed similar disregard for the inevitably asymmetric nature of the political dynamics in negotiations with Brussels after a Brexit vote. Britain would 'hold all the cards' in such talks, Gove bragged in the weeks before the vote. Precisely the reverse was true. The twenty-seven other European Union states accounted for about 50 per cent of Britain's trade. The stakes were much higher for Britain than for the Union. A complete breakdown in the relationship would certainly create difficulties for some continental industries, but overall the economic impact on Britain would be far more damaging. They held all the cards. British ministers struggled to admit this basic reality. Misjudgements were piled atop the misapprehensions. By the account of Whitehall officials intimately involved in the negotiations, what followed during the subsequent years was a calamitous failure of British politics and diplomacy. In the judgement of one senior figure in 10 Downing Street, 'Brexit was a deep, self-inflicted wound. We then proceeded to turn the knife in it.'[4]

Theresa May was a Remainer, albeit slightly reluctantly, during the referendum. After winning the contest to replace Cameron, she spent three years of her premiership trying first to cement support for her premiership among the Brexiters and subsequently to reconcile the ideological certitudes of her party's English nationalists with unavoidable political and economic realities. To the bemusement and frustration of Britain's former partners, May would spend more time negotiating with her own party than with Brussels. The British officials dispatched to negotiate in Brussels privately confessed they were frequently unsure of their own government's stance. Deepening rancour in the Tory Party between Brexit 'ultras' emboldened by the referendum to demand the severing of all European ties and a band of centrist pragmatists seeking an amicable arrangement with Brussels saw ministers veer between serious engagement and threats to quit the Union without any agreement. In the description of De Rynck, it often seemed to Brussels that the British were 'playing chicken' with themselves.

British chaos met unruffled professionalism in Brussels and diplomatic energy in Dublin. Leaders of the European Union appointed Michel Barnier as chief negotiator in talks with Britain. With long experience as a senior French politician and member of the European Commission, the suave Barnier brought confidence, expertise and intelligence to the role. As the commissioner responsible for regional affairs, he had had a significant hand in the European Union's substantial financial support for Northern Ireland to support the Good Friday peace process. A fluent English speaker with a dry sense of humour, he would be unimpressed by the histrionics of the Brexiters. Behind him stood phalanxes of professional trade negotiators, lawyers and experts who had made their careers as negotiators with nations outside the Union. The contrast with the erratic style of David Davis and David Frost – successively the two lead negotiators on the British side for May and Johnson – could not have been sharper. Davis, a long-time Brexiter in the Tory ranks at Westminster, showed little enthusiasm for mastering the detail and complexity of the issues, preferring rhetorical flourishes to granular analysis. Frost, a former diplomat turned political adviser to Johnson, seemed above all intent on building a political career by playing to the gallery of hardline Brexiters. He had left the Foreign Office a few years earlier, after learning he was unlikely ever to be offered a 'big' ambassadorship. It often seemed that he saw Brexit as revenge on the staunchly pro-European stance of his erstwhile department. To Barnier's mind, the consistent mistake on the British side was to confuse hopes with reality.

The reaction in Dublin to the outcome of the referendum was deep dismay. The Irish economy was still recovering from the meltdown of its banking system that had accompanied the global financial crash of 2008. Remaining in the embattled eurozone had come at the price of severe austerity. In spite of the rapid diversification of its economy during its membership of the European Union, Britain remained the Republic's pivotal trading partner. Ireland depended for much of its energy on the interconnectors running under the sea from Britain. Europe, however, had been woven into the bilateral economic relationship. The two nations helped shape the same Europe-wide regulations and obeyed the same rules. And the Republic's political interests reached beyond the existential question of the future of Northern Ireland. In spite of Irish neutrality, the two nations' security was intertwined. During more than forty years of membership Brussels had become a vital rendezvous for their politicians. It was a place where the two leaders, attending regular European summits, could do business together beyond the glare of formal meetings in London and Dublin. The 1985 Anglo-Irish Agreement had been formulated in the margins of these summits. Albert Reynolds and John Major had first struck up their friendship in Brussels. Enda Kenny, the Taoiseach at the time of the referendum, had forged a good relationship with Cameron and had travelled to Britain during the campaign to support him in making the case for a Remain vote among the Irish diaspora.

Unlike Cameron, Kenny had been wise enough to set in train contingency plans for Brexit. The Irish journalist Tony Connelly reported that the strategy ran to 130 pages.[5] The preparations did not soften the shock of the Leave vote. Departure from the European Union would turn on their head the organising assumptions of British foreign policy during the previous forty years. It would do much the same on the other side of the Irish Sea. But Dublin at least had a plan.

The immediate priority of Kenny's government was now to emphasise that the Republic would not follow its neighbour out of Europe. The initial thought in Dublin was to explore nonetheless whether it could strike a bilateral deal with London to protect its economic interests. The idea was dropped as it became clear that for the British, Brexit was a journey with neither map nor clear destination. Kenny instead forged an alliance with Barnier. In an exercise closely coordinated from Dublin, Irish diplomats across the continent set to work to persuade other European Union governments that whatever the terms of Britain's departure, the Good Friday Agreement had to be protected. Kenny's argument struck an emotional chord in many capitals. From the outset, European integration had been founded on Franco-German reconciliation, with the goal of promoting peace on the continent. It had done just that in providing economic aid to cement the peace accord in Northern Ireland.

———

Theresa May's first strategic mistake was an attempt to prove her credentials to the party's Brexiters by promising a decisive break with almost everything European – a hard Brexit, in the jargon. In the immediate aftermath of the June 2016 referendum there had been speculation that Britain would seek to maintain a close economic and political relationship with Brussels – a so-called 'soft' Brexit. Norway, which had access to the single market through membership of the European Economic Area, was a possible model. So too were the slightly different arrangements enjoyed by Switzerland. The truth was that the coalition that had backed Brexit had never agreed on the form it would take: a retreat from the political ambitions of the Union while maintaining close economic integration, or a clean break that would take Britain out of the customs union and single market. Speaking to her party's annual conference in October, May made the choice. Showing all the fervour of the religious convert, she signalled Britain would leave the single market and customs union and would not accept any economic or political arrangements that encroached on its national sovereignty. In particular, it would banish from the United Kingdom the jurisdiction of the European Court of Justice – the bête noire of Brexiters. Beyond that she was vague. Pressed on what would replace the vast panoply of political, economic and social agreements that had for decades defined the country's relationship not just with Europe but also with the rest of the world, May would reply that 'Brexit means Brexit'. The mantra concealed the inconvenient truth that, beyond insisting that the writ of European law would no longer run in

Britain, the government lacked a coherent answer as to what that actually meant.

Her second error was to underestimate the cohesion of the other twenty-seven states. Many Brexiters imagined that Britain's departure would serve as a trigger for a wider unravelling of European integration. Over time Brexit might well be followed by 'Grexit' and indeed 'Frexit' as voters in Greece and France followed the British lead. Britain, Gove would say, would then be the fulcrum for a new European order. In the interim, self-interest (German car exports or sales of Italian prosecco in Britain) would drive politicians in national capitals to break ranks with Brussels' demand for a hard bargain on the terms of Britain's departure. Ireland, for its part, could be bullied into a bilateral deal. Great hopes were invested in Angela Merkel, the German chancellor, who made it clear that she wanted to preserve a cordial relationship with Britain.

This was vainglorious nonsense. Among Britain's erstwhile partners Brexit acted as a centripetal rather than centrifugal force. The twenty-seven governments stuck firmly together. For all her Anglophile instincts, the hard-headed Merkel had a higher priority. She was determined to preserve the rules, the so-called *acquis communautaire*, upon which, as a law-based enterprise, the European Union was built. May then made a third misjudgement. By invoking the European treaty's Article 50, the clause that allows members to leave, she set the clock ticking on a two-year deadline to reach an agreement. The pressure to strike a deal now fell unevenly on Britain. Brussels could afford to wait it out. To add to the stresses, Barnier insisted the negotiations be split into two: the bargaining on the nature of the broad economic and political relationship between Britain and the twenty-seven could begin only after they had first concluded an outline 'Withdrawal Agreement'. This would set in stone London's commitment to meet its outstanding financial obligations to the Union, would establish the rights of European citizens living in Britain and, critically, would guarantee the open Irish border underpinning the Good Friday accord.

Ireland's intense diplomacy reaped its rewards in April 2017, when a summit of European Union leaders announced the framework for Brussels' stance. A communiqué spoke of the central role of the Good Friday Agreement in promoting peace in Northern Ireland and noted that the preservation of the accord would be of 'paramount importance' in a Brexit deal. To the extent that May's government had thought about Ireland, it had assumed that it could separate discussions with Dublin on the border issue from the wider talks about Britain's future relationship with the European Union. Brussels, it imagined, would be obliged to incorporate a bilateral arrangement with Ireland into the overall Brexit bargain. The summit carried a completely different message, closely identifying the interests of the Dublin government with those of other member states and putting the preservation of the terms of the Good Friday accord at the heart of Europe's negotiating position. To add insult to injury, the leaders declared that if Northern Ireland should vote at some future date for Irish unity, the province would be offered automatic entry into the Union. Unionists who had hoped Brexit would weaken all-Ireland integration were now confronted with the prospect that the reverse might well be true.

As Britain blew up its bridges with the continent, Ireland resolved to become more European. By the beginning of 2017 the initial temptation in Dublin to explore the possibility of a bilateral arrangement with Britain – above all to guarantee the common travel area between the two nations – gave way to a more strategic assessment of the Republic's interests. It was articulated by Phil Hogan, the politician serving as the country's commissioner in Brussels. 'There is a real risk that Ireland could allow our relationship with Europe to be defined by our relationship with the United Kingdom,' Hogan wrote. This would be an enormous mistake. 'Instead we should have the confidence and direction to recognise that post-Brexit Ireland will need to have in place a wholly different set of relationships with our European Union partners – relationships that we will forge, advocate, defend and address directly and out of the shadow of our nearest neighbour.' Hogan was fully alive to the implications. 'Unwittingly, Brexit may present Ireland with the chance to seize the next phase in our development and maturity as a sovereign state. It will force us to forge relations and shape our destiny within the European Union without the presence of our nearest and strongest ally since 1973.'[6] Simply put, Britain's break with Europe would see Ireland break further with Britain. Kenny concurred, using a speech on the eve of the opening of formal negotiations to crush remaining British hopes that Dublin would be an ally in the European camp. 'Let me make one thing absolutely clear. Ireland will be on the European Union side of the table when the negotiations begin. We will be one of the twenty-seven.' To cement this arrangement Barnier spoke to a joint sitting of the Dáil and the parliament's second chamber, the Seanad. 'I want to reassure the Irish people that in these negotiations, Ireland's interests will be the European Union's interests.'

The preliminary skirmishes crystallised what European diplomats called the 'trilemma' created by Brexit. The European Union was determined that its new border with the United Kingdom in Northern Ireland would not become an unpoliced back door for goods to enter the single market without the requisite checks. The open Irish economy envisaged in the Good Friday Agreement militated against the imposition of controls on north–south trade. For its part, London wanted to quit the single market and customs union to allow Britain to break out of Europe's regulatory ambit and strike trade deals with other major economies. Something had to give. These three goals could be reconciled only if Northern Ireland was made a special case and a new, east–west customs border was created in the Irish Sea to regulate trade between mainland Britain and Northern Ireland – a barrier to intra-UK trade anathema to unionists. The alternative was to drop May's insistence on making a clean break in the trading relationship with Brussels.

In a joint report on the progress of negotiations agreed in December 2017, May was obliged to concede that one way or another, Northern Ireland would have to remain within the single market and customs union. The dry, technical language of Clause 49 of the report scarcely concealed May's political retreat:

> The United Kingdom remains committed to protecting North–South cooperation and to its guarantee of avoiding a hard border. Any future arrangements must be compatible with these overarching requirements. The United Kingdom's intention is to achieve these objectives through the overall EU–UK relationship. Should this not be possible, the United Kingdom will propose specific solutions to address the unique circumstances of the island of Ireland. In the absence of agreed solutions, the United Kingdom will maintain full alignment with those rules of the Internal Market and the Customs Union which, now or in the future, support North–South cooperation, the all-island economy and the protection of the 1998 Agreement.

Translated, the province would accept continued oversight from Brussels. Northern Ireland would retain frictionless trade with the Republic and the rest of the European Union, even if this meant the creation of a border between Britain and Northern Ireland or the rest of the United Kingdom agreeing to stick to European rules.

The controversy reset the domestic politics of Northern Ireland. The political institutions created by the Good Friday Agreement had not settled the clash of ambitions between unionism and nationalism. Rather, they had set them to one side. Sinn Féin's place at Stormont ensured that nationalist demands for a united Ireland were an ever-present fact of politics. But as the Northern Ireland executive grappled with the more pressing challenges of government – the economy, housing, health and the rest – the case for unification had been pushed into the background. Fervent nationalists would point to the continuing demographic shift in favour of Catholics, alarming more fearful unionists, but Irish unity was for most still an aspiration (or a threat) located well in the future. Brexit changed the calculation. In leaving the European Union, the United Kingdom had raised questions about its own future – and the place of Northern Ireland. Martin McGuinness, Sinn Féin's deputy first minister in the Stormont executive, was quick to declare the referendum had underscored the case for Irish unity.

Britain was leaving the European Union, while Ireland, north and south, wanted to remain. Across the United Kingdom the vote in favour of Brexit was 52 to 48 per cent. In Northern Ireland it was 56 to 44 per cent in favour of staying in the EU. Of the largest parties, only the DUP counted itself in the Leave camp, with the UUP joining the nationalist and Alliance parties on the Remain side. Nationalists overwhelmingly backed continued membership, while a sizeable majority of unionists favoured departure. Catholics voted to stay by a proportion of 85 to 15 per cent, while Protestants voted to leave by 60 to 40 per cent. Similarly, two-thirds of self-described 'unionists' voted to leave, while almost 90 per cent of self-described 'nationalists' voted to remain.[7] Arlene Foster, the Stormont first minister and DUP leader, had campaigned for Brexit, but the expectation of her party was that the Remain camp would win the vote. Once the ballots were counted, the unionist hope became that the outcome would force the restoration of border controls between the province and the Republic. Instead, it was soon apparent that any economic disruption was more likely to fall on Northern Ireland's trade with the rest of the United Kingdom. Unionism was the loser from Brexit.

In the summer of 2017 May sought to avoid a looming deadlock in the House of Commons about the terms of Brexit by calling a snap general election. It was a miscalculation. The Conservatives lost their majority and May was left dependent on the support of unionist MPs at Westminster. The latter's demand was straightforward: an undeliverable rejection of exceptionalism. Northern Ireland must be treated no differently from England, Scotland and Wales in a Brexit deal with Brussels. More specifically, as Nigel Dodds, the leader of the DUP MPs at Westminster, put it: 'The DUP will not tolerate a border on the Irish Sea.'[8]

May attempted to square the circle of the 'trilemma' by proposing a 'backstop' arrangement if no other means could be found simultaneously to protect Ireland's open border, safeguard the integrity of the European single market and avoid disrupting trade between the British mainland and Northern Ireland. In such circumstances, all four parts of the United Kingdom would remain within the ambit of European rules. The prime minister's hope was that the backstop would never come into effect. All manner of alternative arrangements were floated by British negotiators, including automatic data collection, electronic surveillance, 'trusted trader' schemes and 'invisible' customs posts. The pitch was that they would allow traffic to pass unimpeded between Northern Ireland and the Republic, and thus the European Union, and be checked by the authorities without the construction of physical infrastructure. All were untested and none withstood serious scrutiny by Brussels.

For their part, the Brexit ultras on the Tory back benches rejected May's acquiescence in a deal that might, by default, leave Britain as well as Northern Ireland in the customs union and single market. These were the ingredients of political deadlock. The choice facing May's government had become one between a 'soft' Brexit for all of the United Kingdom and a border in the Irish Sea. Faced with the objections of hardliners demanding a hard Brexit and the DUP's insistence that an east–west border would fatally undermine Northern Ireland's place in the United Kingdom, she lacked a parliamentary majority for either. Negotiating deadlines with Brussels came and went. Davis and Johnson resigned rather than accept a cabinet decision to press ahead with a UK-wide backstop. The Tory civil war continued, with the European Union and Ireland largely bystanders in the British psychodrama. In the summer of 2019 two years of trench warfare at Westminster ended in paralysis and parliamentary defeat for May's proposal. Barnier summed up the mood in Brussels: 'It is madness to see the extent to which the future of this great country, and our relationship with it, has for three years now been dependent on the bickering, backstabbing, serial betrayals and thwarted ambitions of a handful of Conservative MPs.' Donald Tusk, the president of the European Council, expressed the same view: 'I've been wondering what the special place in hell looks like for those who promoted Brexit, without even the sketch of a plan about how to carry it out safely.'[9]

May's approach to Brexit was a model of statecraft when set against the reckless and dismal record of her successor, Johnson. His arrival in 10 Downing Street in July 2019 added braggadocio and mendacity in liberal measure to Britain's negotiating posture. Johnson had not won friends in Europe during his spell as May's foreign secretary. Ireland's foreign minister Charles Flanagan spoke for many of his continental counterparts: 'I have to say around the Foreign Affairs table he was a figure of fun. People did not warm to him and he did nothing to ingratiate himself. He was provocative towards the French and the Germans and Italians, and everyone.' In place of a strategy, the new prime minister offered bluster and brinkmanship: if the Northern Ireland problem could not be wished away, Britain would simply quit the European Union without any agreement on trade. Confronted with inconvenient truths, Johnson, in the description of one Whitehall official, would put his hands over ears and hum 'Rule Britannia'. Another official was harsher: 'I think he lies to himself as well as to everyone else.'[10] The 'everyone else' included Queen Elizabeth. When in the late summer of 2019 the House of Commons threatened to close off the option of a 'no-deal Brexit', Johnson persuaded the sovereign to prorogue parliament. The Supreme Court concluded that Her Majesty had been deceived by Downing Street, and parliament was recalled.

Capricious chaos in London was met by calm in Brussels. Barnier was unruffled by the prime minister's shenanigans, sticking to the view he had expressed to the European Parliament in March 2019 that whatever threats Johnson might make, he could not escape Britain's international treaty obligations to Ireland: 'In a no-deal, in all scenarios, the Good Friday Agreement will continue to apply. The United Kingdom will remain a core co-guarantor of that agreement.' As for what was known in Brussels as Johnson's 'mad man' strategy of threatening to abandon negotiations, Barnier was unperturbed, not least because he had heard Johnson admit that he needed a deal. 'I wasn't surprised by the madman strategy. I was told that this strategy was taught at university in the UK.'[11] Privately, British officials gave Johnson the same message. Beyond the damage to the economy that would result from crashing out without an agreement with the European

Union, the nation's standing in the world would be irreparably damaged if it was seen to jettison its international obligations and renege on the peace process.

The comfortable House of Commons majority Johnson secured after a second 'Brexit' election in December 2019 did not change any of these inconvenient truths. Johnson had promised during the campaign to 'get Brexit done'. He had benefited greatly from a lurch to the left of the Labour opposition under the leadership of Jeremy Corbyn – himself no friend of Europe. Wildly, the prime minister pledged that Britain could leave the single market and customs union, maintain a smooth trading relationship with the European Union and avoid any checks on trade between the British mainland and Northern Ireland. Barnier called the bluff. Johnson blinked. Was he prepared to sacrifice the decisive break he had promised with the European Union in order to preserve frictionless trade between the mainland and Northern Ireland? The answer was no. At a meeting with the Taoiseach, Leo Varadkar, Johnson signalled that he was willing to accept a separate, exceptional arrangement for Northern Ireland. In the afterglow of his election victory Johnson in effect tore up his promise to the unionists by consenting to a Withdrawal Agreement with Brussels that included a protocol with unique arrangements for Northern Ireland. Unionists cried foul. Theresa May's proposals had provided for the United Kingdom to remain economically aligned with Europe. Johnson's deal saw Britain breaking free from Brussels while Northern Ireland remained in the single market and customs union. This meant a new border in the Irish Sea, leaving the province economically closer to the Republic than to Britain. The Democratic Unionists had some cause when they charged that the delicate balance between unionism and nationalism struck in the Good Friday Agreement had been tilted in favour of the latter.

A CHOICE OF UNIONS

The prime minister, though he still refused to admit as much, had put a hard Brexit for the rest of the United Kingdom ahead of the interests of unionism. With an eighty-seat majority, Johnson, unlike May, had no need for the votes of DUP MPs at Westminster. So he ignored them.

A clean-break Brexit for Great Britain was prioritised over both the views of unionists and political stability in Northern Ireland. Encouraged by his close adviser Dominic Cummings, 'Johnson calculated . . . that the majority of the British public did not know much or care much about Northern Ireland'.[12] In January 2020 the re-elected Johnson signed the formal Withdrawal Agreement with Brussels, including the Northern Ireland protocol. His response to unionist protests was to pretend that the new border in the Irish Sea would never materialise. Reality imposed itself when the deal came into force. British businesses discovered that goods shipped from the mainland to Northern Ireland now required complex regulatory paperwork. Food and other agricultural products needed particular certification. Many companies decided that doing business with Northern Ireland was not worth the additional costs.

In the minds of the DUP, the long-held fear of betrayal by its friends at Westminster had once again been realised. The Northern Ireland secretary Julian Smith agreed. 'My sense was that Northern Ireland policy was being driven by Brexit . . . There was no humility, no recognition how fragile the Northern Ireland ecosystem was, but arrogance and confusion.'[13] Smith's questioning of Number 10's approach saw him relieved of his job. 'Johnson could not cope with any pushback.' For two years the party had collaborated with the hardline Brexiters on the Tory back benches to thwart Theresa May's plans. Those same Tory MPs then deserted the unionists to back Johnson's decision to concede special status for Northern Ireland. The painful irony here was that the DUP had inadvertently conspired in an outcome it did not want. If it had supported May's proposals, Northern Ireland would have received the same treatment as the rest of the United Kingdom.

Even for Downing Street insiders who had grown accustomed to the delusion and deception that characterised Johnson's premiership, the kaleidoscope of chaos that now followed was unnerving. The Withdrawal Agreement was only part one of the Brexit process. A second accord was needed to set the terms of the future economic and political relationship between Britain and the European Union. Yet even before the ink was dry, Johnson and his lead negotiator, Frost, set about reneging on the protocol. Frost later claimed this had been the intention all along. The object had been to get a withdrawal deal 'over the line' and then force Brussels and Dublin to renegotiate the Northern Ireland dimension. If that were true, it showed that the government had learned nothing from the first round of negotiations. It also exposed its contempt for the long-cherished notion that a nation such as Britain should keep its word.

The eighteen months that followed the signing of the agreement were marked out on the British side by hubris, bluster and, bluntly, lies. The Covid-19 pandemic that swept across the world in the early months of 2020 served to amplify the disarray. Prime ministerial indecision was punctuated by mendacity, private concessions masked by public grandstanding. Senior officials complained that it was impossible to negotiate seriously with Brussels because the prime minister continued to refuse to establish a consistent position. 'How can we do a deal with Barnier when we don't know what Johnson wants?' one senior aide remarked at the time. 'And we don't know if he knows what he wants.'[14] Jonathan Powell, Blair's chief negotiator, spoke for many of his former colleagues in Whitehall when he warned of the dangers of destabilising the peace. 'What I really object to ... is the casual vandalism of the Northern Ireland peace process, something a previous generation of British politicians on both sides spent decades constructing.'[15]

Johnson, backed by Gove, continued to misread the dynamics of the negotiation. Faced with Barnier's refusal to reopen the terms of the agreement, he produced domestic legislation that would allow the government to ignore it. The purpose of the UK Internal Markets Bill was to put pressure on Brussels. The effect was to provoke widespread anger and opprobrium. Brandon Lewis, who had replaced Smith as Northern Ireland secretary, admitted in the House of Commons that the bill would mean Britain breaking international law. It did not help that he added that the breach would be 'limited and specific'. A phalanx of former prime ministers, including John Major and Theresa May, warned that Britain's reputation as a trusted international partner was being squandered. In Major's description, 'For generations, Britain's word, solemnly given, has been accepted by friend and foe. Our signature on any treaty or agreement has been sacrosanct.' The former Conservative leader Michael Howard went further, declaring that breaking its international obligations would put Britain in the same category as Russia, China and Iran.

Barnier and his team did not budge. Johnson ploughed on regardless, describing his deal as Britain's final leap to 'freedom'. Brushing aside the still unresolved argument about Northern Ireland, he deployed his trademark hyperbole by travelling to the Meridian Line in Greenwich to declare the beginning of a second Elizabethan age, in which a reinvigorated 'Global Britain' would make its presence felt again in every corner of the world. Closer to home, businesses trading between Britain and Northern Ireland were faced with an avalanche of paperwork. The Europeans were not about to help by lowering the bureaucratic hurdles that left supermarket shelves in the province empty of some products produced on the mainland – and, for a time, put at risk the trade in essential medicines. Johnson's posturing, however, scarcely encouraged compromise. The prime minister's continuing attempts to override the protocol attracted opprobrium reaching beyond Brussels. Joe Biden, newly installed in the White House, greatly cherished his Irish heritage. He was blunt in his warnings to Johnson that anything that jeopardised the Good Friday Agreement would meet with a strong reaction. Johnson's much vaunted promise of a post-Brexit trade deal with the United States turned to dust. For most of the post-war period British prime ministers had boasted of a 'special relationship' with the United States. In briefings for journalists Biden's aides made it clear that Johnson was unwelcome at the White House.

By the time Britain ended the Northern Ireland stand-off with the European Union with the signature of the Windsor Framework in February 2023, the Conservatives had thrown out Boris Johnson, put Liz Truss in Downing Street, ejected her after only forty-nine days and chosen Rishi Sunak to replace her. Johnson's fall was by his own hand. His promise had been to 'get Brexit done'. He had done so at the cost of a deal that amplified the harm done by the original decision to leave and severely damaged Britain's place in the wider world. The patience of his cabinet and MPs finally snapped, however, at his insouciant dismissal of the basic standards and rules of political life. The disclosure of Downing Street's serial breaches during periods of Covid lockdown of the strict rules imposed on the rest of the country and Johnson's repeated untruths to parliament brought to an end a shameful premiership. Johnson did not go quietly. Some fifty-seven of his ministers had resigned before he was finally prevailed upon to pack his bags. Truss too would soon prove the author of her own destruction, though for different reasons. Chosen largely because she was liked by party activists, Truss produced a populist tax-cutting Budget in the hope of restoring Conservative fortunes. Instead, she provoked a crisis in financial markets. The promise of tens of billions of pounds in unfunded tax cuts saw the value of sterling crash, the cost of government borrowing soar and the economy heading for a slump. Her short spell in Number 10 invited widespread comparisons between her premiership and the shelf life of a supermarket lettuce. She too was bundled out, to be replaced by Sunak, Britain's fourth prime minister in as many years. After all the chaos, Sunak, unexciting but with a reputation as a hard-working chancellor, was deemed a safe pair of hands.

The Windsor deal was hailed by the new prime minister as a qualitative leap from the accord first agreed by Johnson. What was true was that it damped down the Tory hysteria. There were some tangible improvements, notably in reducing the checks on goods being shipped from the British mainland to Northern Ireland. There were provisions also for the Stormont parliament to oversee the trading arrangements. But the essential architecture of the Withdrawal Agreement remained in place. In order to keep open the border between the province and the Republic, the government had consented to the creation of a frontier in the Irish Sea, imposing new frictions on economic relations within the United Kingdom. Confronted with a choice between their political priorities at Westminster and the fortunes of unionism in Northern Ireland, the Conservatives had opted for the former.

For the ever-fearful unionists the codicil to the Brexit saga came with the publication of the 2021 census. The fear that had haunted them for decades – that Protestants in the province would at some point be outnumbered by Catholics – had become a reality. A decade earlier, some 48 per cent of those who responded to the survey had put themselves in the Protestant camp, while 45 per cent identified as Catholic. By 2021 the Catholic cohort had risen slightly to 45.7 per cent, while the number from Protestant or other Christian denominations fell to 43.5 per cent. A fraction under 11 per cent declared no affiliation or adherence to non-Christian religions. The trajectory had been clear since partition – the 1926 census had shown the province 62.2/33.5 per cent Protestant/Catholic. For all that, the crossover was acutely felt – the more so when the political implications were reflected in elections to the Belfast assembly in the summer of 2022. Albeit helped by a split in the unionist vote, Sinn Féin emerged as the largest party, with the DUP trailing in second. The result put Michelle O'Neill, Sinn Féin vice-president, at the head of the Stormont executive as the province's first minister-designate. The DUP leader Jeffrey Donaldson blocked the establishment of the executive, citing his party's demand for further revision of the Brexit arrangements to dismantle entirely the border in the Irish Sea. The boycott was sustained for a year, but like his predecessors, Donaldson could not hold back the tide. Unionism had been confronted again with British indifference. The paradox was that in economic terms, Northern Ireland had secured a better deal from Brexit than had the rest of the United Kingdom. Business in the province retained the easy access to the European single market lost to competitors operating from the rest of the United Kingdom.

For the Republic the deal was an undoubted diplomatic victory. By holding firm against British bombast and threats it had protected a central pillar of the Good Friday Agreement from the impact of Brexit. The border remained open. The Irish, and European, identity of northern nationalists had been safeguarded. And the south's economy was now growing strongly again, in sharp contrast to the stagnation in Britain, where Brexit had provoked a slump in trade flows and overseas investment. But the advance of Sinn Féin was in its way as unsettling to mainstream politicians in the Republic as to unionists. As so many of their predecessors, the leaders of Fianna Fáil and Fine Gael had come to see Irish unity as a long-term goal – a distant aspiration. With the prospect always in the middle distance, there was little pressure to confront the changes it would inevitably bring to the Republic as much as to the north. Brexit and the arguments around it put the issue centre-stage. Sinn Féin's march towards power reached across the border from Northern Ireland. In the Republic's 2020 election it recorded a higher share of the vote than either Fianna Fáil or Fine Gael. In terms of seats in the Dáil it was in second place. Sinn Féin's political campaigning focused on issues closer to the immediate concerns of voters, such as the economy, housing and the condition of the health and other public services, but the party's organising mission was to reverse the partition of the island. Its leader in the Republic, Mary Lou McDonald, called for an all-Ireland vote within a decade. The unanswered question was: what would such unity look like?

11 PAST AND FUTURE

For a good part of a century, an end to partition was the organising emotion of much of Irish nationalism. By the early 2020s reunification of the twenty-six counties of the south with the six of the north had begun to look more plausible than at any time since the Anglo-Irish Treaty. And yet, plausible is not the same as probable. Even as nationalists began to imagine an Ireland at last whole and free, there was precious little sign of a consensus about what a united Ireland would actually look like. The lazy assumption had long been that Northern Ireland's Protestants could simply be absorbed, assimilated into the existing Republic. In truth, the disappearance of the border would create a different Ireland. Here the deal that brought peace to Northern Ireland carried within it a danger. Irish unity, the Good Friday Agreement said, required a simple majority of voters in both parts of the island to support it. Given the consistent backing in the south for removal of the border, this implied that all that was needed was a pro-unity vote in the north. It should also have been obvious to those who had paid attention to the events of the past century that binding the wounds of division between the two communities in Ireland could not be reduced to a question of electoral arithmetic. The 'consent' required to make a success of a thirty-two-county Irish state would require a lot more than a 51:49 per cent vote on one particular day. The nationalist politician Seamus Mallon sounded the warning: 'Just as Northern Ireland proved ungovernable because of the withdrawal of support of a sizeable proportion of its nationalist inhabitants, so an Ireland "united" in this way could prove ungovernable if a large proportion of its new unionist inhabitants were opposed to its very existence.'[1]

Reconciliation, the Irish essayist Hubert Butler wrote more than half a century earlier, demanded that the passage of time be left to work its magic.[2] Partition, Dublin's politicians still insisted at the time of his writing during the 1950s, was an act of English perfidy that must be undone by the English. For their part, the English ruling class preferred the see-no-evil approach that, as James Callaghan discovered, consigned the affairs of Northern Ireland to the department in the Home Office charged with alcohol licensing and taxi regulation. Butler took a long view. In time, he remarked, the border that divided Ireland would 'cease to become a menace and an anxiety'. Instead, 'Either it will become meaningless and will drop off painlessly like a strip of sticking plaster from a wound that has healed or else it will survive in some modified form as a definition which distinguishes but does not divide.' One way or another Ireland had to find an accommodation between nationalism and unionism with which both communities were comfortable.

Butler's was a hope widely shared but rarely publicly voiced among Ireland's elites. Unity was an article of faith for the two parties that emerged from the civil war, and partition a convenient stick with which to beat the English. The injustices of history demanded that on each occasion the Taoiseach met the British prime minister he demanded the return of the Republic's national territory. Yet there was an Augustinian quality to the protest. To adapt the prayer of the Catholic saint: 'Lord make us one nation, but not quite yet.' Nationalism was tinged with performance politics. If Britain was brazen in its neglect of its colonial possession, little was done in Dublin's corridors of power to prepare for political reconciliation. Before the Troubles, in Dublin, as in London, Northern Ireland was mostly out of sight.

PAST AND FUTURE

The low-level but bloody civil war that scarred the province over three decades looked like a rebuff to Butler's reasoned optimism. Partition, it turned out, had entrenched sectarianism. Unionists fought to defend their Protestant citadel and the PIRA picked up its guns in the cause of ending partition. In the exasperated expression of the constitutional nationalist John Hume, the future was handed to those who had never escaped the past. On one side of the ramparts stood unionists trapped in archaic supremacism. On the other side were the militant republicans who declared 'the British are to blame for everything – even their own [the PIRA's] atrocities'.

A quarter of a century after the Good Friday Agreement, the idea of unity has returned to the stage. The march of demographics in favour of the Catholic community in the north, the political success of Sinn Féin on both sides of the border and the constitutional uncertainties in Britain caused by Brexit have injected an unfamiliar immediacy into the debate. Post-Brexit, the economics seem compelling. Ireland remains part of the European Union. So, in all but name, does Northern Ireland. Goods flow freely over the Irish border. Yet now they must be checked before they cross the Irish Sea from Great Britain to Northern Ireland. But where is the offer that might persuade unionists that their identity would be respected in a thirty-two-county Ireland?

By 2024 the seemingly impregnable majority bequeathed to unionism by the Government of Ireland Act of 1920 had disappeared. Among those in Northern Ireland who identified themselves by confessional choice, Catholics outnumbered Protestants. The shift saw unionism lose its majority among MPs elected to the United Kingdom parliament, as well as at Stormont. In the 2024 general election that saw Rishi Sunak's Conservatives swept from office by Labour's Keir Starmer, Sinn Féin won more seats at Westminster than any other Northern Ireland party. The province's first minister was drawn from the party whose leaders had not so long ago carried the caskets of the PIRA's Volunteers at republican funerals. The demographic crossover did not create an automatic majority for nationalism. The province's non-sectarian Alliance Party draws support from Catholics and Protestants alike. Presented with the choice, a significant minority of Catholics back staying in the union. But the pro-union majority is narrowing. On the present trajectory it could disappear within a decade or so.

For some nationalists it has all been happening too fast. You do not have to search far in Dublin to find politicians and policy-makers clinging on to Butler's formula that the wound must be allowed to heal. The unspoken concern is that circumstance, what Harold Macmillan called 'events', might force the pace towards a vote on unification. After all, there is now a road map. The Good Friday Agreement set out for the first time the mechanics: the support of majorities south and north, expressed in concurrent referendums. Britain was not obliged to back unity, but nor could it obstruct it. Presented with credible evidence that a majority in the province favoured scrapping the border, a British secretary of state would be obliged to hold the vote. The Republic's backing is considered a foregone conclusion – about two-thirds of voters have habitually told the opinion pollsters they want the restoration to the national territory of the six counties. Sinn Féin, in power at Stormont, has pushed the issue of unity on to the Republic's political agenda. The erstwhile political wing of the PIRA has reinvented itself as a populist party of the left, but its organising purpose remains Irish unity.

The Republic, it should be said, is a more hospitable place for unionists. The Gaelic mysticism that prompted Seán MacEntee to warn Éamon de Valera that 'every bigot and killjoy' in the south was 'doing his damnedest here to keep them [Protestants] out' was long gone. Emigration has been replaced by immigration. A nation that had shut itself off from the world is now home to scores of nationalities. Kiltimagh boasts Chinese, Indian and Italian cuisine. Maestro's, on Main Street, advertises itself as 'Irish European'. The evisceration of the authority of the Church hierarchy – mostly self-inflicted – and the embrace of liberal attitudes to marriage and divorce, abortion and gender has bequeathed a society as much secular as Catholic. Even Ian Paisley would have struggled in 2024 to call Dublin rule 'Rome rule'. Ironically, the rigid social conservatism that marked the early decades of the Free State is now more often found in the north than the south, and among Protestants more than Catholics. Citizens in Northern Ireland need no longer fear that scrapping the border would drag them into an economic backwater. To the contrary, recent decades have seen economic fortunes reversed. Productivity, employment and investment are all higher in the Republic than in the north. So too are living standards. Dublin's commuter belt spills over the border to towns in the north where housing is cheaper. The Republic is content in its new identity as a modern European state. 'What makes you think we want those people from the Falls Road [Catholic Belfast] in our country?' I once heard an aide to Bertie Ahern remark caustically, in an acknowledgement that unity would carry its own dangers.

The English view of Ireland, veering between condescension, contempt, frustration and indifference (and entirely separate from the much warmer sentiments expressed by Brits towards the Irish people), has lagged far behind the economic and social transformation in the Republic. Attitudes towards the north have not much changed. The successors to the senior Whitehall officials who concluded as long ago as the 1970s that few members of parliament would be 'sad' to lose Northern Ireland reached the same conclusion fifty years later. Politicians on the left instinctively recoil from the record of colonialism, and just as they supported the unwinding of empire in Africa and beyond, they tend to sympathise with the nationalist cause. Few, if any, though, would go as far as Harold Wilson in suggesting the province should be pushed out of the United Kingdom. Keen as it has been to rebuild a good relationship between London and Dublin after the depredations of the Conservatives, Keir Starmer's Labour government (in power from July 2024) has been studiously neutral about Irish unity. On the political right, a handful of Conservatives still hold a candle for unionism for reasons of imperial nostalgia and ideological reflex, much as they insist on the indelible 'Britishness' of Gibraltar and the Falkland Islands. The lesson of the Brexit negotiations, however, was that although they styled themselves the Conservative and Unionist Party, the Conservatives' commitment to the province was now declaratory.

Much less clear is whether Ireland can mark out a straight road to unity and how the journey might be safely navigated. Most obviously, not all Catholics are nationalists. Nationalism in the Republic has its own ambivalences. For all the historical and emotional pull, Northern Ireland per se has remained largely in the Republic's peripheral vision as the latter has grappled with the challenges as well as the successes of modernity. Sinn Féin's emergence as a political force in the Republic should not be mistaken for an upsurge of enthusiasm to throw out the Brits. Its most potent messages, rooted in the political discontent left by the global financial crash, have been about housing shortages for the young and the failures of the health and welfare systems. Fianna Fáil and Fine Gael lost their iron grip on power not because they abandoned nationalist dreams but because of the severe economic hardships that followed the global financial crash. Broad popular support for the idea of unity sits alongside indications that most have yet to think deeply about the consequences. Leo Varadkar, the leader of Fine Gael and former Taoiseach, acknowledged as much when he called during the summer of 2024 for the nation's politicians to begin to make it a practical policy 'objective' rather than an aspiration. And in the November 2024 general election the governing coalition parties renewed their historical commitment. They did so with caution. As long as the ambition is distant, the awkward practicalities can be set to one side. Politicians in Dublin are acutely aware that voters calling for the border to be scrapped also set themselves against any significant change in the way the nation is governed.

The easy answer is to say that Irish unification would be like that in Germany at the end of the Cold War. The six counties would be added to the twenty-six, and life would continue much as before in a new unitary state. The comparison, however, does not withstand cursory scrutiny. East Germany was separated from the Federal Republic not as a result of internal cleavages but because the Soviet Union built a wall. Citizens of the German Democratic Republic did not claim Russian over German identity. When the Berlin Wall came down, they flooded westwards. Entirely absent was the confessional and cultural divide that set Northern Ireland apart from the Republic. Even so, German unification has proved anything but seamless. The vast resources poured by the federal government into reconstruction in the former German Democratic Republic have failed to bridge a yawning psychological divide between east and west. It is no accident that the right-wing populism of the Alternative for Germany party has taken root in the old GDR.

There is nothing resembling a national consensus on the constitutional and political architecture of a united Ireland. The ARINS project, a research programme established in 2020 by the Royal Irish Academy in collaboration with the University of Notre Dame to explore Ireland's constitutional and political future, has illuminated the tensions and complexities. Its first annual surveys, published in the *Irish Times*, record that almost two-thirds of voters in the Republic would back unification in a referendum, with the remainder roughly divided between those opposed and self-declared 'don't knows'. Pro-unity respondents, however, are reluctant to accept that this would demand any compromises with unionism. There is no enthusiasm for changes to the constitution, and hostility to the idea of a new flag to replace the Republic's tricolour or a new anthem to acknowledge the British allegiance of what would still be a sizeable community in the unified state. One respondent to an ARINS survey offered a commonplace view: 'I just figured they join us and that would be that.' This is scarcely a compelling pitch to unionists in the north who cherish their British and Protestant traditions.

The economic and social consequences of unity are likewise largely unexplored. Northern Ireland, as British prime ministers have often complained, is a financial burden on the British Exchequer. Responsibility for the £10 billion-plus annual subvention to Stormont from the British Treasury would pass to Dublin. So too would the cost of equalising the levels of pension and other social benefits in the province with those prevailing in the Republic. Who would pay? What would a single Irish welfare system look like? Would the south import the British National Health Service or would the north lose it? A report from the Dublin-based Institute for International and European Affairs has estimated that the overall cost to the Republic of unification could amount to about €20 billion annually – a figure that would imply a sharp fall in living standards. That is probably a worst case and there are countervailing arguments. By leaving both parts of Ireland within the ambit of the European single market, Brexit has reinforced the logic of closer economic integration between north and south. Unity would bring productivity and competitive gains. And the Dublin government could expect to agree transitional arrangements with Britain to phase in the costs. In the long term, a united Ireland might well be a richer Ireland. But the initial economic shock that would be delivered by removing the border cannot simply be wished away.

It's unclear also how the British would behave. By introducing the British question into Irish politics the elimination of the border would change irrevocably the nature of the state. The new Ireland would count about one million Protestants, many, if not most, professing allegiance to Britain, among a population of a little over seven million. Westminster might expect a say in the treatment of the unionist community, just as Dublin now speaks for nationalists in the province. In any event, under the terms of the Good Friday Agreement these 'Brits' in Ireland would inherit by right all the guarantees around identity, equality and civil rights now afforded to the north's Catholic nationalists. They would be promised 'the principles of full respect for, and equality of, civil, political, social, and cultural rights, of freedom from discrimination for all citizens, and of parity of esteem and of just and equal treatment for the identity, ethos, and aspirations of both communities'. They would have the right to remain British citizens or to assume both nationalities. If they so chose, they could presumably continue to march each summer in celebration of Protestant victories in centuries gone by. It is hard to see how such provisions would sit easily inside an Irish constitution that starts with the preamble 'In the name of the Most Holy Trinity, from whom is all authority' and goes on to afford a special place for the Catholic Church in the life of the nation.

Much as the present political discourse tends to offer a binary choice between the status quo and a 'they-join-us-and-that-will-be-that' unitary Irish state, it was not always so. Look back over the past century and several different models of unity have been considered by political leaders on both sides of the Irish Sea.

When Lloyd George's government drafted the Government of Ireland Act of 1920 it foresaw (eventually) an Ireland with two centres of power – Dublin and Belfast – with a Council of Ireland sitting above them to affirm Ireland's essential unity. Michael Collins's Free State's constitution made room for such an arrangement, leaving Stormont in place but transferring to Dublin powers reserved to Westminster. De Valera's replacement constitution did likewise. In his contacts with the British before and during the Second World War, the Taoiseach was clear that Northern Ireland could hold on to its control of domestic affairs through a parliament at Stormont as long as sovereignty was transferred from Dublin to London. His irresolvable argument with Churchill was about sovereignty and neutrality rather than the political architecture.

Irish leaders have also explored the choices beyond the unitary and two-parliament models. The New Ireland Forum, the public consultation undertaken by Garret FitzGerald that so irritated Margaret Thatcher during the 1980s, floated the possibility of a federal or confederal thirty-two-county state in which northern Protestants retained a significant degree of local autonomy. It also imagined, at least as a starting point, the possibility of shared political authority in the province between Britain and the Republic. Nationalists might also look further afield to federal systems such as those in Germany or Switzerland.

The prior question is how to describe, beyond the arithmetic, what is meant by the 'consent' principle central to the reconciliation that ended the war. Nationalists say this was settled in the

Good Friday Agreement. In legal terms, they are indisputably correct. The referendums north and south provided for in the accord are to be decided by simple majorities. All nationalists need do is secure the votes of 50 per cent plus one in Northern Ireland and the Good Friday bargain would be kept. And yet, how well would the new united Ireland function if hundreds of thousands of resentful citizens were unwilling to accept the transfer of sovereignty to Dublin? Would a vote so closely won, and one in which by definition unionists overwhelmingly rejected citizenship of the Republic, confer indisputable legitimacy on the new state? 'Few southern Irishmen', Butler wrote in his essay, 'would wish to absorb Ulster like greenfly invading a neglected tree.' For good reason: 'Ulster would no longer be of value to Ireland if she were robbed of her rich history, her varied traditions.'[3] The more decentralised the proposed structures in a united Ireland, the fewer the likely fears among unionists of losing their identity. Whatever the model, unity secured by a narrow numerical majority would struggle to underwrite a stable, prosperous Ireland.

Closer to a referendum, the practical advantages and drawbacks would test the solidity of the nationalist vote on both sides of the border. A cold look at the implications for living standards, taxation and public services might well mute enthusiasm. One of the striking results of the ARINS surveys is that many pro-unity citizens in the Republic do not rank unity as a burning imperative. Half would 'happily accept' a referendum outcome that saw the north remain within the United Kingdom. Another 40 per cent say that, unhappy as they might be, they could live with such a decision. Intriguingly, some 59 per cent of Catholics in the north say they would be content with a vote for the status quo. Only 6 per cent of Catholics in the south and 4 per cent in the north say they would find a lost referendum 'impossible to accept'. The lines are drawn more sharply among unionists. Nearly a quarter of Protestants say they would find it all but impossible to come to terms with a decision to leave the United Kingdom. Nationalists, of course, could choose to be ruled by the heart rather than the head. The Brexit vote, though it is an inexact parallel, showed what can happen when emotional impulses push aside political realities and a sober assessment of national interests.

Much as the underlying trends point in the nationalists' favour, support for unity as yet has fallen short of the sustained shift in public opinion needed to persuade a British secretary of state to call a referendum. The snapshot surveys of the ARINS project in 2022 and 2023 suggest that the overwhelming majority of Protestants back staying within the United Kingdom. About a fifth of Catholics say they would back the union. The mistake for nationalists would be to set as their overriding ambition winning over this Catholic cohort. The temptation is clear. This might be enough to meet the terms of the Good Friday Agreement. It would surely also fall short, however, of securing the loser's consent needed to make a success of a united Ireland. It would risk, as Mallon warned, a transfer of the sectarian discontent that has scarred Northern Ireland to the new thirty-two-county state.

Northern Ireland's nationalists and unionists have stopped fighting each other, but it would be hard to say they are properly at peace. Schoolchildren remain segregated and communities are separated by the euphemistically named peace walls built during the Troubles. Confessional affiliation often remains the first point of reference. Ironically, the political arrangements at Stormont, designed to entrench the rights of each community, unconsciously perpetuate their differences.

Unionists such as David Trimble understood that Northern Ireland will remain part of the United Kingdom only if they persuade enough Catholics in the province that they are better off with the status quo. Likewise, a united Ireland will prosper only if nationalists persuade sufficient unionists that their identity and Protestant faith will be fully respected within a united Ireland. Britain cannot abdicate its role here.

Generations of British politicians have decided to forget Northern Ireland. Others have been tempted by the notion of simply cutting and running. The lesson of the past century, however, has been that the former colonial power cannot shrug off its responsibilities if the Irish question in Britain is replaced by the British question in Ireland. For as long as the north remains part of the United Kingdom, the British government has an unavoidable role in translating the absence of war into reconciliation between the two communities. In the event of a vote for unity, the task of making a success of a new constitutional settlement would fall on the London as well as the Dublin government. Politicians at Westminster should have learned by now that things go wrong in Ireland when they look the other way. And who knows? Constitutional upheaval in Ireland might persuade the English to look again at their relationship with Scotland and Wales. A commonwealth of the Isles?

Ireland has become less divided. It will escape its troubled past, as F. S. L. Lyons said, when it ceases to live in it. Much as unity now looks possible, even likely, during the coming decades, the mistake would be a leap in the dark – a headlong and, in the case of unionism, deeply resented rush onto unprepared ground. If Irish nationalism is to achieve its goal, the first step, in the phrase of Jonathan Powell, will be to 'demystify' the constitutional options. Unionism made a grievous error in imagining that it could forever exercise hegemony over the nationalist population of Northern Ireland. Nationalism would make an equally bad mistake in thinking that the interests and identity of the province's unionists could be easily assimilated. Majoritarianism has been tested to destruction in Ireland.

Partition may have the look of an anachronism, but ripping off the sticking plaster prematurely is the wrong answer. The numerical disappearance of the Protestant majority in Northern Ireland is not the foundation for a new Irish state. Receiving his Nobel Peace Prize, David Trimble said that unionism had built a 'cold house' for Catholics. Nationalists should avoid the same mistake. The culture of mutual respect for Ireland's two traditions sought long ago by Yeats is still a work in progress. The wound has yet to heal.

SHORT BIBLIOGRAPHY

Forests have been torn down in the task of chronicling the long, difficult history of Britain and Ireland since Norman warriors crossed the Irish Sea during the twelfth century. The official archives in London, Dublin and Washington are piled high with documents charting the more recent course of the conflict, the tragedy, diplomacy and, eventually, the quest for peace that are the focus of this book.

So below is a summary of other readings I have enjoyed and found useful in the research for this book. The thoughts, and suggestions, are of necessity incomplete. There is a lifetime of reading on offer to those seeking to dig deeper into the procession of events – Cromwell's plantations, recurring Irish rebellion, the Great Famine, Home Rule, the Easter Rising, the Anglo-Irish and civil wars, partition and the Troubles – that leap from the pages of this tumultuous relationship.

Turning to the past century, it is impossible to understand how Ireland and its leaders thought about Britain and the world without delving often and deep into the superb collection of official documents on Irish foreign policy edited and assembled in print and online by the Royal Irish Academy and National Archives of Ireland. Harder to navigate, the UK National Archives at Kew provide another essential window into history as it happened and a useful antidote against seeing the past through the lens of the present. The Cain Archive is an indispensable source for events in Northern Ireland, as is the Margaret Thatcher Foundation for the Lady's always robust views.

SHORT BIBLIOGRAPHY

There are so many good histories and revealing memoirs that it is invidious to single out particular choices. That said, Roy Foster's *Modern Ireland* is a vital starting point and Diarmaid Ferriter's several books on the events of the past century are insightful as well as comprehensive. Ronan Fanning's account of the decade surrounding the Easter Rising and partition is as gripping as it is authoritative. Those looking for an insight into British condescension and indifference should pick up John Peck's memoir of his time as ambassador in Dublin. David Goodall provides the inside story on the Anglo-Irish Agreement. The facsimile Irish newspapers reproduced in *The Revolution Papers* are a reminder, like the archives, that perspectives change. Frank Pakenham (Lord Longford) offers a ringside seat at the negotiations for the 1921 Anglo-Irish Treaty. Fast-forwarding, Stephen Collins and Tony Connelly have produced excellent accounts of how Irish governments handled Brexit. Tim Pat Coogan's biography of Michael Collins is gripping. Hubert Butler's essays, published as *Grandmother and Wolfe Tone*, are a journey into wisdom. Cecil Woodham-Smith's *The Great Hunger* is as fresh today as half a century ago. Fintan O'Toole's personal journey in *We Don't Know Ourselves* tells brilliantly the story of modern Ireland. David McKittrick and David McVea do likewise in making sense of the Troubles.

Websites

Cain Archive: cain.ulster.ac.uk/bibdbs/index.html
Hansard: hansard.parliament.uk
John F. Kennedy Presidential Library: jfklibrary.org
Margaret Thatcher Foundation: margaretthatcher.org
National Archives of Ireland: www.nationalarchives.ie
National Archives, Kew: nationalarchives.gov.uk
National Security Archive, Washington: nsarchive.gwu.edu
Office of the Historian, State Department: history.state.gov
RIA/NAI, Documents on Irish Foreign Policy: difp.ie
Royal Irish Academy: ria.ie
US National Archives: archives.gov

SHORT BIBLIOGRAPHY

Books

Ahern, Bertie, and Aldous Richard, *The Autobiography* (London, 2009)
Andrew, Christopher, *The Defence of the Realm: The Authorized History of MI5* (London, 2009)
Bartlett, Thomas, *Ireland: A History* (Cambridge, 2010)
Bew, Paul, *Ancestral Voices in Irish Politics: Judging Dillon and Parnell* (Oxford, 2023)
——, *Churchill and Ireland* (Oxford, 2016)
——, *Ireland: The Politics of Enmity 1789–2006* (Oxford, 2007)
—— (ed.), *A Yankee in de Valera's Ireland: The Memoir of David Gray* (Dublin, 2012)
Blair, Tony, *A Journey* (London, 2011)
Bowman, John, *De Valera and the Ulster Question 1917–1973* (Oxford, 1989)
Butler, Hubert, *Grandmother and Wolfe Tone* (Dublin, 1990)
Callaghan, James, *A House Divided: The Dilemma of Northern Ireland* (London, 1973)
——, *Time and Chance* (London, 1987)
Campbell, John, *Roy Jenkins: A Well-Rounded Life* (London, 2014)
Carroll, Rory, *Killing Thatcher: The IRA Manhunt and the Long War on the Crown* (London, 2023)
Catterall, Peter (ed.), *The Macmillan Diaries*, Vol. 2, *Prime Minister and After* (London, 2011)
Churchill, Winston, *The World Crisis*, Vol. 4, *The Aftermath* (London, 1929)
Collins, Stephen, *Ireland's Call: Navigating Brexit* (Dublin, 2022)
Colville, John, *The Fringes of Power: Downing Street Diaries 1939–1955* (London, 1985)
Connelly, Tony, *Brexit and Ireland: The Dangers, the Opportunities, and the Inside Story of the Irish Response* (London, 2023)
Connolly, S. J. (ed.), *Oxford Companion to Irish History* (Oxford, 2004)
Coogan, Tim Pat, *The IRA* (London, 2002)
——, *Michael Collins* (London, 1991)
Cooney, John, *John Charles McQuaid: Ruler of Catholic Ireland* (Dublin, 1999)
Crowe, Catriona, et al. (eds), *Documents on Irish Foreign Policy*, vols 1–13 (Dublin, 1998–)
Daly, Mary E. (ed.), *Brokering the Good Friday Agreement* (Dublin, 2019)
De Rynck, Stefaan, *Inside the Deal: How the EU Got Brexit Done* (Newcastle, 2023)
Deane, Seamus, *Small World: Ireland 1978–2018* (Cambridge, 2021)
Dolan, Anne, and William Murphy, *Michael Collins: The Man and the Revolution* (Cork, 2018)
Donoghue, David, *One Good Day: My Journey to the Good Friday Agreement* (Dublin, 2022)

SHORT BIBLIOGRAPHY

Donoughue, Bernard, *Downing Street Diary: With Harold Wilson in No. 10* (London, 2005)
English, Richard, *Armed Struggle: The History of the IRA* (London, 2012)
———, *Irish Freedom: The History of Nationalism in Ireland* (London, 2007)
Fanning, Ronan, *Fatal Path: British Government and Irish Revolution 1910–1922* (London, 2013)
———, *Éamon de Valera: A Will to Power* (London, 2016)
Farren, Sean (ed.), *John Hume: In His Own Words* (Dublin, 2018)
Ferriter, Diarmaid, *Between Two Hells: The Irish Civil War* (London, 2022)
———, *The Border: The Legacy of a Century of Anglo-Irish Politics* (London, 2019)
———, *The Revelation of Ireland 1995–2020* (London, 2024)
———, *The Transformation of Ireland 1900–2000* (London, 2005)
FitzGerald, Garret, *All in a Life: An Autobiography* (Dublin, 1991)
Foster, Peter, *What Went Wrong with Brexit* (Edinburgh, 2023)
Foster, Roy, *Luck and the Irish: A Brief History of Change, c.1970–2000* (London, 2008)
———, *Modern Ireland 1600–1972* (London, 1989)
———, *Vivid Faces: The Revolutionary Generation in Ireland 1890–1923* (London, 2015)
Gibney, John, *A Short History of Ireland 1500–2000* (London, 2013)
Godson, Dean, *Himself Alone: David Trimble and the Ordeal of Unionism* (London, 2004)
Goodall, David, *The Making of the Anglo-Irish Agreement of 1985: A Memoir*, ed. Frank Sheridan (Dublin, 2021)
Grey, Chris, *Brexit Unfolded* (London, 2023)
Haines, Joe, *The Politics of Power* (London, 1977)
Hayden, Tom (ed.), *Irish Hunger: Personal Reflections on the Legacy of the Famine* (Dublin, 1997)
Healy, John, *No One Shouted Stop* (Achill, 1988)
Heath, Edward, *The Course of My Life* (London, 1998)
Hennessy, Peter, *Having It So Good: Britain in the Early 1950s* (London, 2006)
———, *Winds of Change: Britain in the Early Sixties* (London, 2019)
Howe, Geoffrey, *Conflict of Loyalty* (London, 1994)
Hurd, Douglas, *Memoirs* (London, 2003)
Jackson, Alvin, *Home Rule: An Irish History 1800–2000* (London, 2003)
Jeffery, Keith, *Field Marshal Sir Henry Wilson: A Political Soldier* (Oxford, 2006)
Jenkins, Roy, *Churchill* (London, 2017)
———, *A Life at the Centre* (London, 1992)
Jones, Thomas, *Whitehall Diary*, Vol. 3, *Ireland 1918–1925*, ed. Keith Middlemas (London, 1971)
Jordan, Anthony, *W. T. Cosgrave 1880–1965: Founder of Modern Ireland* (Dublin, 2006)

SHORT BIBLIOGRAPHY

Joyce, James, *A Portrait of the Artist as a Young Man* (1916; repr. London, 2000)
Kavanagh, Dennis, and Anthony Seldon, *The Major Effect* (London, 1994)
Lenihan, Conor, *Albert Reynolds: Risk Taker for Peace* (Newbridge, 2021)
Loughlin, James, *Ulster Unionism and British Identity since 1885* (London, 1995)
Lyons, F. S. L., *Ireland since the Famine* (London, 1985)
McCullagh, David, *De Valera: Rule 1932–1975* (Dublin, 2018)
MacDonagh, Oliver, *States of Mind: A Study of Irish Conflict, 1780–1980* (London, 1983)
McKittrick, David, and David McVea, *Making Sense of the Troubles* (London, 2012)
Major, John, *The Autobiography* (London, 2000)
Mallie, Eamonn, and David McKittrick, *Endgame in Ireland* (London, 2001)
———, *The Fight for Peace: The Secret Story Behind the Irish Peace Process* (London, 1996)
Mansergh, Martin, *The Legacy of History* (Cork, 2003)
Meagher, Kevin, *A United Ireland: Why Unification Is Inevitable and How It Will Come About* (London, 2022)
———, *What a Bloody Awful Country: Northern Ireland's Century of Division* (London, 2021)
Millar, Frank, *David Trimble: The Price of Peace* (Dublin, 2004)
Mitchell, George, *Making Peace* (California, 2001)
Moloney, Ed, *A Secret History of the IRA* (London, 2002)
Moore, Charles, *Margaret Thatcher*, Vol. 1, *Not for Turning* (London, 2013)
———, *Margaret Thatcher*, Vol. 2, *Everything She Wants* (London, 2015)
Mowlam, Mo, *Momentum: The Struggle for Peace, Politics and the People* (London, 2002)
Mullin, Chris, *A Walk-On Part: Diaries 1994–1999* (London, 2011)
Needham, Richard, *Battling for Peace* (Co. Down, 1998)
———, *One Man, Two Worlds* (Newtownards, 2021)
O'Brien, Conor Cruise, *States of Ireland* (London, 2015)
O'Clery, Connor, *The Greening of the White House* (Dublin, 1996)
O'Connor, Steven, and Ian Kenneally Ian (eds), *The Revolution Papers* (Dublin, 2015–18)
O'Leary, Brendan, *Making Sense of a United Ireland* (London, 2022)
O'Toole, Fintan, *Heroic Failure: Brexit and the Politics of Pain* (London, 2019)
———, *We Don't Know Ourselves: A Personal History of Ireland since 1958* (London, 2021)
Ohlmeyer, Jane, *Making Empire: Ireland, Imperialism and the Early Modern World* (Oxford, 2023)
Pakenham, Frank (Lord Longford), *Peace by Ordeal: The Negotiation of the Anglo-Irish Treaty, 1921* (London, 1992)
Patten, Chris, *Not Quite the Diplomat: Home Truths about World Affairs* (London, 2005)

SHORT BIBLIOGRAPHY

Patterson, Glenn, *The Last Irish Question: Will Six into Twenty-Six Ever Go?* (London, 2021)
Patterson, Henry, *Ireland since 1939: The Persistence of Conflict* (Dublin, 2006)
Peck, John, *Dublin from Downing Street* (Dublin, 1978)
Powell, Jonathan, *Great Hatred, Little Room: Making Peace in Northern Ireland* (London, 2008)
———, *Talking to Terrorists: How to End Armed Conflicts* (London, 2014)
Price, Dominic, *The Flame and the Candle: War in Mayo 1919–1924* (Cork, 2012)
Reynolds, Albert, *My Autobiography* (Dublin, 2010)
Seldon, Anthony, and Raymond Newell, *Johnson at 10* (London, 2023)
Shearman, Hugh, *Anglo-Irish Relations* (London, 1948)
Spencer, Graham (ed.), *The British and Peace in Northern Ireland* (Cambridge, 2015)
Stephens, Philip, *Tony Blair* (New York, 2004)
———, *Britain Alone: The Path from Suez to Brexit* (London, 2021)
Stewart, Anthony, *The Narrow Ground: Aspects of Ulster, 1609–1969* (Dublin, 1997)
Taylor, Peter, *The Provos: The IRA and Sinn Fein* (London, 1997)
Thatcher, Margaret, *The Downing Street Years* (London, 1993)
Tobin, Fergal, *The Irish Difference: A Tumultuous History of Ireland's Breakup with Britain* (London, 2022)
Tóibín, Colm, *Bad Blood: A Walk Along the Irish Border* (London, 2001)
Townshend, Charles, *The Partition: Ireland Divided 1885–1925* (London, 2021)
———, *The Republic: The Fight for Irish Independence, 1918–2023* (London, 2013)
Woodham-Smith, Cecil, *The Great Hunger: Ireland 1845–1849* (London, 1987)

NOTES

Prologue

1. Royal Irish Academy/National Archive (Ireland) (hereafter RIA/NAI), Documents on Irish Foreign Policy, No. 29 NAI 2006/39.
2. National Archives, Kew, FCO 160/191/31.
3. Jonathan Powell, *Great Hatred, Little Room: Making Peace in Northern Ireland* (London, 2008), p. 36.
4. Conor Cruise O'Brien, *States of Ireland* (London, 2015), p. 27.
5. RIA/NAI, Documents on Irish Foreign Policy, No. 29 NAI 2006/39.

1 A Divided Peace

1. Thomas Jones, *Whitehall Diary*, ed. Keith Middlemas, Vol. 3, *Ireland 1918–1925* (London, 1971), p. 181.
2. Quoted in Diarmaid Ferriter, *The Border: The Legacy of a Century of Anglo-Irish Politics* (London, 2019), p. 9.
3. Quoted in Roy Foster, *Modern Ireland 1600–1972* (London, 1989), p. 431.
4. www.nidirect.gov.uk/articles/about-ulster-covenant.
5. Keith Jeffery, *Field Marshal Sir Henry Wilson: A Political Soldier* (Oxford, 2006), pp. 122, 273.
6. Steven O'Connor and Ian Kenneally (eds), *The Revolution Papers* (Dublin, 2015–18), no. 1.
7. Quoted in Roy Foster, *Vivid Faces: The Revolutionary Generation in Ireland 1890–1923* (London, 2015), p. 260.
8. *Irish Independent*, 26 April–4 May 1916.
9. Quoted in Foster, *Vivid Faces*, p. 260.
10. Ronan Fanning, *Fatal Path: British Government and Irish Revolution 1910–1922* (London, 2013), p. 152.
11. Jones, *Whitehall Diary*, Vol. 3, p. 150.
12. Ibid., p. 69.
13. Quoted in Fanning, *Fatal Path*, p. 211.
14. Ibid., p. 21.
15. Ibid., p. 60.
16. Jones, *Whitehall Diary*, Vol. 3, p. 16.
17. RIA/NAI, Documents on Irish Foreign Policy, No. 141. Reprinted from *Official Correspondence Relating to the Peace Negotiations June–September 1921* (Dublin, 1921).

NOTES

18 RIA/NAI, Documents on Irish Foreign Policy, No. 146. NAI DFA ES Box 27 File 158.
19 Jones, *Whitehall Diary*, Vol. 3, p. 83.
20 Ibid., pp. 85–7.
21 RIA/NAI, Documents on Irish Foreign Policy, No. 147. Reprinted from *Official Correspondence Relating to the Peace Negotiations*.
22 Speech to the Dáil, 19 December 1921.
23 Jones, *Whitehall Diary*, Vol. 3, p. 160.
24 Ibid., pp. 259–65.

2 Best of Enemies

1 Quoted in Frank Pakenham, *Peace by Ordeal: The Negotiation of the Anglo-Irish Treaty, 1921* (London, 1992), pp. 111–12.
2 Quoted in Paul Bew, *Churchill and Ireland* (Oxford, 2016), p. 95.
3 *Hansard*, House of Commons, 15 December 1921.
4 Bew, *Churchill and Ireland*, p. 103.
5 Quoted in Roy Jenkins, *Churchill* (London, 2017), p. 363.
6 Quoted in Pakenham, *Peace by Ordeal*, p. 103.
7 Ibid., p. 111.
8 Quoted in Tim Pat Coogan, *Michael Collins* (London, 1991), p. 164.
9 Jones, *Whitehall Diary*, Vol. 3, p. 83.
10 Quoted in Coogan, *Michael Collins*, p. 242.
11 RIA/NAI, Documents on Irish Foreign Policy, No. 147. Reprinted from *Official Correspondence Relating to the Peace Negotiations*.
12 Dáil debate, 19 December 1921.
13 Ibid.
14 Quoted in Coogan, *Michael Collins*, p. 226.
15 *Hansard*, House of Commons, 15 February 1922.
16 Ibid.
17 Ibid.
18 Ibid.
19 Ibid.
20 National Archives, CAB 24/136/14, 30 March 1922
21 Quoted in Bew, *Churchill and Ireland*, p. 129.
22 Jones, *Whitehall Diary*, Vol. 3, p. 215.
23 Quoted in Coogan, *Michael Collins*, p. 256.

3 A Border of the Mind

1 *Irish Times*, 23 August 1922.
2 Diarmaid Ferriter, *Between Two Hells: The Irish Civil War* (London, 2022), p. 95.
3 Foster, *Modern Ireland*, p. 516.

NOTES

4 RIA/NAI, Documents on Irish Foreign Policy, No. 218, NAI DE 4/5/13.
5 NAI No. 27 Cab 1/7.
6 Quoted in John Bowman, *De Valera and the Ulster Question 1917–1973* (Oxford, 1989), p. 110.
7 RIA/NAI, Documents on Irish Foreign Policy, No. 88, UCDA P150/2349.
8 RIA/NAI, Documents on Irish Foreign Policy, No. 28, NAI DT S10389.
9 *Hansard*, House of Commons, 5 May 1938.
10 Ferriter, *The Border*, p. 10.
11 For a vivid description, see Colm Tóibín, *Bad Blood: A Walk Along the Irish Border* (London, 2001).
12 Ferriter, *The Border*, p. 20.
13 National Archives, CAB 24/134/73, March 1922.
14 Quoted in Ferriter, *The Border*, p. 32.
15 Quoted in ibid., p. 41.
16 RIA/NAI, Documents on Irish Foreign Policy, No. 154, TNA DO 130/170.
17 RIA/NAI, Documents on Irish Foreign Policy, No. 155, UCDA P150/2632.
18 RIA/NAI, Documents on Irish Foreign Policy, No. 160, NAI DFA 305/392.
19 RIA/NAI, Documents on Irish Foreign Policy, No. 588, NAI DFA Secretary's Files, A2.
20 RIA/NAI, Documents on Irish Foreign Policy, No. 196, NAI DFA Secretary's Files, A2.
21 National Archives, CAB WP (40) 233, 29 June 1940.
22 RIA/NAI, Documents on Irish Foreign Policy, No. 208, NAI DFA Secretary's Files, p. 13.
23 National Archives, CAB WP (40) 251, 5 July 1940.
24 RIA/NAI, DOC 147, 10/8/1921, reprinted from official correspondence relating to the peace negotiations, June–Sept. 1921.
25 RIA/NAI, Documents on Irish Foreign Policy, No. 88, UCDA P150/2349.
26 RIA/NAI, Documents on Irish Foreign Policy, No. 68, NAI DFA Secretary's Files, P12/14/1.
27 RIA/NAI, Documents on Irish Foreign Policy, No. 350, UCDA P150/2571.
28 National Archives, CAB WM (39), 66th conclusions.
29 RIA/NAI, Documents on Irish Foreign Policy, No. 76, NAI DFA Secretary's Files, A3.
30 National Archives, CAB WP (44) 156, 10 March 1944.
31 RIA/NAI, Documents on Irish Foreign Policy, No. 4, UCDA P150 2676.
32 National Archives, CAB CP (45) 152, 7 September 1945.
33 Cited in *Irish Independent*, 27 January 1999.

NOTES

4 De Valera's Ireland

1. John Healy, *No One Shouted Stop* (Achill, 1988).
2. 'From the Archives', *Irish Times*, 19 September 2015.
3. Quoted in David McCullagh, *De Valera Rule 1932–1975* (Dublin, 2018), p. 46.
4. RIA/NAI, Documents on Irish Foreign Policy, No. 8, UCDA P 150/2701.
5. John Cooney, *John Charles McQuaid: Ruler of Catholic Ireland* (Dublin, 1999).
6. Foster, *Modern Ireland*, p. 538.
7. RIA/NAI, Documents on Irish Foreign Policy, No. 461, NAID T5 82 B.
8. 'Irish Emigration Patterns and Citizens Abroad', https://www.dfa.ie/media/dfa/alldfawebsitemedia/newspress/publications/ministersbrief-june2017/1--Global-Irish-in-Numbers.pdf.
9. For an interesting account of the statistics and political debate, see Henrietta Ewart, 'Caring for Migrants: Policy Responses to Irish Migration to England, 1940–1972', PhD thesis, Warwick University, 2012.
10. RIA/NAI, Documents on Irish Foreign Policy, No. 25, NAI DFA 6/402/222.
11. McCullagh, *De Valera Rule*, p. 324.
12. RIA/NAI, Documents on Irish Foreign Policy, No. 104, NAI DFA A/5/313 31D.
13. RIA/NAI, Documents on Irish Foreign Policy, No. 161, NAI DFA 417/33.
14. RIA/NAI, Documents on Irish Foreign Policy, No. 207, NAI DFA 305/34.
15. National Archives, CP (45) 152, 7 September 1945.
16. RIA/NAI, Documents on Irish Foreign Policy, No. 8, UCDA P150/2701.
17. RIA/NAI, Documents on Irish Foreign Policy, No. 224, NAI TSCH/3/5/14544/A.
18. Quoted in Ferriter, *The Border*, p. 50.
19. RIA/NAI, Documents on Irish Foreign Policy, No. 319, NAI DFA/10/P203.
20. National Archives, CAB 128/15/34.
21. National Archives, CP (45) 152, 7 September 1945.
22. Fintan O'Toole, *We Don't Know Ourselves: A Personal History of Ireland since 1958* (London, 2021), p. 41.

5 Trapped by History

1. National Archives, CAB 128/15/34.
2. James Callaghan, *A House Divided: The Dilemma of Northern Ireland* (London, 1973), p. 1.
3. Quoted in David McKittrick and David McVea, *Making Sense of the Troubles* (London, 2012), p. 72.
4. Peter Catterall (ed.), *The Macmillan Diaries*, Vol. 2, *Prime Minister and After* (London, 2011), p. 550.

5 Ibid., p. 104.
6 John Peck, *Dublin from Downing Street* (Dublin, 1978), p. 18.
7 Ibid., p. 20.
8 Quoted in Christopher Andrew, *The Defence of the Realm: The Authorized History of MI5* (London, 2009), p. 602.
9 National Archives, CP (70) 19, 20 July 1970.
10 Callaghan, *A House Divided*, p. 117.
11 National Archives, CJ4/184. NI 18/28/12.
12 Quoted in Ferriter, *The Border*, p. 62.
13 RIA/NAI, Documents on Irish Foreign Policy, No. 447, NA 99/1/283.
14 Ibid.
15 Peck, *Dublin from Downing Street*, p. 122.
16 Callaghan, *A House Divided*, p. 163.
17 Peck, *Dublin from Downing Street*, p. 133.
18 National Archives, CP (72) 26, 3 March 1972.
19 Quoted in McKittrick and McVea, *Making Sense of the Troubles*, p. 120.
20 Quoted in ibid., p. 122.
21 Garret FitzGerald, *All in a Life: An Autobiography* (Dublin, 1991), p. 243.
22 National Archives, PREM 16/148, 30 May 1974.
23 Bernard Donoughue, *Downing Street Diary: With Harold Wilson in No. 10* (London, 2005), p. 130.
24 National Archives, PREM 16/959, 9 January 1976.
25 Donoughue, *Downing Street Diary*, p. 619.
26 Ibid., p. 252.
27 Edward Heath, *The Course of My Life* (London, 1998), p. 436.
28 National Archives, CAB 301/904.
29 FitzGerald, *All in a Life*, p. 218.
30 National Archives, FCO/160/181/50.
31 FitzGerald, *All in a Life*, p. 185.

6 The Americans Are Back

1 Cruise O'Brien, *States of Ireland*, p. 45.
2 David Langbart, 'Ireland: The Easter Rising, 1916: Follow-Up on Eamon de Valera', US National Archives blog, 28 April 2016, https://text-message.blogs.archives.gov/2016/04/28/ireland-the-easter-rising-1916-follow-up-on-eamon-de-valera.
3 O'Connor and Kenneally (eds), *The Revolution Papers*, p. 22.
4 RIA/NAI, Documents on Irish Foreign Policy, No. 96, NAI DFA Secretary's Files P48A.
5 RIA/NAI, Documents on Irish Foreign Policy, No. 98, NAI DFA Secretary's Files P48A.
6 RIA/NAI, Documents on Irish Foreign Policy, No. 108, NAI DFA Secretary's Files P48A.

7 RIA/NAI, Documents on Irish Foreign Policy, No. 96, NAI DFA Secretary's Files P48A.
8 US State Department, Office of the Historian, European Policy and Economic Developments, Vol. III, No. 611.40A/8/1550.
9 Ibid., Vol. IV, Part 1m, No. 230.
10 RIA/NAI, Documents on Irish Foreign Policy, No. 413, NAI DFA/10/P/277/2.
11 US State Department, Office of the Historian, Foreign Policy of the US 1969–76, Vol. XLI, Western Europe, No. 171.
12 Quoted in Mary E. Daly (ed.), *Brokering the Good Friday Agreement* (Dublin, 2019), p. 16.
13 10 Downing Street, note for the record, 23 August 1979. Margaret Thatcher Foundation.
14 Letter to President Carter, 20 July 1979. Margaret Thatcher Foundation.
15 Conversation with the author.
16 Conversation with the author.

7 The Lady Turns

1 Margaret Thatcher, *The Downing Street Years* (London, 1993), p. 384.
2 Quoted in David Goodall, *The Making of the Anglo-Irish Agreement of 1985: A Memoir*, ed. Frank Sheridan (Dublin, 2021), pp. 68, 134.
3 National Archives, CAB 128/72/7, 2 July 1981.
4 National Archives, Prem 19/81, August 1979.
5 National Archives, Most confidential record to CC(81) 26th CONCLUSION, Cab Office, 7 July 1981.
6 Goodall, *The Making of the Anglo-Irish Agreement*, p. 5.
7 Ibid., p. 30.
8 Quoted in *Financial Times*, 2 January 2014.
9 Goodall, *The Making of the Anglo-Irish Agreement*, p. 9.
10 National Archives, PREM 19/1286/f56.
11 Quoted in 'Thatcher and FitzGerald Talks: Redrawing of Northern Ireland Border Was Discussed', BBC News, 27 September 2014, https://www.bbc.co.uk/news/uk-northern-ireland-30610096.
12 FitzGerald, *All in a Life*, p. 568.
13 Goodall, *The Making of the Anglo-Irish Agreement*, p. xiii.
14 Ibid., p. 183.
15 Ibid., p. 89.
16 Ibid., p. 149.
17 Quoted in Daly (ed.), *Brokering the Good Friday Agreement*, p. 76.
18 Richard Needham, *One Man, Two Worlds: Memoir of a Businessman in Politics* (Newtownards, 2021), p. 160.
19 Quoted in Daly (ed.), *Brokering the Good Friday Agreement*, p. 93.

NOTES

8 Talking to Terrorists

1 Conversation with the author.
2 Powell, *Great Hatred, Little Room*, p. 167.
3 Quoted in McKittrick and McVea, *Making Sense of the Troubles*, p. 217.
4 Ibid., p. 228.
5 Albert Reynolds, *My Autobiography* (Dublin, 2009), pp. 348–9.
6 Ibid., p. 354.
7 Quoted in Daly (ed.), *Brokering the Good Friday Agreement*, p. 116.
8 Ibid.
9 https://clinton.presidentiallibraries.us/files/original/16581db376221ea-3ceef915f0600787c.pdf.
10 Quoted in Reynolds, *My Autobiography*, p. 379.
11 Quoted in Conor O'Cleary, *The Greening of the White House* (Dublin, 1997), pp. 21–2.
12 Quoted in McKittrick and McVea, *Making Sense of the Troubles*, pp. 235–6.

9 The End of History

1 O'Toole, *We Don't Know Ourselves*, p. 526.
2 Tony Blair, *A Journey* (London, 2010), p. 158.
3 Ibid., p. 157.
4 Powell, *Great Hatred, Little Room*, p. 3.
5 Blair, *A Journey*, p. 167.
6 Quoted in Frank Millar, *David Trimble: The Price of Peace* (Dublin, 2004), p. 66.
7 Quoted in McKittrick and McVea, *Making Sense of the Troubles*, p. 253.
8 Interview with the author.
9 Ibid.
10 Ibid.
11 Ibid.
12 Daly (ed.), *Brokering the Good Friday Agreement*, p. 147.
13 Interview in the *Irish Times*, 10 April 2023.
14 Quoted in Chris Mullin, *A Walk-On Part: Diaries 1994–1999* (London, 2011), p. 460.
15 Roy Foster, *Irish Times*, 26 May 1998.
16 Powell, *Great Hatred, Little Room*, p. 236.
17 Ibid., p. 211.
18 Ibid., p. 307.
19 Needham, *One Man, Two Worlds*, p. 186.
20 Quoted in Daly (ed.), *Brokering the Good Friday Agreement*, p. 113.

NOTES

10 A Choice of Unions

1. Interview with the author.
2. Rory Carroll, 'Karen Bradley Admits Ignorance of Northern Ireland Politics', *Guardian*, 7 September 2018.
3. Stefaan De Rynck, *Inside the Deal: How the EU Got Brexit Done* (Newcastle, 2023), p. 123.
4. Interview with the author.
5. Tony Connelly, *Brexit and Ireland: The Dangers, the Opportunities, and the Inside Story of the Irish Response* (London, 2023), p. 30.
6. Quoted in Stephen Collins, *Ireland's Call: Navigating Brexit* (Dublin, 2022), pp. 50–1.
7. John Garry, 'The EU Referendum Vote in Northern Ireland: Implications for Our Understanding of Citizens' Political Views and Behaviour', https://www.qub.ac.uk/brexit/Brexitfilestore/Filetoupload,728121,en.pdf.
8. Collins, *Ireland's Call*, pp. 147, 157.
9. *Financial Times*, 20 November 2023.
10. Interviews with the author.
11. Quoted in Peter Foster, *What Went Wrong with Brexit: And What Can We Do about It* (Edinburgh, 2023), p. 105.
12. Anthony Seldon and Raymond Newell, *Johnson at 10: The Inside Story* (London, 2023), p. 401.
13. Interview with the author.
14. Ibid.
15. Jonathan Powell, 'The UK Approach to Northern Ireland Is One of Casual Political Vandalism', *Financial Times*, 15 October 2021.

11 Past and Future

1. Quoted in *Irish News*, 17 May 2019.
2. Hubert Butler, *Grandmother and Wolfe Tone* (Dublin, 1990), p. 68.
3. Ibid.

INDEX

Unless otherwise indicated, references to 'Ireland' relate to the Republic of Ireland.

Act of Union (1800), 5
Adams, Edward, 149
Adams, Gerry, 167, 185–6, 190, 191, 201–2, 215, 227, 230–1
Addison, Viscount, 108
adoption, forced, 96
agricultural economy, Ireland, 90, 92, 98, 99, 118
Ahern, Bertie, 203, 210, 216, 217, 219, 220, 221, 231
Alderdice, John, 207
Alibrandi, Monsignor Gaetano, 143
Alliance Party, 207, 228, 264
American Civil War, 147, 148
Anglo-Irish Agreement (1985): Fianna Fáil's response to, 181; limited impact on violence, 184; provisions, 163–4, 178–9; signing, 160, 163; talks and negotiations, 160–1, 172–8; unionists' response to, 164, 181; US support of, 160–1, 182; Westminster's response to, 180–1
Anglo-Irish Free Trade Agreement (1965), 118
Anglo-Irish Intergovernmental Conference, 179, 181
Anglo-Irish Trade Agreement (1948), 108
Anglo-Irish Treaty (1921): creation of Irish Free State, 43, 58, 59, 61; Dáil Éireann debate and ratification, 54, 55–6, 57–8; different perspectives on, 11–12, 16–17, 44–5; establishment of Provisional Government, 43–4, 58; immediate responses to, 43, 54–6, 57, 59; negotiations, 15–16, 36–43, 47–8, 49, 51–2, 53–5; provisions, 43, 57, 58, 59, 69; signing, 15, 43, 47; UK Parliament debate and ratification, 56–7
Anglo-Irish War *see* War of Independence (1919–21)
anti-Treaty IRA, 44, 60 *see also* Irish Civil War (1922–3)
Apprentice Boys of Derry, 120
Arcy, Charles Frederick d', 22
ARINS project, 268, 271–2
Armstrong, Robert, 173, 174, 177
army, British *see* British army
Asquith, Herbert, 17–18, 19, 21, 22–4, 32, 56
Attlee, Clement, 86–7, 107, 110, 115
aviation industry, Ireland, 99

Baldwin, Stanley, 67
Balfour, Arthur, 32–3
Barnier, Michel, 240–1, 242, 244, 246, 250, 251, 252
Barrington, Donal, 125
Barry, Peter, 174
Barton, Robert, 15, 52, 55–6
Battle of Kinsale (1601–2), 6
Battle of the Boyne (1690), 6–7
Begley, Thomas, 191
Belfast: Anglo-Irish Intergovernmental Conference, 179, 181; Maze prison, 164–6, 211–12; Northern Bank robbery, 228 *see also* Northern Ireland Assembly; Parliament of Northern Ireland (1921–72); Troubles (1969–98)
Belfast Agreement *see* Good Friday Agreement (1998)
Beveridge, William, 96–7

289

INDEX

Bevin, Ernest, 111
Biaggi, Mario, 157
Biden, Joe, 256
Birkenhead, Lord, 42–3, 47
Black and Tan War *see* War of Independence (1919–21)
Black and Tans, 31, 50, 53
Blair, Tony: addresses Dáil Éireann, 222; and Brexit referendum, 239; on changing fortunes of Ireland and Northern Ireland, 207–8; electoral victory, 203, 209; first visit to Belfast, 214–15; global ambitions, 208–9; and Good Friday Agreement, 214–16, 219, 220, 221, 225, 227, 229, 231; on Irish conflict being 'old-fashioned', 208; Irish roots, 208; resigns as PM, 230; self-belief, 203, 208, 209, 213; statement at 150th anniversary of Great Famine, 213–14
Blaney, Neil, 129
Bloody Sunday (Derry, 1972), 130–1, 166, 219; Saville Inquiry, 131, 219
Bloody Sunday (Dublin, 1920), 34–5, 53
Boland, Frederick, 85, 152
Boland, Harry, 38, 150
Bonar Law, Andrew, 19, 22, 37
border (between Ireland and Northern Ireland): as arbitrary and unenforceable, 70–1; as 'border of the mind', 70–1, 72; border poll, 133; boundary commission's shelved work on, 71–2, 73; and Brexit, 245, 246–7, 249–50, 252, 258, 263; as 'sticking plaster', 262, 274; Thatcher's redrawing idea, 175–6; during Troubles, 124, 164
border (in Irish sea), 247, 249, 250, 252, 253, 255–6, 257, 263
boundary commission, 71–2, 73
Bradley, Denis, 191
Bradley, Karen, 238
Brenchley, Frank, 139–40
Brennan, Denis, 85
Brennan, Robert, 151, 152
Brexit: and argument for reunification, 269; border issues, 238–9, 245, 246–7, 249–50, 252, 253, 255–6, 257, 263; and Ireland, 241–2, 245–6, 258–9; negotiations with Brussels, 239–41, 243–5, 246–7, 249–53, 254–6; and Northern Ireland, 13, 235, 246–50, 252–4, 255–6, 258; referendum campaigns and vote (2016), 234–7, 248; reputational damage to Britain, 250–2, 254–5, 256; UK Internal Markets Bill (2020), 255–6; Windsor Framework (2023), 256, 257; Withdrawal Agreement (2020), 244–5, 252–3, 257
British army *see* military, British
British attitudes towards Ireland/Northern Ireland and the Irish: Andrew Bonar Law, 37; Arthur Balfour, 32; 'beyond the pale', 3; Boris Johnson, 4, 237; 'choreographed private disagreement' over Ireland's new constitution, 67–9; conquest, colonialism and proprietorship, 3–4, 5–7, 9–10, 17, 19, 44, 50, 86, 129; contentment with status quo, 103; disregard and indifference, 9, 10, 44, 115–18, 180, 238, 262, 265; distancing during First World War, 28; distancing during Troubles, 168–9; goodwill gestures on Easter Rising fiftieth anniversary, 118–19; hardened attitude towards nationalism, 107–8, 109; Harold Wilson, 135–6, 177; ignorance and prejudice, 100, 102, 119, 123–4, 175, 180–1, 238, 265; Irish question as problematic, 4, 17, 31, 56–7, 123, 138; Ivor Stanbrook, 180; James Anthony Froude, 19; John Maffey, 87; Karen Bradley, 238; Margaret Thatcher, 174–5, 176, 177, 187–8; monarchy, 1–2, 106; Neville Chamberlain, 67–8; Nicholas Budgen, 180; Northern Ireland as drain on resources, 72, 74, 177, 237, 268; politics before principle, 8, 17,

INDEX

18–19, 23–4, 29–30, 257; prejudice towards Irish immigrants, 100, 102; Reginald Maulding, 116, 123; respect for Irish arts and literature, 102; Roy Jenkins, 138; strategic role of ports, 69, 77, 78; threat of RUC, 74; Tony Blair, 208; William Thackery, 2; Winston Churchill, 10, 36–7, 48, 49–51, 56–7, 72, 86

British Empire and Commonwealth: Churchill's views on, 48, 50, 57; Commonwealth immigrants to Britain, 100; dismantling, 30–1, 67, 97, 100, 108–9, 113; Dominion status of Ireland (considered), 17, 36, 39, 42; Dominion status of Northern Ireland (considered), 137, 139; expansion and extent, 22, 31; Ireland as within, 3, 16, 17, 18, 19, 32, 35, 54, 55, 57, 68, 87, 107; Ireland becomes a Republic, 100, 107, 108; Irish diaspora to wider Empire, 10, 91; Kipling's views on, 50; United States calls for decolonisation, 30

British intelligence: collusion with loyalist paramilitaries, 185; MI5 assesses security problem in Northern Ireland, 122; MI5 hosts journalists, 198–9; MI5 surveillance during Troubles, 199; MI6 appoints Richard Moore as chief, 2; MI6 has secret talks with IRA, 189, 191, 192

British rule (pre-Anglo-Irish Treaty), 3–11

Brooke, Basil, 110
Brooke, Peter, 186–8, 189–90
Browne, Noel, 97
Bruton, John, 200, 201
Buckley, Jack, 2–3
Budgen, Nicholas, 180
Bush, George W., 229–30
Butler, Hubert, 262, 271

Callaghan, James, 115, 122, 123–4, 128, 140, 158, 163, 168–9
Cameron, David, 131, 185, 234–5, 237, 242

Cameron, Lord: Commission on the Disturbances report, 122–3
Carey, Hugh, 156, 159
Carson, Edward, 18, 22, 23, 28, 32, 34, 42–3, 57
Carter, Jimmy, 145, 146, 155–8, 159
Casement, Roger, 1, 26, 119
Catholicism: anti-Catholic discrimination in Northern Ireland, 74, 75, 119, 120, 121, 171; and Brexit referendum, 248; and censorship, 63, 96; decreasing influence in Ireland, 205–6, 265; dominance in Ireland, 66, 75, 92, 93, 95–6, 97, 143, 205; growth in Northern Ireland, 211, 248, 257–8, 263; John Charles McQuaid, 95–6, 97; linked to nationalism/republicanism, 22, 27–8, 66, 92, 93, 143; MacBride Principles, 159–60; penal laws against Catholics, 6; pope visits Ireland, 205; pope's audience with FitzGerald, 143; during the Reformation, 5; and RUC/PSNI, 226; sexual abuse of children, 96, 205; social cachet in upper-middle-class Britain, 102; views on possible reunification referendum, 271–2
censorship, 63, 96
Chamberlain, Austen, 15, 47, 52
Chamberlain, Neville, 67–8, 69–70, 78, 79
Charlestown, County Mayo, 91
Chastelain, John de, 227
children of unmarried mothers, 96, 205
Churchill, Randolph, 19, 48, 49
Churchill, Winston: on Anglo-American relations, 31; and Anglo-Irish Treaty, 15, 36–7, 41, 51, 56–7, 58, 59–60; attitudes towards Ireland, 10, 36–7, 48, 49–51, 56–7, 72, 86; character, 49, 60; on de Valera, 86; Irish roots, 48; on Michael Collins, 60; nudges Herbet Asquith towards partition, 32; and Second World War, 76–7, 78, 79–81, 84, 86, 151; on settlement with de Valera, 70; shares a platform with John Redmond, 49

291

INDEX

Clann na Poblachta (political party), 107
Clinton, Bill: involvement in peace process discussions, 201, 212–13, 220, 221, 227, 229, 231; Irish roots, 212; lifts visa ban on Sinn Féin leaders, 195–7; on Martin McGuinness, 217; warm relations with Blair, 209
Cold War, 118, 139, 146, 155
Collins, Michael: admits north cannot be won over, 72; and Anglo-Irish Treaty, 15, 39, 41, 43, 47, 48, 51–2, 53, 54, 55–6, 58; arrest, 25; celebrity status, 48; chair of Provisional Government, 43–4, 58; character, 41, 47–8, 49, 51–2, 53, 60; Craig–Collins pact, 59; death and legacy, 44, 60, 62; early life, 47; electoral pact, 58; Gaelic League membership, 21, 47; IRA commander, 52–3, 54; IRB and Volunteers membership, 47; Kiltimagh hideout, 92; on Lloyd George, 60; perspective on Anglo-Irish Treaty, 17; republicanism, 47; sanctions IRA attacks after Anglo-Irish Treaty, 58–9; takes charge of IRA Volunteers, 30; on Winston Churchill, 60
Commission on the Disturbances report, 122–3
Common Market, 113 *see also* European Economic Community (EEC) and European Union (EU)
Commonwealth *see* British Empire and Commonwealth
Connelly, Tony, 242
Conradh na Gaeilge (Gaelic League), 20, 21, 40, 47, 66
'consent' to partition/unity: and Anglo-Irish Agreement (1985), 161, 178; and Brexit, 238; and Downing Street Declaration (1993), 193–5; and Good Friday Agreement (1998), 220–1, 238, 264; and Government of Ireland Act (1920), 34; and Ireland Act (1949), 111–12; and practicalities for the future, 261, 264, 270–2

contraception, prohibition in Ireland, 206
Cook, Judith, 142
Cooney, John, 96
Cosgrave, Liam, 133–4, 141
Cosgrave, William T., 61, 62, 63, 64, 72
Costello, John, 96, 107, 108, 109, 153–4
Council of Ireland: under Government of Ireland Act (1920), 34; under Sunningdale Agreement, 134
Covid-19 pandemic, 254, 256
Craig, James, 15, 36, 42, 59, 73, 76
Cremin, Con, 101–2, 103
Cromwell, Oliver, 6
Cumann na mBan (women's militia), 21, 24
Cumann na nGaedheal (political party, later Fine Gael), 61, 63
Cummings, Dominic, 253

Dáil Éireann (Assembly of Ireland): Anglo-Irish Treaty debate and ratification (1922), 54, 55–6, 57–8; de Valera abandons abstentionism policy, 64–5; election results (1921), 36; election results (1932), 65; election results (1948), 96; election results (1951), 153; election results (1954), 153; election results (1973), 141; election results (1977), 142; election results (1982), 169; election results (1994), 200; election results (1997), 203; election results (2020), 259; electoral pact (1922), 58; Michel Barnier addresses, 246; northern nationalists refused representation in, 75; presidents and Taoiseachs, 30, 44, 58, 61, 65, 96, 114, 124, 134, 141, 153, 169, 184, 200, 203, 224, 233, 242, 252; as single-chamber parliament (1919), 30; Tony Blair addresses, 222 *see also individual presidents and Taoiseachs*
d'Arcy, Charles Frederick, 22
Davis, David, 241, 250
de Chastelain, John, 227
De Rynck, Stefaan, 239

292

INDEX

de Valera, Éamon: and Anglo-Irish Treaty (1921), 37–9, 42, 43, 53–5, 58, 81; approves First Programme of Economic Expansion, 113–14; believes British coercion is needed to solve partition, 75–6, 80; calls on anti-Treaty IRA to dump arms, 62, 64; Catholicism, 28; character, 40, 67; commuted prison sentence, 148–9; complains about conditions facing Irish workers in Britain, 101; creates new constitution for Irish Free State (as Éire), 65–6; denies being dictator, 153; early life, 40; election loss, 96; electoral pact, 58; establishes Fianna Fáil, 63, 64–5; fundraising in the US, 52, 83, 149–50; Gaelic League membership, 21; Gray's allegations about, 151–2; and 'Irish Ireland', 90, 92–5, 104; in Irish Volunteers, 40; Lloyd George on, 38; Lord Granard on, 67; Macmillan hosts at Downing Street, 117; negotiates with Chamberlain, 69–70; offers condolences on death of Hitler, 85; popularity in County Mayo, 92; as president and Taoiseach of Dáil Éireann, 30, 44, 58, 65, 66, 113–14, 153; as president of Sinn Féin and Irish Volunteers, 27; refuses to abandon wartime neutrality of Ireland, 76–8, 80–2, 151; refuses to attend George VI's coronation, 1–2, 10; republicanism, 40, 81, 105, 117; Stanley Baldwin on, 67; wartime rift with US, 83–5, 151–3

Democratic Unionist Party (DUP): and Brexit, 248–9, 250, 253–4; growth after Good Friday Agreement, 228, 229; at Westminster, 249, 250, 253 *see also* Donaldson, Jeffrey; Foster, Arlene; Paisley, Ian

Derry, 119, 120, 121, 130–1, 166, 219, 239

Devlin, Bernadette, 196

Devonshire, Duke of, 124–5

Dillon, John, 26–7

direct rule in Northern Ireland (1972–98), 132 *see also* Sunningdale Agreement (1973)

Disraeli, Benjamin, 16

divorce, prohibition in Ireland, 93, 206

Dodds, Nigel, 249–50

Donaldson, Jeffrey, 258

Donlon, Sean, 156, 157, 160, 172

Donoughue, Bernard, 137, 138

'Doomsday Scenario' planning for Northern Ireland, 136–7

Dorr, Noel, 174

Douglas-Home, Alec, 138

Downing Street Declaration (1993), 183, 189–95

Dublin: Bloody Sunday *see* Bloody Sunday (Dublin, 1920); Dáil Éireann *see* Dáil Éireann (Irish Assembly); Easter Rising *see* Easter Rising (1916); Four Courts occupation, 44, 58, 59; Queen Elizabeth II visits, 1, 2, 224

Duddy, Brendan, 189

Duffy, George Gavan, 15

Duggan, Eamonn, 15

Dulanty, John, 106, 111

Easter Rising (1916), 7, 24–5, 26, 27–8; execution of leaders, 1, 11, 25–6, 28, 50, 148–9; fiftieth-anniversary events, 118–19, 120, 121; and shift towards revolutionary republicanism, 26–7, 50, 166

'economic war' (1932–8), 69

Eden, Anthony, 118

Edward VIII, King, 65

Éire (Ireland) *see* Republic of Ireland

Elizabeth II, Queen: Irish ministers and officials debarred from coronation events, 106; meets Martin McGuinness, 224; prorogues parliament, 251; visits Dublin, 1, 2, 224

emigration from Ireland *see* Irish diaspora, Britain; Irish diaspora, elsewhere

293

INDEX

Ervine, David, 198, 212
European Court of Human Rights, 129
European Economic Community (EEC) and European Union (EU): Brexit *see* Brexit; Britain and Ireland join (1973), 183, 204; Britain blocked by France (1963), 118; expansion, 208; investment in Ireland, 204; investment in Northern Ireland, 224, 240, 242–3; Ireland requests to join (1961), 114; Maastricht Treaty (1992), 192, 201, 234
Ewart-Biggs, Christopher, 142
Executive Authority (External Relations) Act (1936), 65, 68

Falklands War (1982), 169–70, 172
Fanning, Ronan, 33, 34
Farage, Nigel, 234, 236
Faulkner, Brian, 132
Fenian Brotherhood (United States), 21, 148
Ferris, Martin, 216
Ferriter, Diarmaid, 71, 73
Fianna Fáil (political party), 63, 64–5, 93, 94, 129, 142, 190, 266–7 *see also* Ahern, Bertie; de Valera, Éamon; Haughey, Charles; Lynch, Jack; Reynolds, Albert
financial crisis and austerity, 233, 236, 241, 266
Fine Gael (political party): decline, 266–7; electoral victory (1948), 96 *see also* Bruton, John; Cosgrave, Liam; Cosgrave, William T.; Cumann na nGaedheal (political party, later Fine Gael); FitzGerald, Garret; Kenny, Enda; Varadkar, Leo
Finucane, Brendan (Paddy), 83
First World War, 11, 18, 28, 50, 148 *see also* Treaty of Versailles (1919)
FitzGerald, Desmond, 104
FitzGerald, Garret: and Anglo-Irish Agreement, 160–1, 172, 173, 174, 176, 177, 178, 181, 184; audience with pope, 143; on importance of defeating PIRA, 142, 170–1; nationalism, 170–1, 172; New Ireland Forum, 270; on Noraid, 157; on Sunningdale, 134, 141; on Wilson's government, 136
Flags and Emblems (Display) Act (Northern Ireland) (1954), 172
Flanagan, Charles, 250–1
Foster, Arlene, 248–9
Foster, Roy, 25, 28, 99, 223
Four Courts occupation (1922), 44, 58, 59
'Four Horsemen', 156
Framework Documents (1995), 218
Free State *see* Irish Free State (1922–37)
French, John, 35
Frost, David, 241, 254
Froude, James Anthony, 19

Gaelic Athletic Association (GAA), 20–1
Gaelic language, 20, 21, 63, 66, 87, 92–4
Gaelic League, 20, 21, 40, 47, 66
Gaelic Revival, 9, 20–1
Galsworthy, Arthur, 142–3
general strike (Northern Ireland, 1974), 135
George V, King, 37, 73
George VI, King, 1–2, 10, 65, 106
German reunification, 267
Gladstone, William, 16, 18–19
Good Friday Agreement (1998): likened to Sunningdale Agreement, 134; Mitchell Principles, 217–18; negotiators and behind-the-scenes players, 210–14; Nobel Peace Prize, 228–9; provisions, 218, 220–1, 225–6, 227; ratification, 221, 222; success of, 12; talks and negotiations, 5, 212, 213, 215–20, 225; threatened by Brexit, 13, 238–9, 242, 246–7, 256; twenty-fifth anniversary, 217
Goodall, David, 173, 174, 177
Gove, Michael, 236–7, 238, 244, 255
government of Ireland *see* Dáil Éireann (Assembly of Ireland)

INDEX

Government of Ireland Act (1914), 17–18, 19–20, 21–2
Government of Ireland Act (1920), 32–4, 270
Government of Ireland Act (1949), 133
government of Northern Ireland *see* direct rule in Northern Ireland (1972–98); Northern Ireland Assembly (1998–2002); Northern Ireland Assembly (2007–17); Parliament of Northern Ireland (1921–72); power sharing in Northern Ireland
Gow, Ian, 181
Granard, Lord, 67
Gray, David, 83, 84, 151–2
Great Famine (1845–51), 8, 22, 92, 147; Tony Blair's statement at 150th anniversary, 213–14
Grey, Edward, 31
Griffith, Arthur: and Anglo-Irish Treaty (1921), 15, 39, 43, 47, 52, 54; character, 47, 52; death, 4, 60; founds Sinn Féin, 21, 41; prison sentence, 41; other mentions, 27, 58

Hattersley, Roy, 30
Haughey, Charles, 129, 142, 169–70, 181, 184
health and welfare provision: in Ireland, 97; in Northern Ireland, 96, 112
Healy, John, 91
Heath, Edward, 127–8, 132–4, 135
Hempel, Eduard, 85
Higgins, Michael, 233
Higgins, Tom, 91
Hitler, Adolf: death, 85 *see also* Second World War
Hogan, Phil, 245–6
Holmes, John, 213–14, 215, 216, 217
Home Rule Act (1914), 17–18, 19–20, 21–2
Home Rule Bill (1886) (defeated), 9, 16, 18
Home Rule Bill (1912) (passed), 19, 21, 22–4, 29

Home Rule movement: Winston Churchill addresses rally, 10
Howard, Michael, 255
Howe, Geoffrey, 171, 174, 177, 181–2
Hughes, Frank, 92
Hume, John, 156, 190, 191, 210, 228–9, 231
hunger strike protests (1981), 164–6
Hunt, John, 137, 138, 140
Hurd, Douglas, 195
Hutchinson, Billy, 198
Hyde, Douglas, 20, 66, 93–4

immigrants to Britain: from Ireland *see* Irish diaspora, Britain; from other Commonwealth countries, 100
India, 31, 97
intelligence services *see* British intelligence
IPP (Irish Parliamentary Party), 18, 19, 23–4
IRA (Irish Republican Army): aligns with Nazi Germany and bombs Britain, 81; anti-Treaty IRA, 44, 60; attacks on Northern Ireland (1950s), 126; changing leadership and split, 126–7; division after Anglo-Irish Treaty, 44; outlawed in Treason Act (1939), 81; recognised as threat in build-up to Troubles, 122; response to Anglo-Irish Treaty (1921), 43 *see also* Collins, Michael; Irish Civil War (1922–3); Provisional IRA (PIRA); Real IRA; Sinn Féin; War of Independence (1919–21)
IRB (Irish Republican Brotherhood), 21, 47, 148 *see also* Irish Volunteers
Ireland Act (1949), 111
Ireland/Éire *see* Republic of Ireland
Irish Citizen Army, 21, 24
Irish Civil War (1922–3): beginnings, 57, 58–9; brevity, 61–2; casualties, 62; Craig–Collins pact, 59; executions, 62; Four Courts occupation, 44, 58, 59; long legacy, 62–3; and population decline, 91–2; Winston Churchill on, 59–60

INDEX

Irish diaspora, Britain: and Brexit referendum, 242; holidaying in Ireland, 89–91, 114; and Irish economy, 91, 98; living and working conditions, 99, 100–1; middle classes, 102, 103; and population decline in Ireland, 9, 91–2, 101; prejudice towards, 100, 102; rights of emigrants, 3, 99–100; during Second World War, 11, 88; and shared cultures, 3; unskilled men, 98–9, 101–2; voting practices, 103; women, 11, 98, 101, 102
Irish diaspora, elsewhere: British Empire, 10, 91; United States, 8, 21, 31, 83, 91, 103, 104
Irish Free State (1922–37): constitution, 43, 59, 270; creation of, 43, 58, 59, 61; under Éamon de Valera, 65–6; 'economic war' with Britain, 69; new constitution as Ireland (Éire), 65–6; northern border *see* border (between Ireland and Northern Ireland); Protestants as minority in, 74–5; under William T. Cosgrave, 61, 62–4 *see also* Anglo-Irish Treaty (1921); Provisional Government (1922); Republic of Ireland
Irish National Liberation Army (INLA), 127, 164–5
Irish parliament *see* Dáil Éireann (Assembly of Ireland)
Irish Parliamentary Party (IPP), 18, 19, 23–4
Irish Potato Famine (1845–51), 8, 22, 92, 147; Tony Blair's statement at 150th anniversary, 213–14
Irish Republican Brotherhood (IRB), 21, 47, 148 *see also* Irish Volunteers
Irish Volunteers (later IRA), 24, 27, 40, 47
Irish War of Independence *see* War of Independence (1919–21)

James II, King, 6
Jenkins, Roy, 138
Johnson, Boris: attitudes towards Ireland and Northern Ireland, 4, 237; and Brexit negotiations, 250–6; and Brexit referendum campaign, 236; end of premiership, 256
Jones, Thomas, 29–30, 38, 39–40
Joyce, James, 63

Kelly, Gerry, 216
Kennedy, Edward, 156
Kennedy, John F., 154–5
Kenny, Enda, 242, 246
Kiernan, Thomas, 154–5
Kiltimagh, County Mayo, 89–91, 92, 114, 206, 265
King, Frank, 135
Kipling, Rudyard, 50

Lascelles, Alan, 106
League of Nations, 64
Lemass, Seán, 114, 117, 121, 125, 204
Lewis, Brandon, 255
Lillis, Michael, 155–6, 160, 173, 174, 179, 213
Lloyd George, David: and Anglo-Irish Treaty (1921), 15–16, 36, 37–40, 41–2, 47, 51, 53–5, 81; character, 39, 60; and Government of Ireland Act (1920), 33; Henry Wilson accuses of cowardice, 23; leads wartime and post-war coalitions, 28, 29–30, 32–3; on Michael Collins, 47–8, 60; nudges Herbert Asquith towards partition, 32; response to insurrection, 35; views on unionists, 29
Logue, Cardinal Michael, 27
Long, Walter, 33
loyalists *see* unionists and loyalists
Lynch, Jack, 124, 127–9, 132–3, 155, 157
Lyne, Roderic, 192
Lyons, F. S. L., 14, 273

Maastricht Treaty (1992), 192, 201, 234
McAleese, Mary, 224
MacBride Principles (for US companies in Northern Ireland), 159–60
MacBride, Seán, 107, 109–10, 159
MacDonald, Malcolm, 68, 69, 79

INDEX

McDonald, Mary Lou, 259
MacEntee, Seán, 76, 264
McGuinness, Martin: and Brexit, 248; and Downing Street Declaration, 191; and Good Friday Agreement, 215–17, 230–1; involvement in PIRA, 215–17; in London talks, 127; meets Queen Elizabeth II, 224; reassesses republican options, 185–6; shared leadership with Paisley, 230–2; stance on PIRA disarmament, 201–2, 227
McMichael, Gary, 212
Macmillan, Harold, 97–8, 117, 118
McQuaid, John Charles, 95–6, 97
Maffey, John, 76, 78, 87, 112
Major, John: background, 184; and Brexit, 239, 255; desire to take on Northern Ireland project, 184; difficult relationship with Clinton, 196, 197; and Downing Street Declaration, 183, 191–3; and Framework Documents, 200; and Maastricht Treaty, 192, 201; rapport and arguments with Albert Reynolds, 183–4, 191–2; targeted by PIRA, 185
Mallon, Seamus, 134, 226, 261–2
Manning, David, 160
Mansergh, Martin, 220
martyrs, Irish, 9, 11, 25–6, 28, 31, 35, 165–6
Maryfield Secretariat (Anglo-Irish Intergovernmental Conference), 179, 181
Mason, Roy, 165
Maudling, Reginald, 116, 123, 132
Maxwell, General John, 25, 27, 28, 149
May, Theresa, 237, 240, 243–5, 247, 249–50, 255
Mayhew, Patrick, 191, 195
Maze prison, Belfast: hunger strike protests (1981), 164–6; Mo Mowlam visits (1998), 211–12
Merkel, Angela, 244
MI5 (Security Service): assesses security problem in Northern Ireland, 122; hosts journalists (1995), 198–9; surveillance during Troubles, 199

MI6 (Secret Intelligence Service): appoints Richard Moore as chief, 2; has secret talks with IRA, 189, 191, 192
military, British: Bloody Sunday events (1972), 130–1; first casualty of Troubles, 126; Irishmen and women serve with during world wars, 11, 28, 50, 82–3, 86, 88; presence in Northern Ireland during Troubles, 123–4, 126, 130–1, 141, 160, 167–8; refusal to break blockades of general strike, 135; refusal to face down UVF, 23
military, Irish: independence from the Crown, 63–4, 69–70; serving with British in world wars, 11, 28, 50, 82–3, 86, 88
Mitchell, George, 201, 212, 217
Mitchell Principles, 217–18
Molyneaux, James, 181
Moore, Richard, 2
Morrison, Danny, 167
Mountbatten, Earl, 168
Mowlam, Marjorie (Mo), 211–12
Moynihan, Daniel Patrick, 156

Nally, Dermot, 174
National Army, 59 *see also* Irish Civil War (1922–3)
nationalists and republicans *see* Cumann na mBan (women's militia); Easter Rising (1916); Fenian Brotherhood; home rule movement; IRA (Irish Republican Army); IRB (Irish Republican Brotherhood); Irish Citizen Army; Irish Parliamentary Party (IPP); martyrs, Irish; Provisional IRA (PIRA); Sinn Féin; *individual people*
Nationality Act (1948), 99–100
NATO (North Atlantic Treaty Organisation), 105, 106, 152
Neave, Airey, 164
Needham, Richard, 180, 231
New Ireland Forum, 270
Nobel Peace Prize, 228–9

INDEX

Noraid (Irish Northern Aid Committee), 157, 170
Northern Ireland: absence of wartime conscription, 81, 82; Anglo-Irish Agreement *see* Anglo-Irish Agreement (1985); anti-Catholic discrimination, 74, 75, 119, 120, 121, 171; Apprentice Boys of Derry, 120; border poll (1973), 133; and Brexit, 13, 235, 246–50, 252–4, 255–6, 258; British exit scenario consideration (1974–6), 136–40; British subsidies, 177, 268; disinvestment and deindustrialisation during Troubles, 206–7; Downing Street Declaration (1993), 183, 189–95; electoral boundary gerrymandering, 73, 120, 121; European investment in, 224, 240, 242–3; first summit with Ireland, 121; Flags and Emblems (Display) Act (1954), 172; Framework Documents (1995), 218; 'The Future of Northern Ireland' Green Paper (1972), 132–3; general strike (1974), 135; Good Friday Agreement *see* Good Friday Agreement (1998); government *see* government of Northern Ireland; growing Catholic population, 211, 248, 257–8, 263; health and welfare provision, 96, 112; Home Office neglect, 115–16; increasing prosperity, 112; legacy of Troubles, 224–5; Orange Order and marching season, 7, 21–2, 73, 120, 208, 210–11, 227; Police Service of Northern Ireland (PSNI), 226; regeneration and investment, 180; RUC, 73–4, 158, 167, 168, 225–6; secured by Ireland Act (1949), 111; southern border *see* border (between Ireland and Northern Ireland); unionist control and paranoia, 73–4; US investment in, 159–60, 197 *see also* Belfast; Derry; peace process; Troubles (1969–98); Ulster
Northern Ireland Assembly: difficulties, 226–8; establishment, 221; narrowing pro-union majority, 263–4; shared leadership of Paisley and McGuinness, 230–2; suspension periods, 228, 258
Northern Ireland Civil Rights Association, 121

Ó Ceallaigh, Dáithí, 172, 181
Ó hUiginn, Seán, 194, 232
oath of allegiance to British Crown: and Anglo-Irish Treaty (1921), 39, 42, 55, 58, 64; removal (1933), 65
O'Brien, Conor Cruise, 147
Oireachtas (Irish parliament): lower house *see* Dáil Éireann (Assembly of Ireland)
Omagh bombing (1998), 221–2
O'Neill, Hugh, 6
O'Neill, Michelle, 258
O'Neill, Terence, 121
O'Neill, Thomas 'Tip', 156, 158
Orange Order and marching season, 7, 21–2, 73, 120, 208, 210–11, 227
orphans, 96
O'Toole, Fintan, 114

Paisley, Ian, 121–2, 198, 218, 219, 221, 226, 228, 230–2
parliament of Ireland *see* Dáil Éireann (Assembly of Ireland)
Parliament of Northern Ireland (1921–72): and 'consent' to partition, 111–12, 125; first election and inauguration, 34, 36, 37, 73; move to Stormont Castle, 72; prime ministers, 36, 110, 132; suspension and imposition of direct rule, 132 *see also* Northern Ireland Assembly
Parnell, Charles Stewart, 8–9, 19–20
Partition Act (1920), 32–4, 270
partition of Ireland: Anglo-Irish Treaty *see* Anglo-Irish Treaty (1921); Government of Ireland Act (1920), 32–4, 270 *see also* border (between Ireland and Northern Ireland); 'consent' to partition/unity; unification of Ireland (in future)

298

INDEX

Patten, Chris, 225–6
peace process: both sides recognise military stalemate, 185–8; ceasefires, 127, 141, 195, 197–8, 199–200, 215; Downing Street Declaration (1993), 183, 189–95; Framework Documents (1995), 200; Good Friday Agreement *see* Good Friday Agreement (1998); PIRA refuses to disarm prior to negotiations, 200–2; role of women's movements, 212; unsung heroes, 189, 213–14
Pearse, Patrick, 21, 24–5, 27–8
Peck, John, 119, 127, 130, 131
PIRA (Provisional IRA): ceasefires, 127, 141, 195, 197–8, 199–200, 215; 'cellular' structure, 168; creation, 127; fixation on Second World War, 188; and Good Friday Agreement, 215–19, 227; hunger strike protests, 164–6; John Hume on, 189; judicial bar on extradition to Britain, 164, 172, 174; legal measures against, 133; Libyan weapons supply, 217; Northern Bank robbery, 228; Peter Brooke's coded message to, 186–8; prisoner release, 227; refuses to disarm prior to negotiation, 200–2; secret talks with British intelligence, 189, 191, 192; spying on Northern Ireland Assembly, 227; strengthening, 128, 129, 131; talks leading to Downing Street Declaration, 190–1; US funding, 148, 157, 170, 217; weapons decommissioning, 227–8, 230 *see also* Adams, Gerry; McGuinness, Martin; Sinn Féin; Troubles (1969–98)
Police Service of Northern Ireland (PSNI), 226
ports, Irish: British desire to regain control, 77, 78, 84; British withdrawal from, 66, 69–70
Powell, Charles, 177–8
Powell, Enoch, 164, 181, 237–8
Powell, Jonathan, 5, 189, 209, 209–10, 213, 219, 229, 230, 254–5, 273

power sharing in Northern Ireland: Framework Documents (1995), 200; Good Friday Agreement *see* Good Friday Agreement (1998); Sunningdale Agreement (1973) (failed), 133–5
Price, Major I. H., 149
Protestantism: and Brexit referendum, 248; and future unification of Ireland, 269; linked to unionism, 21–2; Orange Order and marching season, 7, 21–2, 73, 120, 208, 210–11, 227; in pre-partition Ulster, 5–7, 22; stronghold in Northern Ireland, 73–4, 171; views on possible reunification referendum results, 272; William of Orange's victory, 6–7
Provisional Government (1922): establishment and chair, 43–4, 58
Provisional IRA *see* PIRA (Provisional IRA)

Reagan, Ronald, 146, 158, 160, 182
Real IRA: Omagh bombing (1998), 221–2
Redmond, John, 18, 28, 29, 49, 200 *see also* Irish Parliamentary Party (IPP)
Reid, Alec, 189
Republic of Ireland: agricultural economy, 90, 92, 98, 99, 118; Anglo-Irish Agreement *see* Anglo-Irish Agreement (1985); aviation industry, 99; becomes a Republic (1949), 100, 107, 108; and Brexit, 241–2, 245–6, 258–9; Catholicism's decreasing influence, 205–6, 265; Catholicism's dominance, 66, 75, 92, 93, 95–6, 97, 143, 205; children of unmarried mothers, 96, 205; constitution (1937), 65–7, 68–9, 75, 92–3, 270; constitutional amendment after Good Friday Agreement (1998), 220–1; creation, 100, 107, 108; currency, 104–5, 205, 233; de Valera's vision of 'Irish Ireland', 90, 92–5, 104; deliberate distancing from Britain, 105–6, 108; economic

INDEX

dependence on Britain, 104–5, 112, 204–5; economic independence and growth, 203–5, 265; education system, 114, 124, 203; European investment in, 204; exclusion from constitutional discussions concerning Northern Ireland, 127–8; exclusion from Treaty of Versailles talks, 150–1; financial crisis (2008), 233, 241; First Programme of Economic Expansion (1958), 113; first summit with Northern Ireland, 121; Gaelic as official language, 94; government *see* Dáil Éireann (Assembly of Ireland); healthcare provision, 97; immigrant population, 203–4, 206, 265; inclusion in constitutional discussions concerning Northern Ireland, 132–3, 134, 142–3, 183, 189–95; joins EEC (1973), 183, 204; joins IMF and World Bank (1957), 113; joins United Nations (1955), 106, 113, 153; Kennedy visits (1963), 154–5; naming (Ireland/Éire/Republic of Ireland), 106, 223; neutrality during Falklands War, 169–70; neutrality during Second World War, 76–82, 83, 86, 87–8, 104, 108, 151, 152, 153; northern border *see* border (between Ireland and Northern Ireland); as outside NATO, 105, 106; population changes, 91–2, 98, 99, 101, 117; post-war emigration, 98–100; poverty, 90–1, 98, 99, 112; public support for Good Friday Agreement, 221, 223; public views on reunification, 124, 133, 264, 268; Queen Elizabeth II visits, 1, 2, 224; Reagan visits, 146, 160; repeal of prohibitive laws, 206; requests to join EEC (1961), 114; as 'rural idyll', 89–91, 92, 99; settlement with Britain over free trade and return of ports, 66, 69–70; shares wartime intelligence with Britain, 82, 83, 88; thawing relations with US, 153–4; trade agreements with Britain, 108, 109, 118; US investment in, 204; wartime rift with US, 83–5, 151–3; women *see* women, in Ireland; *see also* Irish Free State (1922–37)

republicans *see* nationalists and republicans

reunification of Ireland *see* unification of Ireland (in future)

Reynolds, Albert, 183–4, 191–4, 195

Rimington, Stella, 198–9

Robinson, Séumas, 55

Roosevelt, Franklin D., 83, 84, 151

Royal Irish Constabulary (RIC) (later Royal Ulster Constabulary), 30, 31, 34, 50, 53, 122, 126, 135

Royal Ulster Constabulary (RUC) (formerly Royal Irish Constabulary), 73–4, 158, 167, 168, 225–6

Rutter, Jill, 184

Ryan, Richard, 180

Sands, Bobby, 165, 166, 167, 168

Saville Inquiry, 131, 219

Scotland: referendum on independence (2014), 237, 239

Scullion, John, 120

SDLP (Social Democratic and Labour Party), 133, 156, 170, 226, 228 *see also* Hume, John

Second World War: absence of conscription in Northern Ireland, 81, 82; British desire for control of Irish ports, 77, 78, 84; build-up to, 67–8, 69–70, 78; de Valera offers condolences on death of Hitler, 85; IRA aligns with Nazi Germany and bombs Britain, 81; Ireland shares intelligence with Britain, 82, 83, 88; Ireland–US rift, 83–5, 151–3; Irish labour, 11, 88; Irish soldiers, 11, 82–3, 86, 88; neutrality of Ireland, 76–82, 83, 86, 87–8, 104, 108, 151, 152, 153; post-war reconstruction, 97–8; US involvement, 77, 84, 151

Seitz, Raymond, 196

Sheinwald, Nigel, 159

INDEX

Sinn Féin: abstentionism policy, 41, 64, 166–7; and Anglo-Irish Treaty, 15, 37–9, 41, 43, 51; boycotts border poll, 133; changed electoral strategy, 167, 168, 186; Clinton lifts visa ban for leaders, 195–7; Dáil Éireann election success, 36, 259; founding, 21, 41; growth after Brexit, 258, 259, 263; growth after Easter Rising, 27; growth after Good Friday Agreement, 228, 229; Northern Ireland Assembly election success, 229, 258, 264; seats in Westminster, 29, 167, 168, 263; shifting priorities, 266; talks leading to Good Friday Agreement, 215–17; US support for, 149–50 *see also* Adams, Gerry; de Valera, Éamon; Griffith, Arthur; IRA; McDonald, Mary Lou; O'Neill, Michelle; PIRA (Provisional IRA)
Smith, Julian, 253
Smuts, Jan, 53
Social Democratic and Labour Party (SDLP), 133, 156, 170, 226, 228 *see also* Hume, John
Soderberg, Nancy, 197
Spence, Gusty, 198, 212
Stanbrook, Ivor, 180
Starmer, Keir, 263, 266
Statute of Westminster (1931), 64
Steele, Frank, 189
Stephens, Philip: childhood and family, 89–90, 91, 92, 102–3; visits MI5, 198–9
Stormont *see* Northern Ireland Assembly (1998–2002); Parliament of Northern Ireland (1921–72)
Sunak, Rishi, 256, 257, 263
Sunningdale Agreement (1973), 133–5

Teilefís Éireann (TV channel), 154
Thackery, William, 2
Thatcher, Margaret: and Anglo-Irish Agreement, 160–1, 163–4, 173–9, 181–2, 184; attitudes towards the Irish, 163, 169, 173, 174–5, 176, 177, 187–8; difficult relationship with Haughey, 169–70; and Falklands War, 172; meets Carter, 159; resigns, 186; response to US ban of arms sales to RUC, 158–9; security concerns, 164, 168, 174, 182; stance on republican prisoners' hunger strike protests, 165–6; stirs rebellion against John Major, 192; targeted by PIRA, 175; unity with Reagan, 160
Tóibín, Colm, 71
Tone, Theobald Wolfe, 7–8
Treason Act (1939), 81
Treaty of Limerick (1691), 6
Treaty of Versailles (1919), 30, 150–1
Trevelyan, Charles, 8
Trimble, David, 210–11, 215, 219, 226–7, 228–9, 231
Troubles (1969–98): Anglo-Irish Agreement *see* Anglo-Irish Agreement (1985); attacks on British mainland, 131, 137, 141, 142, 164, 175, 181, 185, 199–200; attacks south of border, 141–2; Bloody Sunday, 130–1, 166, 219; border patrols and watch towers, 124; both sides recognise military stalemate, 185–8; British army presence in Northern Ireland, 123–4, 126, 130–1, 141, 160, 167–8; build-up to, 12, 119–23; Carter's statement and beginnings of US involvement, 145, 146, 155–8, 159; casualties and statistics, 129, 130, 131, 141–2, 164, 168, 175, 181, 185, 188, 191, 221–2, 231; Catholics flee south, 124; ceasefires, 127, 141, 195, 197–8, 199–200, 215; Downing Street Declaration (1993), 183, 189–95; Framework Documents (1995), 200; Good Friday Agreement *see* Good Friday Agreement (1998); internment and mistreatment of republican suspected terrorists, 128, 129; Lynch places responsibility with British, 124; Omagh bombing, 221–2; 'peace walls' dividing communities, 207, 272; PIRA refuses to disarm prior to negotiation, 200–2;

INDEX

republican prisoners' hunger strike protests (1981), 164–6; resumption of violence, 199–200, 202; state collusion with loyalist paramilitaries, 185; US non-intervention policy, 155 *see also* peace process; PIRA (Provisional IRA)

Truman, Harry, 151–2

Trump, Donald, 236

Truss, Liz, 256–7

Tusk, Donald, 250

UK Internal Markets Bill (2020), 255–6

UKIP (United Kingdom Independence Party), 234 *see also* Farage, Nigel

Ulster: as Protestant stronghold before formal partition, 5–7, 22; provisions of Government of Ireland Act (1920), 33 *see also* Northern Ireland

Ulster Defence Association, 131

Ulster Defence Regiment, 168, 171

Ulster Unionist Party (UUP): and Brexit, 248; and Good Friday Agreement, 215, 226, 228; leaders/prime ministers, 121, 179, 181, 198, 210 *see also* Carson, Edward; Faulkner, Brian; Powell, Enoch; Trimble, David

Ulster unionists: Northern Ireland election results (1921), 36; Orange Order and marching season, 7, 21–2, 73, 120, 208, 210–11, 227; Ulster Defence Association, 131; Ulster Volunteer Force (UVF) (founded 1912), 22–3; Ulster Volunteer Force (UVF) (founded 1966), 120, 122, 126, 131, 227 *see also* Craig, James

Ulster Workers' Council: general strike (1974), 135

unification of Ireland (in future): ARINS project, 268, 271–2; British role in, 14, 273; British views on, 265–6; Catholic/Protestant views on, 271–2; comparison with German reunification, 267; and 'consent', 261–2, 264, 270–2; economic and social aspects, 263, 268–9; models for, 270; nationalist views on, 262, 264, 271; not to be rushed, 12–13, 267, 273–4; pro-unity support in Republic of Ireland, 268, 271; and Protestant population, 269; unionist views on, 272

unionists and loyalists: control and paranoia in Northern Ireland, 73–4; linked to Protestantism, 21–2; Lloyd George's views on, 29; narrowing majority in Northern Ireland Assembly, 263–4; response to Anglo-Irish Agreement (1985), 164, 181; response to Anglo-Irish Treaty (1921), 43, 57, 59; response to creation of Republic of Ireland (1949), 111; response to de Valera's constitution for Éire, 66–7; response to Good Friday Agreement, 228; response to PIRA ceasefire (1994), 197–8; seats in Westminster (1918), 29; stance on Brexit, 248–9, 252, 253–4, 258; views on Home Rule Bill/Act (1912/14), 18, 22–3 *see also* 'consent' to partition/unity; Troubles (1969–98); Ulster unionists; *specific people*

United Nations (UN), 106, 113, 153

United States: American Civil War, 147, 148; Anglo-American relations, 31, 38, 118, 145–6, 155, 195–6, 197, 209, 256; bans sales to RUC, 158–9; and Brexit, 256; Carter's statement and beginnings of involvement in Northern Ireland, 145, 146, 155–8, 159; Clinton's initiative to promote investment in Northern Ireland, 197; Cold War, 118, 139, 146, 155; de Valera's fundraising in, 52, 83, 149–50; demonstrations, 120; discussions about PIRA disarmament, 201; Fenian Brotherhood, 21, 148; financial support for PIRA, 148, 157, 170, 217; and First World War, 148; and Good Friday Agreement

(1998), 212–13, 220, 221, 227; investment in Ireland, 204; Irish diaspora, 8, 21, 31, 83, 146–8, 155, 158, 165, 196, 212; Irish heritage politicians, 145, 146, 154, 160, 229, 256; lifts visa ban on Sinn Féin leaders, 195–7; MacBride Principles (for US companies in Northern Ireland), 159–60; naval disarmament negotiations with British, 38, 150; Noraid, 157, 170; privileges own interests over Irish, 150–1; refusal to intervene during Troubles, 155; refusal to sell weapons to Ireland, 152; and Second World War, 77, 84, 151; St Patrick's Day events, 151, 153, 160; supports Anglo-Irish Agreement (1985), 160–1, 182; and talks following Good Friday agreement, 229–30; thawing relations with Ireland, 153–4; unease over hunger strike protests, 165; wartime rift with de Valera, 83–5, 151–3; Wilson calls for decolonisation (1919), 30; withdraws economic aid to Ireland, 153 *see also individual presidents*
UUP *see* Ulster Unionist Party (UUP)
UVF (Ulster Volunteer Force) (founded 1912), 22–3

UVF (Ulster Volunteer Force) (founded 1966), 120, 122, 126, 131, 227

Varadkar, Leo, 252, 267

Walshe, Joseph, 77, 79, 83, 85, 95
War of Independence (1919–21), 3, 34–5, 37, 50–1, 52–3 *see also* Anglo-Irish Treaty (1921)
Whitaker, Thomas, 113, 125, 142
Whitelaw, William, 127, 132–3, 189
Widgery, Lord, 130–1
William III (William of Orange), King, 6
Wilson, Harold, 103, 135–8, 140, 177
Wilson, Henry, 23, 35, 44
Wilson, Woodrow, 30, 148, 149, 150–1
Windsor Framework (2023), 256, 257
women, in Ireland: as belonging at home, 92, 93; contraception, 206; demanding equality, 205; divorce, 93, 206; emigrating to Britain to work, 11, 98, 101, 102; unmarried mothers and their children, 96, 205–6
women's movements (Ireland and Northern Ireland), influence on peace process, 212

Yeats, William Butler, 3, 20, 21, 26, 76
Young Ireland movement, 21